HOLD FAST

A NOVEL

Book 1 Of The HOLD FAST Series

CYNTHIA HARRIS

For my **mother,**

who, by teaching me to read, inspired

a love of storytelling that became a career

before it became a calling

CONTENTS

ABOUT THE AUTHOR
FROM THE AUTHOR

ONE
The Council Of Brothers

Dunmara Castle
Isle of Skye, Scotland
April 1766

Tha e nas fheàrr a dhol tro bheatha na aonar na droch cheangal
It is better to go through life alone than with bad company

I am used to being on my own—in fact; I prefer it. It is unfortunate that the ancient Scots Gaelic, spoken by so many in Clan MacLeod, has eluded me. I may be the only person on Skye that struggles with the beautiful language of our land and people. I understand more than I can speak myself and often confuse it with my own rudimentary understanding of French and Latin from my studies. Whatever the language, however, the meaning of the proverb is universal. I have taken it to heart and made it my mission to live the truth of it.

In the sheltered confines of Dunmara Castle, I never let many people get close to me outside of my family. From a young age, I knew I could make my own way in this life. I was always one to wander off on my own

1

adventures when allowed, and I was not one to conform to the traditional expectations placed on young women. I knew early on that I was not destined to be anyone's wife or mother, and I made my personal declarations of independence to my family as often as I could. I was unyielding on this point.

Some may see independence for a young woman as a rejection of men or a blind resignation to live a life destined for gray-knit shawls and loneliness—the life of the dreaded spinster. I knew, however, that my independence was a force of strength. It was about preserving myself within the power of the clan and preparing myself for what my family may need from me going forward. It was about holding fast and raising my shield to protect my family, my future, and even my own heart.

I imagine there was an unspoken belief amongst my family that I would grow out of this line of solitary thinking as I matured and came of age. As I approach my twentieth year, I realize I may not be alone forever, but I have no intention of going through life with *bad company*.

With the first bite of fish pie, I leaned back in my chair and closed my eyes. It has been a while since we had such fine fare for supper, and I wanted to savor every salty morsel of cod and tatties encased in a flaky crust on my plate.

The fishermen have clearly taken advantage of the fine weather of late and brought in a significant haul of cod for us to have such a feast. They always set aside a portion of the catch each night for smoking or salt curing to keep the clan fed during the winter months. For them to have enough fresh fish to feed the entire hall this night was an unexpected treat. We would normally reserve a meal this fine for a special occasion.

My eyes closed again as I silently praised Missus Gerrard's cooking and the gifts from a bountiful sea. I opened my eyes and looked ahead at the crowded room before me and then at the empty seats next to me.

Chewing slower now, I examined all corners of the room, searching for the familiar faces of my uncle Laird Graham MacLeod or perhaps even a hopeful sighting of my aunt Lady Margaret. After my mother's death, when I was just six, my father went to study at the University of Edinburgh and left me in their care. Surely, they must be on the way to join me. I know I am not at supper early. That would be an unexpected triumph! I am not always late, but I am *never* early.

My focus soon became the natural waves of movement and sounds within the room. Much like the sea's pulsations that surround the castle perched above the western coast of the Isle of Skye, I became adrift and entranced by the people coming in and out of the Great Hall.

In and out.

In and out.

From the steady movement of food and drink delivered to tables to the amplified voices and conversations echoing throughout the hall, the natural rhythm and pulse of the room became soothing. The appreciation for the unexpected fare heightened the noise in the room. It did not take long for me to become more focused on the sounds in the room than on my own plate.

In and out.

In and out.

Facing the Great Hall on my own was not something I have ever done before. As I snapped out of the trance the busy room had me under, I felt my cheeks grow red, staring down at the faces of my kinsmen before me. *Why am I sitting here alone?*

At that moment, I heard a small, breathless voice in the distance. A voice struggling to be heard above the conversations and booming clatter of cutlery on plates resonating off of the stone walls in the acoustic wonder that is the Great Hall of Dunmara Castle.

"Erm, excuse me! Excuse me, Mistress Alexandra!" said the soft voice, heading straight for me. His voice breaking the spell of the people, the room, and my own thoughts of sitting alone.

"Aye!" I said with a cheerful smile to the lad as I reached out to smooth his thick and tangled curls. "Hello, my wee Robbie!"

Robbie MacLeod, a boy of nine, is my cousin. I love this darling lad with all of my heart, and I cannot help but smile whenever I see him. Just a year ago, Robbie gained his post here in the castle as a messenger and errand boy for Laird Graham and Missus Gerrard. Robbie started working in the stables the summer before he turned eight. One day, the lad made a serious error by taking out an unbroken colt to impress his friends. On his boastful ride, and one he was woefully unprepared for, the lad was thrown from the horse and landed hard on the rocky ground below.

By an absolute miracle—granted by the grace of God Himself— Robbie survived the fall. We all took turns spending day and night praying at his bedside for healing, tending to his care, and giving his mother my Auntie Sarah the support she needed. Precious Robbie became our own wee bairn during this time.

But there is another reason I love this lad. Robbie has always had the most gorgeous head of thick, curly hair in the color of deepest auburn.

His mother's legacy, to be sure. As he has grown, his ginger locks have grown brighter, thicker, and even more unruly.

I challenge anyone within arm's reach of Robbie MacLeod's curls not to touch them when speaking to the boy. It is a completely involuntary response. His glorious ringlets invite you to do so. As he has grown older, he naturally dislikes the attention and affection.

The *tamin' of the locks* as we started calling it within our family cannot be stopped. Men and women alike revere Robbie's tousled red hair. Despite knowing it will make him twist and turn his head and body away from your hands in many extraordinary ways, you cannot help it. You touch his hair anyway.

"Och, stop it," he said, squirming underneath my hands and officially discharging his honorable duty. "The laird is asking for ye, cousin."

"Is he?" I asked, while trying to look around the room for the man myself. "I dinnae see him here at the head table where he should be at this hour."

Leaning in with a little laugh and a wink, I asked, "Is Laird Graham hiding in the Great Hall, lad? *Give me a hint, will ye?*"

I realized in that moment that this summons meant I was not early to supper. There was a reason I am here alone. Something else must be more important than supper this night.

Sounding a little frustrated with me now, Robbie said, "The laird is asking you to meet him upstairs in his chamber. Now, cousin!"

"Fine! I will go!"

I stood up from my chair and could see Robbie stealing bites from what I left on my plate with his fingers. "It is all yers, lad!" I said while touching his gorgeous head of hair once more. He rolled his eyes at me but had such a large mouthful of food, he could not protest my attention.

"Consider it for luck, will ye?" He cocked his head at me once, acknowledging my question, as the crumbs fell from his mouth. I leaned down and whispered in his ear, *"Do ye not think I might need some luck being summoned by Laird Graham in the middle of supper?"* I stood tall and straightened my skirts.

As I left, I touched his shoulder, facing backward from the room and said, laughing, "C'mon, lad, yer at the head table! Slow down or the entire clan will think we dinnae feed ye at all!"

I lost wee Robbie's attention the minute he fulfilled his task and set his sights on my unfinished plate. I am convinced the lad made the sign of the cross as I reached the back stairs. So, I took a deep breath, said a prayer myself, and marched ahead to answer the summons of Laird Graham of Clan MacLeod.

I walked slowly down the long hall to the laird's chamber, mostly to catch my breath from climbing two flights of stairs and out of the sudden realization that he was not alone. As I approached, I could distinctly hear several male voices on the other side of the half-open door.

I know better than to appear to be eavesdropping on a private conversation in the castle and I immediately stepped into the room to show that I was here, as summoned.

"Ye sent fer me, my laird?" I asked as I opened the door wider. I revealed that the other voices in the room belonged to my father, Alexander, and my other uncle, and youngest of the MacLeod brothers, Duncan.

This brotherly assembly startled me to my core, and I fear that I just walked into a scolding I am unprepared for.

+++

Dunmara Castle is the heart and soul of Clan MacLeod. Dunmara means *'castle by the sea,'* and despite the often moody and bitter Scottish weather that can change at any moment, the design of the castle and surrounding buildings on the grounds are as beautiful as functional against the weather, the sea, and potential threats.

Perched high above the adjacent promontory of Cairn's Point and facing the Sea of the Hebrides ahead and the Atlantic Ocean beyond, the original builders of the castle in the Sixteenth Century captured both the natural light of the outdoors while blocking the bitter sea breeze from the interior walls.

The location above the ocean on one side and surrounded by a high wall and tower on the land side, ensures Dunmara is an impenetrable fortress. Without a doubt, Dunmara Castle is an architectural wonder.

"Father?" I asked, when I saw him. He seemed frozen in place himself. The time between our last meeting has been several years and made us both uncertain if we should embrace each other.

As my mind raced, Laird Graham said with a smile, "Aye, Alexandra! Come in, lass. Join yer father and yer uncles."

Laird Graham became the laird of the clan when his father, Norman, left Skye under a cloud of controversy for other pursuits in London and died there. True to his nature, the laird has always operated from a sense of responsibility, duty, and service to the kinsmen and home he loves. He is respected and revered for his firm, but fair, leadership. The clan lands have also prospered under his time as chief. It is hard to challenge a laird that keeps you and your family protected and fed.

+++

This trio, this council of brothers, is a force to reckon with. They are a tall and imposing group. Dark-haired with blue-gray eyes, these handsome men reflect the Norse influence across the Scottish Isles. Laird Graham, being the oldest, has a beard and more gray hair, but there is no mistaking their relation.

I smiled and bowed my head slightly to the laird. Before I could speak, he said, "Close the door behind ye, Alexandra."

I followed his direction slowly, unsure of what meeting I had just walked into. As I turned to close the door, I said under my breath, *"This cannae be good."*

Staring at the door, unable to turn back around, my mind began racing over the events of the last month.

> *What could I have done to get in trouble with my father and my uncles?*
>
> *Did they find out I scolded Mean Old Mary MacAskill for being hateful to a kitchen maid?*
>
> *Did they discover I smuggled a half-empty bottle of claret from the kitchen to Cairn's Point?*

I told myself that none of these minor transgressions would warrant my father being here from Edinburgh unannounced. I let go of the door handle and turned to face all three of them, determined to accept my unknown fate head-on.

Luckily, my father could read my face and my mind. He put an end to my internal torment, saying, "All is well, Alexandra! Dinnae fash! We just want to talk with you."

"Sit, lass," said the laird, pointing to the only open chair in the room.

As I pulled my skirts beneath me and sat, I looked each of them directly in the eye for a clue. The silence—which was only a few seconds—was almost unbearable. I wrenched my mouth to bite the inside of my lip, signaling my nervous uncertainty once again for all to see. My face always betrays my thinking.

Finally, the laird raised his glass and said with an enormous smile, "To Alexandra Flora MacLeod, my beloved niece… and as of this day… my heir and the next Chief of Clan MacLeod."

All three stood proudly with their glasses and said in unison, *"Sláinte mhath!"*

I looked up at each of them, wide-eyed—and certainly wide-mouthed—with confusion. I stood up with them slowly to receive this moment that was still not clear to me. Before I could question them, my father shoved a glass of whisky in my hand and smiled while placing his arm around my shoulders. He looked from me to each of his brothers, beaming with pride.

"What… is… happening?" I asked through my forced smile as I slowly brought the glass to my lips.

"Why is her first response always a question?" Duncan asked with a nudge to my father's ribs. They clinked their glasses and took another sip, laughing at my expense. I cocked my head and gave them all a sideways look of annoyance, not unlike the one Robbie gave me just moments ago at this family joke—this tedious game.

Before I could tell them off, as I truly wished, the laird spoke again, "My brothers and I have much to tell ye, lass."

+++

TWO
Heir Apparent

Laird Graham walked in front of his desk, leaned back on its edge, and stared at me.

"My dear, ye already ken how much Lady Margaret and I love ye."

We have always talked of family bonds and responsibility to the clan and each other, but I am not sure how often *love* came up in our conversations.

I answered him quickly, "I do, sir!" I looked at my father, who nodded for me to continue speaking. "Erm, I hope ye ken that I feel the same. Ye and Lady Margaret have provided fer my care, protection, and education these many years since my... since my father went away."

I glanced at my father again for reassurance. I almost said, *since my father left me,* which, while true, was not a fair response. He is fulfilling his own duty to the clan in Edinburgh. Thankfully, I caught my words before saying them aloud.

"Every day, I become more and more aware of what a gift education is… especially as a woman."

I had to take a pause on this point as much as it pained me. I gathered myself and said, with my glass held before me, "I can speak for my father when I say that we are both grateful for what ye and our beloved Lady Margaret, have done fer me… and *my future*."

Everyone raised their glass and drank one more sip in honor of the mention of Lady Margaret. She has been battling sick headaches for many months and is confined to her bedchamber most of the time. The light and sound of the castle became too much for her to bear. I visit her when she can bear to have company in her darkened room, where often only soft whispers and prayers are spoken. On the occasion she has a good day, she will venture out of her chamber, but those days have become rare.

This moment was a point of reverence for an incredible woman who has served her husband, the clan, and me with honor and grace. She is the only mother I have ever truly known. I can see the brief smile of approval on my father's face at my response and the respect it afforded both my aunt and uncle for their guardianship over the last fourteen years.

My uncle responded, "That is precisely what this is about—*the future*. Ye have proven yer own ability to lead with a natural sense of diplomacy and fairness. Ye also understand and appreciate the inner workings—and dare I say, the politics of the castle. More than that, I believe yer kind heart along with yer keen mind will carry Clan MacLeod forward."

There was a silent pause in the room on these words and I looked around in case there was more to say. With all eyes on me, I spoke up,

"Ye honor me, but… I still dinnae understand. Why me? Why not one of yer brothers or…"

"It is a fair question, lass. I have been working with my brothers on this fer many months now," he said, looking at each of them respectfully, acknowledging their silent agreement one-by-one, as he walked back to his chair behind the large wooden desk.

"We have been talking about how to find the best path forward fer the clan in these changing times." His tone turned serious as he stared ahead. It was as if we were listening to his inner thoughts. "We need new thinking. I believe we, here on Skye, are facing what our Highland brothers and sisters have endured over these last few years. We need to preserve what we can, change what we need to, and help our kinsmen make the best choice fer themselves and their families. Choices that may, in fact, take them away from Skye or even from Scotland."

He continued, leaning back in his chair, now looking at each of us, "I believe ye can help me here, Alexandra. I believe ye can help us all! However, I will be honest and tell ye that if we dinnae get this right, I am not certain how long we can maintain our place here. We are going to have to rethink how to manage our lands, support our people, and pay our increasing taxes to the Crown. If we cannae, there may be a time we have to let it all go." We looked at each other with concern at his words. "Is that not the ultimate irony when ye think about that possibility of letting go of all we know and hold dear against the clan motto of *Hold Fast?*"

We all paused and said nothing. Each of us sipped our dram at the thought of letting go. And for me, I had the silent hope that I will never have to make such a decision for Clan MacLeod.

He continued, "If that unfortunate time comes, and I pray to God it doesna, I want it to be with compassion fer the families under our care and the lands we inhabit. Either way, it will take a strong and compassionate leader to guide the way."

"But again, why me? How is it even possible? I am…" I said, rethinking my words for a second. "I am not yer daughter. I am… a woman, and I am not yet twenty years of age."

Laird Graham would not let me diminish myself by noting my sex or my age and ignored my question. I admired him all the more for it.

"It is simple. I have no direct heirs of my own."

"I still…" I said as I started to ask the same question again. He did not let me finish and cut me off abruptly.

"I am not well, lass," he said, looking into my eyes. The entire room shifted beneath my feet. I cannot imagine both my aunt and uncle being unwell at the same time.

I blinked back the tears immediately forming in my eyes on his words, as I moved to the edge of my seat and said, "I didna ken. I…"

"None of us are guaranteed another day in this life and I am not looking to leave this world any time soon. Ye ken what Father Bruce teaches us."

"Aye, Father Bruce says that we should be grateful for each day we are on this Earth and live a life that we can be proud of."

"That is right. Ye, ken I trust my brothers completely. I believe if we do this right, and we do this *together as a family*, we can try to protect our lands and the clan for the generations to come. Yer father and uncle believe the same. So much so that they are not contending for the position themselves. That should tell ye something, Alexandra! We all believe in ye."

After centuries of brothers, cousins, and rivals battling each other for power and control of Clan MacLeod, this is a unique and unexpected event. I thought about his words—the *brothers are not contending for the role themselves*. Three brothers, serving as a unified front, and supporting a young woman to lead is nothing short of remarkable.

"I ken more than anyone what I am asking of ye, and the responsibility can be a burden, to be sure. It takes a special person to take such a task on. I did so out of necessity when our father left Skye, and I have had the support and counsel of my brothers and my beloved wife along the way. I have also had yer support and counsel, lass, and it has made all the difference in the world!"

I am certain that despite the tears forming in my eyes and the returned smile, I still looked confused. He reassured me, "Aye m'dear, ye have been a valuable partner. Ye didna realize, but ye have not just transcribed the decisions over the last year, but have also provided guidance on those decisions. Ye helped me review the complaints in the Great Hall and ye gave me a new perspective on how the decisions we make an impact the men, women, and children on our clan lands."

I nodded silently, now recollecting the memories of our discussions here in this very chamber. I can see now that our conversations were part of my education. While I was building my relationship with Laird Graham, he was also guiding and testing my ability as a leader.

"My ask is that ye no longer just advise me here in this chamber, but that ye also stand by my side in the Great Hall from this moment on," he said. "The entire clan will see that we are reviewing and providing judgment and direction *together*. We must move quickly. I want to go before the Fine tomorrow and assuming we have an agreement, we can announce to the rest of the clan in tomorrow's Great Hall."

The Fine—the *daoine uaisle* in Gaelic—is essentially the clan gentry. My eyes welled up with tears at both the responsibility before me and the validation that I was worthy, as each man—men I love and respect—nodded to me in support.

I breathed in deeply and raised my head proudly and said, "I will do what ye ask of me, my laird. I will serve Clan MacLeod with the same honor, faith, and conviction ye have for the rest of my days."

+++

The ceremony and celebration of the decision was fleeting. Laird Graham smiled and spoke quickly of action. "Time is of the essence here, brothers. Tomorrow is the last Great Hall before the summer lads arrive and I need to clear this before we have to put all of our focus on the shearing. We have barely had a moment of rest from the lambing."

"Aye," Duncan and my father agreed in unison.

"I can defend my choice, but we ken well enough that there will be at least three areas where we will get the most resistance. I believe these are some same questions ye had yourself, Alexandra. First, ye are not my child. Alexander has helped here by giving me official guardianship under Scottish law from this day forward."

I gave my father an immediate look of shock at this, but he reassured me directly by winking at me, "You ken I am your father, lass. Nothing changes that. We simply acknowledged the fact that I have been in Edinburgh and away from Dunmara for some time. In fact, we should have done this long ago as Laird Graham and Lady Margaret have fulfilled the role as guardians for nearly fourteen years in my absence. Now, we are just making it legal."

15

"If ye will excuse me, and I am sorry to ask this uncle," I said, looking directly at the laird and then back at my father, "and when he dies?"

"Again, I will always be your true father, but upon the laird's death your guardianship will transfer to Duncan until ye turn twenty-one." He then he answered the question I had in my mind before I could ask it. "It will never come back to me, lass."

I could tell with these words he felt the same twinge of loss and separation that I did. My heart was in my throat. I stared at him with the uncertainty of what I was hearing. Before I could protest or react, Father quickly reinforced his own position with a smile, "I know what you are thinking, Alexandra. We need this to protect you under the law. It changes nothing between us and when you reach twenty-one, you will have no need of a guardian."

The laird continued, "I believe the second objection will focus on ye being a young woman. Ye noted this yerself. Clan MacLeod has not had a woman serve as chief since our tenth... Mary, and that was over five-hundred years ago. There are many in the clan who still believe in the old war chief mentality and dinnae believe a woman can lead men."

My father finished his brother's thought, "Or at least, dinnae want to give a woman *the power* to lead men—in war or in their daily life."

Duncan then added, "A woman in power can be seen as a threat to them... to what they ken."

I opened my mouth to argue that the men before me were instilling me with anything but confidence, but before I could, Laird Graham said, "Ye have to be honest with yerself here, Alexandra. This is the reality of the world we are in and the sooner ye accept that the hearts and minds of men are not always as open and accepting as yer own, the better off ye will be. By understanding the foundation of the objection, ye can help counter it in yer actions and words. Do ye understand?"

"Aye," I said, though in my heart I was already ready for the fight to challenge the narrow expectations confining women to their place. I will be damned if my being a woman would hold me back from serving my family. While belligerent and rebellious on one hand, I can see the ask before me for what it is—a chance to serve and not from the back or in the shadows. Not just in a support role. A true leader.

"And finally, I believe the biggest objection will be that yer unmarried, as that puts ye and the clan at risk."

Startled by this, I blurted out innocently, "At risk of *what*?"

My father stepped in to explain. "First, by naming you heir, you will be at risk of unwelcome and unworthy suitors—inside and outside the clan—who may see an advantageous marriage as the method to gain property and power they could not have otherwise. Any suitor may be a threat to you, and your personal risk becomes a risk to the entire clan. You can expect that those with an objection will note this straight away."

"Well, ye all seem to have thought all of this out," I said, leaning back in my chair and sounding somewhat resigned to my status as the unmarried heir posing risks to her own clan. I knew for a fact that none of these men were going to let me sulk my way through this discussion. We sat silently as they all waited for me to say something.

Finally, looking up from the thoughts lingering at the bottom of my glass, I said, "Erm, I have one more question."

Duncan drained the last of his glass on my words and said, clearly annoyed, "Of course ye do!"

I would not give him the satisfaction of a look or response on his reprimand and said, directly to my father, our own MacLeod legal counsel.

"To yer point, Father, what if I marry? Do I lose Dunmara Castle and the clan lands? Do I lose everything because I am a woman?"

They all looked at each other in silence and I leaned back in my chair, arms folded, certain that I had confounded them all with this simple question. When the silence lasted a little too long, I could not help but lash out. "Och! I get it! Ye all believe that I could not *possibly find a man to marry me!*"

It is completely ironic that I have fought against the confines of marriage for so long, and suddenly seemed challenged by those that knew me best for thinking I *could not* marry. This response was not rational, and I am certain was not inspiring much confidence in the choice these three brothers just made. I am not sure I could sink deeper in my chair, but I tried while forming the distinct and insolent pout these poor gentlemen have seen more than once.

+++

Duncan is the only one in the council of brothers who will not let me behave like a petulant child for very long. He has no patience for sulking and pouting and never refrained from jerking me out of a foul mood or disrespectful temperament when needed.

Duncan is only ten years older than me. In some ways, we have grown up together, and he has always been honest with me. I see Duncan's love and care for me, much like my own devotion to wee Robbie. Like Missus Gerrard, Duncan is a massive gossip. He knows everyone and everything. But ultimately, he is a man of principle who

18

values family and loyalty above anything else. He has fought hard in his life. That sense of duty, coupled with his intensely close relationship with his brothers, means that he loves and protects me as his own. He always has.

He stepped forward to me and spoke directly, "No one is questioning whether ye *could* marry. We have looked at this from all angles. We have a draft marriage contract to appease any naysayers in the room tomorrow just in case we need it."

"Ye have a *what*!?" I said, as I stood up in immediate protest, right in his face.

"Hold on, lass," he continued while gently guiding me back to my chair by my shoulder.

"Ye can stop talking now, uncle," I said disrespectfully, with my frustration and belligerence on full display for the entire room. He ignored my immature response and walked away from me with a smirk, grabbing his glass and filling it again. I could see the look of disapproval on my father's face.

Though it took all I had to say the words, I immediately corrected myself with a new tone of contrition, "*I apologize*. Please explain it to me. I just dinnae understand."

"The document has no name on it but yers, Alexandra. We just want to have in case we need to show that Laird Graham, or upon his death, his brothers—myself and Alexander—if still living, will have to approve who ye can marry. The document also includes requirements on what yer betrothed can and cannae gain with such a union, as that union is not just with ye, but with the entire clan."

My father smiled at me reassuringly and said, "This is simply a precaution as we expect the Fine to ask the same question you just did, and we want to show that we are protecting Dunmara Castle and the clan lands to the best of our ability under the law. Any match would have to be beneficial to the clan, and the provisions set forth would limit undue, outside influence. Do you understand, lass?"

"I do. But if I ever marry, and I am not saying I will, mind! Will I have any say in who I wed, or will ye force me into marriage? Perhaps one ye all deem—as ye said—beneficial or advantageous to the clan?"

My father walked to me and put my face in both of his hands and kissed me on the forehead, as he always has. Since I was a wee bairn, his gentle forehead kisses brought me comfort and immediately calmed me. I closed my eyes and thought about all the kisses he had given me over my life and how I have dearly missed them in his absence.

"My dear lass, no one will force you into a marriage you dinnae want. I can speak for my brothers when I say that as long as we are alive, we will advise and counsel on what is best for the clan *and* for you. But, my daughter, you will have the final say on who you marry—or as you say—if you marry at all."

He walked away from me and said as he looked out of the window to the sea before us, "I will say I hope that you will find someone you love and one who is deserving of that love. I pray, every day, that you find what I had with your beloved mother. *I loved her so!*"

I felt ashamed for fighting and bringing sadness back to my father. I now understand the depth of his love and that of my uncles. They only want the best for me, even if I was uncertain I wanted it myself. Even if I was uncertain, I *deserved* it myself.

I walked to him and wrapped my arms around him and said, "Och, Father, I love ye so much for these words. But that does not answer my original question. If I marry, will everything I have become my husband's because I am a woman?"

"We will try to keep everything secured and in MacLeod hands to the best of our ability and under the law. We will want to ensure that we have our papers in order so, I have declared that the office of Master Campbell Forbes, Esquire in Edinburgh, will follow through on the contract when that time comes. Campbell is my most trusted friend and advocate and will see that you and the clan are well cared for."

In some ways, I thought if he said yes, that would solidify my already declared intent to not marry. I would never want to put the clan at risk. But he did not. Then I asked, "So, Father, I must ask this… when ye die? Will I also not be *yer* heir?"

"Ah, that is the best of it, lass," he said, beaming again with his lawful pride. "I have set up a separate trust under the supervision of your guardians until you turn twenty-one. At that age, the trust will entitle you to the money and property that I *choose* to leave to you."

He continued in his education of a trust, "As long as I am alive, you will have an annual allowance. This is in line with what I have provided Laird Graham for your care these many years in my absence. The difference is that at twenty-one, you will decide how to use that money for yourself. I have also set aside some personal property that will be yours upon my death, and what you choose to keep is yours. If you sell anything, the proceeds go to you directly."

"As a woman, I can have such a thing?"

"Ye can!" he said. "Scottish law is very generous to women in some areas, and I can designate ye as the beneficiary of my estate, as I have no male heirs of my own."

Laird Graham took the meeting back, and said, "If we may proceed, brothers. There is a small formality of process here and fer this we will need the *uisge beatha*."

The Gaelic *uisge beatha*, *'water of life'* means the whisky, but in this case, the laird stood up and replaced his glass with the ancient, ceremonial, silver quaich from the shelf behind him.

I knew this process must be serious for Laird Graham to be speaking Gaelic and grabbing the whisky himself. On most occasions, Duncan is in charge of the *uisge beatha*. But the quaich meant he was going to make us swear an oath. This family discussion was about to become formal and one that I will have to record in the ledger.

"Alexandra Flora MacLeod, I will ask ye this only once. As my heir, will ye commit to lead Clan MacLeod into the future? I cannae promise it will be easy. In fact, I believe ye will navigate challenges none before ye have. But ye have my full support fer the rest of my days. I believe in ye, as do each of my brothers standing here. What say ye, lass?"

"Ye have my personal commitment, my laird. I will do what ye ask of me to the best of my ability in honor of the clan," I said, taking the quaich from his hands, raising it to my lips and sipping in tribute. After I agreed, I handed the vessel back, and we all sat in brief silence before he began the ceremony for the council of brothers.

"My brother, Alexander Ewan MacLeod, I ask ye as the true father of Alexandra that ye will provide the legal counsel, instruction, and guidance she will need fer the rest of yer days. That ye will protect her and the clan under the law of the land. Will ye do this fer me, fer your daughter, and fer Clan MacLeod?"

"You have my solemn pledge, my brother, my laird, and my daughter," he said, smiling at Laird Graham and then to me before taking his sip.

The laird continued as he refilled the quaich, "My brother, Duncan Baird MacLeod. While the role of *war chief* is no longer needed in this time, I ask ye as Alexandra's uncle to be vigilant and see to her protection and safety fer the rest of yer days. Will ye do this fer me, fer her, and fer Clan MacLeod?"

"Ye have my solemn pledge, my brother, and my laird," he said mirroring the same gestures as my father, though he chose not to sip the whisky. True to form, he emptied the entire thing.

"Yer pledge to me, brothers—and to our daughter of Clan MacLeod—is received and is binding. Now, we just need to have the approval of the Fine."

Looking tired now, the laird said to me, "We will have to make our intentions known tomorrow. I have summoned all members of the Fine to meet prior to the Great Hall. Ye will need to be prepared to say to them why ye will take on this ask before we can announce it to the clan after. We also need to prepare for the expected objections. I am certain yer father and uncle will give ye their thoughts on that. Meet me here at midday tomorrow to preview the notices and actions. Ye will now stand with me in the review of each item in front of the room to show yer involvement and leadership on the decisions passed. I must leave ye all fer now."

He headed to the door slowly as the events of the day clearly made him wearisome. I moved to stand in front of him, blocking his retreat to the comfort of his warm bed. I bowed my head in reverence and said, "I thank ye for yer belief in me and for giving me this honor, sir. I intend to make ye proud. I intend to make this council of brothers proud."

"I would expect nothing less from ye, my darlin' lass," he said as he kissed me tenderly on the cheek. "That is why ye are our choice for this important task."

He walked past me and out the door as I placed my fingers on the still-wet spot of affection he left on my cheek. I had not noticed it before now, but he was moving slower. Perhaps it is just the knowing that he was unwell that it looked like he was bone-weary, but I stood watching this giant of a man, this man who has meant so much to me, shrink before me as he faded into the dark shadows of the stairs.

THREE
Sprigs Of Juniper

I was not having it! Once the laird walked out of the room, I spun around to the remaining brothers, who I no longer needed to be formal with.

"Ye could not give me some *warning*?" I said, scolding them both.

Duncan did not give me a moment to argue and said, "Grab the whisky lass, we need to write yer remarks."

He moved behind Laird Graham's desk, took the quill, paper, and opened the ink well to get started right away. Before I could act on the request or speak again, my father already gathered our original glasses and a new whisky bottle in his hands.

"Wait just one second! I have questions and ye two will answer them before we write a single word!" I quickly grabbed the bottle from Father's hand and intentionally held it out of his reach. I am certain that the anticipation of another pour will buy me at least a moment of their attention.

"What just happened here?" I asked with my eyes directed at my father first. "Ye returned to Dunmara without any notice... only to give me up?"

Normally, the exchange of letters would have preceded his visit, sharing our excitement at connecting again. I was now sulking like a child with the genuine pain and sadness at not knowing that he was going to be here.

"No! I wanted to surprise you, lass," he said, laughing. He placed the glasses on the desk and grabbed my hands for emphasis, and said, "I am—and always will be—your father and you will always be my own wee bairn. This is nothing more than a legal maneuver to ensure that all the documents are in place to secure your rights as the heir to the laird and to be chief of the clan. With Graham unwell and no direct line of succession, the clan lands are at risk. Duncan and I make no claim here against those that think they do. There are also many who will not want a woman as clan chief. We have called upon yer reputation and the letter of the law to combat these objections. That was my role here—ensuring you and the clan—are protected—now and in the future."

"I understand."

"And just so we are clear on this point, this is not about *us*, or the brothers *rejecting* something," he said, pointing to Duncan and himself. "You earned this because of your own capability and talents. I am proud of you, lass!"

"I thank ye both. I do."

"Also, I want to reiterate what we said about the marriage contract, Alexandra."

"Aye, *please!*" I said with a shaky voice. "Because ye ken that made me especially nervous!"

"I told my brothers that it would cause you the most heartache," he said as he squeezed my hands tighter. "As Duncan said before, the draft of the contract is blank except for your name. Only Laird Graham or Duncan can approve the name of the betrothed. If I am still living, I also have a say. While not a legal requirement, I trust my brothers will allow me to provide counsel. All brothers who are living at the time will essentially approve any union."

"*Do I get a say at some point?*" said, still in an argumentative sulk.

Before he answered me, Duncan, either annoyed by my behavior, the constant repetition of questions, or simply the lack of whisky in his glass, brought us back to the task at hand.

"*Chriiiisssttt!* Aye, Alexandra! Tomorrow is upon us, brother. We need to move forward or none of us will sleep tonight."

I released the whisky bottle and with a quick refresh of the glasses, we continued on our task. As we raised our glasses at the start, I said, "I hope ye brothers live forever and I never have to marry!"

+++

I finally made it to my bedchamber. Outside my window was the blue glow of morning's first light, with the first subtle flecks of orange sunlight dancing across the water. I have always loved the view from my room and often sit within the window nook to stare across the sea to the horizon and listen to the waves on the rocks below. I take strength and peace from the sea, and hope that I can channel the calm I feel now in the hours ahead.

Between the events of the previous evening and the anticipation of the Great Hall, I tossed and turned. On a regular night, this would not be any different. I have always been a restless sleeper. This morning, I surrendered at some point, grabbed my robe, and sat on the floor in front of the fire.

One day, I will be Lady MacLeod.

One day, I will be Chief of Clan MacLeod.

Both are honored and sacred roles. As I thought about what was ahead this day, the expected reaction to the announcement tonight of a young woman as heir scares me more than the responsibility of the role itself.

I thought about Duncan's advice. He said plainly to me in a tone of seriousness that I have not heard very often from him that I had to remain calm in the face of objections. He looked me in the eye and said, *"Men with thwarted ambitions can be a danger. Dinnae give in to yer own emotions and inclinations to fight 'em, lass!"*

His lesson was an important one. I am uncertain what disturbed me more—the idea of *men with thwarted ambitions,* or the pressure to keep my face and reactions from reflecting my inner thoughts. This has proven to be difficult to manage on more than one occasion.

This *legal maneuver* now seems more political and personal than I understood from our family meeting the night before. There may be more to this plan of succession than the brothers are telling me. But I cannot worry about that now. I have to trust that those who have loved and protected me my entire life will not only help me succeed, but keep me safe. I need the support of the council of brothers now, more than ever.

+++

I stayed in my bed for most of the day and only walked out of my room briefly to join the laird at midday, as planned, to discuss the items for review in the Great Hall.

"Ye ken that we have items for the Great Hall tonight, but lass before ye transcribe the list. I want to talk with ye about the meeting with the Fine." Much like Duncan the evening before, his manner turned serious, and I listened to his direction intently. He set himself on the corner of his desk and looked at me.

"I ken we talked about the objections to expect and that yer father and Duncan talked with ye about keeping yer reactions—yer emotions—in check."

His reminders of this lesson told me that all the brothers are a little more concerned about my behavior being an issue this night. "Aye, they did, sir. I understand that showing my reaction on my face or speaking up could bring about even more objections, as members of the Fine may see me as insolent, therefore showing that I am not deserving of the honor."

"That is correct, lass. As I expect the objections from men in the family, we must allow them to be heard and respected for the role that they have—as the gentry of our clan—even if we might disagree with their choice of words or their tone."

"I understand, sir. No matter what they say about me, I will not disrespect ye or the clan. *I promise!*"

"My ask for this self-control continues into the Great Hall. The clan will accept the decision of the Fine and not reject it. But I cannae predict how the room will react on the announcement, and ye need to be prepared for all manner of response, particularly from some men in the room."

"I understand. Even if I have to bite my lip for two hours, I willna fail ye."

"Then this matter is settled, lass. We have an understanding," he said with a slight smile and a tap on my shoulder. The laird crossed around his desk and sat down for the items before the Great Hall.

I picked up the quill and transcribed the plan as expected. We discussed each item together. Outside of my announcement, it was mostly tenant notices. I expected both of our speeches this night would refer to the increasing migrations from MacLeod lands in favor of life in the cities or the colonies, and the items tonight were proving this out with real examples of the change happening before the clan.

Great Hall of Dunmara Castle—30 May 1766

- **Announcement:** *Master Gordon MacClure is vacating his post in the Forge, to join his brother in the colony of North Carolina.*
- **Announcement:** *Master Caleb Norman, his wife Elise, and their two children are vacating Glen Heath croft, to start a new life in Glasgow city.*
- **Announcement:** *Master Geordie MacAskill and his wife Charlotte, are vacating Hawthorn croft, to start a new life in Glasgow city.*
- **Announcement:** *Pending approval from the Fine prior, announcement of Alexandra Flora MacLeod as heir to Laird Graham MacLeod and the next chief of Clan MacLeod upon his death.*

I said, "I notice that the Hawthorn and Glen Heath crofts are close to each other. Do ye think the Norman's and the MacAskill's coordinated their departure?"

"I suspect they did."

"So are we just landlords, sir? Are we beholden completely to the tenants' rents on our lands or do we think about income more in the goods and services these clan lands offer?"

"Yer a fast learner, lass! It is a bit of both. First, we need to look at the map to see what a vacancy of these crofts will do to the lands, the herds, and the security of the castle or borders. This is in addition to accounting for lost rents to our own coffers."

The map, sitting atop another table in the laird's chamber, was a crude depiction of the castle grounds, all the crofts, and border checkpoints that encompass the whole of MacLeod lands. It includes on the side the names of the people, where they live, their responsibility to the clan, and their annual rent. Maintained regularly, the laird and estate factor can see the clan lands before them whenever they need.

"Sometimes, a vacancy can be a problem. In those cases, lairds have denied the request to vacate."

"Ye can do that?" I asked, astonished that someone would stand in the way of the personal happiness of another. I cannot imagine living anywhere other than Dunmara Castle, Skye, or even neighboring Dunmara Village. This land is my home. Many years ago, the thought of joining my father in Edinburgh crossed my mind, but I never left. I am happy here. This is where I belong.

"Aye, ye can," he said, continuing to educate me. "But I could never stop someone unless we were at war, or the change would cause undue harm to others. In those cases, I would work with them to delay—not deny—their departure." I nodded my head in agreement with his kind approach, should I need to do the same. It was fair.

"I do not want to assume the risk of a vacancy, but there is also the risk of having someone on yer lands that doesna want to be there. Ye have to weigh *all* the risks as chief, Alexandra. Ye can also take the time to move families to fill the gaps. That may mean giving a growing family more room with a larger croft or moving kinsman, who are doing well by giving them greater responsibility and larger herds."

"Ye and yer estate factor have to keep the map current, lass," he said, and I nodded in agreement. "This will now be yer responsibility with Auld Knox, do ye ken?"

"Aye," I said, while thinking that this ancient map and system of accounting for rents looks incredibly complicated. I was already thinking of ways to possibly simplify it.

"Knox is assuming this responsibility as estate factor and will learn with ye. I believe he will have to turn over the stables to another to manage this fully at some point."

I started thinking that it would be hard for Auld Knox to lose the stables he loved to another. The laird read my thoughts and said, "He is thinking the same thing ye are—how he can try to do both."

"Somehow, I cannae think about Auld Knox being anywhere but his stables, sir." We nodded in agreement. Knox is going to have to think about his changing role and the future at the same time I do.

"I hope our MacLeod kinsman can find what they are looking for elsewhere. I pray they do, in fact. It would be a benefit to the clan for them to be successful wherever they go, would it not?"

"Aye, lass. It verra well could."

I ran back to my room the minute we finished, and before my nerves got the best of me. The Great Hall had been humming all day. More so than usual. It was as if someone had given the entire clan a preview of the topics this evening. I became more and more anxious. I tried not to look down into the room from the balcony every ten minutes. But, of course, that is *exactly* what I did!

On an afternoon return, when the room was bustling before supper, I slammed the door behind me and jumped on my bed. With my head buried in my linens, I screamed, *"Och! I dinnae want to do this!"*

"Alexandra… get up, lass!"

I lifted my head to see Missus Gerrard standing next to my large wardrobe. Missus Maggie Gerrard, an Irish woman, runs the household at Dunmara Castle. That includes the kitchen, bakehouses, and every other aspect of the household within the walls of the castle—including me. She is married to Auld Knox Gerrard, the stable master and new estate factor.

I am convinced that the woman does not sleep, and it is a known fact that she has many eyes and spies throughout the grounds. She knows everything that happens within the castle walls—and out. Occasionally, she likes to share this knowledge, but we do not dare call it *gossip*.

This day, she did not have the time or the patience to let me wallow in self-pity or insecurities, but I could see she was not just admonishing me but beaming with pride. Behind her, hanging off the mirrored door of the chest, was the most beautiful dress I had ever seen.

The dark blue velvet top had a regal high collar at the back of the neck on top of a gray wool skirt, with thin blue plaid lines complimenting the bodice.

I jumped up and gave Missus Gerard an enthusiastic hug. I touched every stitch and seam as I asked, "Where did this beauty come from? It is stunning!"

"'Tis," she said with a slight pause as she turned from the dress to me, "as are ye, lass. I ken this blue will complement yer beautiful brown hair and eyes! I cannae wait to see ye in it."

"I am not sure I deserve such a fine garment, madam, but I thank ye just the same. *How...?*"

"Ye have grown into a fine young woman! Yer father and uncles are so proud, and I ken that Lady Margaret..." she said and paused in a moment of reverence with her kerchief to her nose as if to hold back a tear. "She ordered that we make the new dress for ye on this occasion, and she would smile at the sight of ye!"

"Then I must get dressed quickly so that we can show her this finery before going down to the Great Hall."

"Aye! She would love that, lass!"

"I can clean and dress myself, though ye might need to tighten the laces for me. But find out if we can visit Lady Margaret, say, in about twenty minutes?"

"Let me see what I can do!"

I smiled as she left the room, and I started undressing immediately. I ran my hands over the dress once more. The gift that Missus Gerrard delivered today will make me look every bit of the lady I am about to become.

+++

I barely had the dress on when Missus Gerrard returned to my bedchamber. Lady Margaret can see us, but we need to go now. She was tired and expecting Father Bruce for her nightly prayers.

The ritual of nightly prayer had become an incredible comfort to her. Despite the herbs and tinctures from Master Morrison, who practiced the art of healing at Dunmara Castle and the village, her greatest relief came from her darkened room, soft whispers, and nightly prayer.

Father Bruce has been a constant comfort for Lady Margaret, and we do not want to interrupt their nightly ritual. We set out quickly. Missus Gerrard tightened my laces, and I put up my dark, tangled curls as we walked together across the upper halls to the lady's bedchamber.

The door was open for us, and we walked right in a little out of breath. Lady Margaret was propped up on her pillows, waiting for us. She seemed so frail, but lit up the minute we walked in the room. I ran for her embrace immediately.

"Och, my lady," I whispered as I kissed her multiple times on the cheek and grabbed her cold, frail hands. *"This dress is bonnie! I cannae thank ye and Missus Gerrard enough. It is perfect! Absolutely perfect!"*

She looked at me and touched my cheek before brushing a wayward curl from my face. "My dear lass, how did ye grow up so fast? Ye look so beautiful." We smiled at each other, and I felt the color rise in my cheeks. I do not think anyone other than my father had ever called me beautiful before.

"Stand up! Stand up! I want to see ye and the fine dress, lass."

I stood up and spun around so she could see the amazing velvet and woolen handiwork she commissioned, and Missus Gerrard immediately set to finishing tightening the laces behind me so that it fit perfectly.

"Alexandra, bring me the jewelry box from the chest there."

I have always admired Lady Margaret's heavily carved wooden jewelry box. When I was younger, I would sit on the edge of her bed and watch her get ready for important visitors or events by pulling out some sort of magic from this box. She rarely wore more than her wedding ring every day, so when she added new sparkle and shine, it transformed her from my Lady Margaret into the Lady MacLeod. The box itself seemed ancient and tonight it revealed a silver broach.

"This is an important night, and this bonnie dress is missing something," she said as she handed the broach to Missus Gerrard. "Will ye help pin this on the lass?"

I beamed with pride that my aunt would let me wear such an important piece representing our family and clan. The broach design was a simple silver circle. The bottom part was thicker than the top and engraved with the MacLeod clan motto, *Hold Fast'* surrounded on both sides by sprigs of juniper. There was a small, but perfect Scottish pearl at the top.

"Och! Thank ye, Lady Margaret!" The dress already made me feel grown, but now the broach makes me feel sophisticated. We smiled at each other for a moment as I thought about how she was reinforcing the confidence I sorely needed this night. I ran straight for the mirror and admired the shine and sentiment now displayed on my chest.

"This is my gift to ye this night. One day, ye will be the Lady MacLeod and will have need of the broach."

Her generosity touched me. Lady Margaret was not just letting me borrow her broach, she was passing me a mantle. She was preparing me to be the next Lady MacLeod. I wanted to tell her in that very moment how I wished she could be there with us tonight as a family, but I did not have the words. She was clearly tiring from this brief visit, so I swallowed my tears and returned to her.

"Wish me luck!" I said as I kissed her again on the cheek. With resignation of my limitations in this area and a slight pout, I continued, "According to the MacLeod brothers, I must not to show *too much emotion* tonight."

"That *is* a tough ask for ye, lass!" she said with a slight wink.

"Ye ken me well!" I said, giving her a side glance and said with all the drama I could muster, "Perhaps I need more than luck, my lady. Please *pray* for me this night!"

Just then, Father Bruce walked through the open door for his scheduled evening prayer session with Lady Margaret. I threw my hands up in the air and said, "There is my salvation now! I asked for prayer and Christ Himself sent me Father Bruce!"

The poor man looked confused as he walked into a room of three women laughing hysterically, but as quietly as we could. He stopped dead in his tracks in front of the door, unsure how he should proceed.

Father Bruce has served Clan MacLeod for generations. The man is revered by all in the family, as so many have grown up with him. In times of worry or doubt, Father Bruce brings peace and calm to all who meet him. He is a man of few words, but when he speaks, his words are powerful. He has a standard line to offer comfort in times of trouble or worry: *If ye have peace in yer heart, this trial is a minor inconvenience.* It was not meant to diminish emotion, but was about knowing how faith can carry you through life's unexpected hardships.

"I am so sorry," I said, trying to hush my tone back to a soft whisper after such a loud exchange of laughter.

Lady Margaret whispered, "Come in, Father. Alexandra and Missus Gerrard were just providing me some much-needed entertainment this evening."

She turned to me, grabbed my hand once more, and said, "Go, my dear lass, and show Clan MacLeod who ye are and that ye are ready to lead!"

I nodded in receipt of her direction, kissed her hand, and walked away. I said on my way out the door, "Pray for me, Father Bruce."

"I pray for ye every day, lass," he said in all the earnest reassurance of his role. I thought for a moment what a comfort his prayers were.

"Well, if ye and Lady Margaret could also pray for my face, that is also needed this night," I said, bringing laughter back to the women in the room.

"Aye, come now, lass. We will leave ye to yer prayers, Lady Margaret," Missus Gerrard said, grabbing me by the arm to usher me out of the bedchamber.

I turned back to her from the hall, "I am sure my uncles will let ye ken if the prayers worked, my lady. Goodnight!"

Our shared laughter faded as we progressed down the hall. Neither of us could speak the words, but I know we both wondered how we could ever let Lady Margaret go. I held Missus Gerrard's hand all the way back to my room for strength, and she held mine.

+++

My father met me at the bottom of the stairs to the Great Hall. I stood on the last step and looked down at him. He smiled, brought his hand to his heart, and said, "I am struck each time I see you, lass. You are the absolute bonnie image of your mother."

I smiled and immediately rebuffed the compliment and nervously started running my hands over my skirts. "This is all because of the magic Lady Margaret imagined and Missus Gerrard conjured with her handiwork. The dress is beautiful, is it not?"

"'Tis," as he nodded in agreement. As he held my hand out to admire the dress from afar. He pulled a sprig of juniper out of his pocket and placed it behind the MacLeod broach on my chest. Juniper is our clan badge and looked as fine against the blue velvet as it would have on our old plaid sash or a man's cap.

"This broach was my mother's, and I always loved it."

I smiled at him, unaware of the history of the family broach, and immediately wanted to know more. He placed his arm out for me to take for the walk straight to the small dining room off of the Great Hall. We used the room only for formal meals when important guests visited the castle, and for meetings with the Fine.

Father and I were the last to arrive and quickly took our place at the front of the room. Standing to the right of the laird was first my father, then my uncle Duncan, and me. I raised my head, squared my shoulders, and waited for Laird Graham to speak.

FOUR
Ghosts Amongst The Ruins

Our assembled presence was a signal for the Fine to come to order. This was a small audience, seated around the table quickly became quiet in anticipation of the laird's remarks and what could have required this assembly before tonight's Great Hall.

If I were not standing here in front of the Fine with the Council of Brothers by my side, I would be even more nervous than I am now. I would feel the embarrassment I felt seated before the Great Hall at supper alone. Tonight, however, with my new dress and the support of my family, I feel empowered. I feel proud. I feel ready!

Laird Graham spoke in a clear and booming tone, with all the weight of his title and position, "To ye, my MacLeod kin, I thank ye. Thank ye… for yer respect, yer strength, and yer loyalty!"

The room responded immediately, in unison, *"Hold Fast!"*

Laird Graham was an imposing figure and the gravelly bass tone to his voice resonated off the stone walls with all the weight of his authority as a respected leader. He has a genuine love for the land and the people he serves. He believes the leadership of the clan is an act of service and is not about advancing himself or his own ambitions. I can only hope to serve Clan MacLeod the same way my uncle taught me.

I smiled slightly at this realization, as he continued, "Time has given us the grace to settle into a new way of living and working. Like all Scots, we have adapted to the changes and restrictions on our way of life since Culloden and the uprising. But I tell you this with the greatest sense of urgency and duty, as yer laird, we must prepare ourselves for a new future. A future that will reshape our lives and our livelihood even more in the years ahead."

Watching the faces before us, I can see that the room is following his thinking with the occasional head nods in agreement as he continued speaking.

"Our world has changed before our verra eyes. Ignoring it and wishing change away will bring failure upon this land and this clan." He garnered some applause on this sentiment, and he continued, "We need to salvage what we can, and we need to let go of what no longer works. To do this, we need to think about having a fresh voice, a new leader, to guide us into the future."

The room rustled slightly on these words, uncertain of where he might go with the talk of a new leader. He recognized the already brewing conversations before him, but continued with his announcement. "Today, I announce that I have named my niece, Alexandra Flora MacLeod, my heir and, upon my death, the next chief of Clan MacLeod."

Gasps erupted in the room immediately, but he continued unnerved by the brewing opposition and said over the room, "With my brothers, standing here today, we have full confidence that Alexandra is the leader we need to guide us on the right path to the future."

If I have learned anything in the last few years within the walls of the castle, it is how gossip spreads with incredible speed. The knowledge Missus Gerrard and Duncan have of all the secrets on Skye and within these walls was proof enough of that. So, I have to admit that I am genuinely astonished by this reaction from the people before me. The shock shows that the active gossip apparatus has missed a significant story. I also thought to myself, *have they not noticed me at the head table for the past fourteen years?*

I nodded to the laird—and now officially my guardian—with a quick smile and he continued to call the bluff of the audience, "Ye have seen her seated at the head table with me and Lady MacLeod for nearly fourteen years. I have worked with Alexandra to address the matters on the clan lands, and many of you have independently sought her advice and counsel. This announcement cannae be a complete *shock* to ye!"

I smiled slightly and bit my lip in recognition that Laird Graham's initial response to this objection was the same as mine. We continued to show our alignment within the hypocrisy and incredulity of the reactions on display before us. The room rumbled in murmurs and visible objection as key members of the Fine moved forward to the front of the room in protest and their chance to speak. I just kept the words of warning my father and Duncan in my head from the night before and continued to bite my bottom lip. It took everything I had to keep my thoughts from showing on my face on their words and betraying my growing nerves.

"I believe Alexandra represents the future. These verra clan lands raised a headstrong lass into a formidable woman. She is your kin. And she will serve by my side for the rest of my days. When I am gone from this world, she will be your chief. With all honor to my beloved wife, we will be proud to call her Lady MacLeod."

He stepped back and waved his hand slightly to me to move forward. I knew that this was my chance to say my remarks. For a moment, I breathed in. I must sound confident, when deep down I was absolutely trembling with fear. My insides felt like liquid as I stepped slightly forward.

Before I could speak, the objections to my appointment came in loudly from members of the crowd, causing me to step back slightly again, in deference to the laird.

A distant cousin, John MacLeod, shouted the first objection angrily, "The lass is no' yer blood—no' yer *sliochd...*"

This statement incensed Laird Graham and did not let the man finish his objection. "Alexandra is not my child. That is correct, sir! But she is my blood family. She is the daughter of my brother, Alexander, standing here with me this night. My brother could not see to Alexandra's care by no fault of his own after his wife's tragic death. I sent him to Edinburgh to gain the education needed to support you, to support Clan MacLeod, through every protection Scots law provides. Lady Margaret... who could not be with us this evening," he said as he bowed his head, and we all followed doing the same, "and I have raised Alexandra as our verra own for nearly fourteen years. She is not my own bairn, but ye are *wrong,* John! The lass is *blood* through and through, not only as my niece, but as the daughter of my heart!"

I smiled at this impassioned defense from my uncle. I caught his eye at the end of his last, unexpected line. His words warmed my heart, for I also saw him as both an uncle and a father. I have never told him that, but I loved him all the more for saying that he felt the same to the entire room.

We all waited, standing resolutely in line as a family, for the next objection from the audience. I glanced out of the side of my eye and realized we had all raised our heads and put our shoulders back, ready to take the next blow as it came as a unit. I bit my lip to keep from smiling at this show of a unified family.

The second objection came from Fergus MacLeod, the great-uncle of the MacLeod brothers. I could almost predict his response and it shocked me he waited until the laird finished talking before shouting, "She's nuthin' but a woman… and an unmarried one at that!"

The man of nearly eighty spit the words out in pure disgust at the thought. In his opinion, sadly that of many others in this room and in the Great Hall beyond us, is that there is nothing worse than being a woman. But a woman not fulfilling her only truly valuable contribution to the world—serving a husband and having his bairns—was an aberration, indeed! I bit my lip again, to the point of generating the metallic taste of blood. One day, I hope to tell Fergus exactly what I think of him.

"We dinnae need our own Flora MacDonald here at Dunmara, and not one that could lose everything with marriage," said James MacLeod, another distant cousin adding to Fergus' complaint. This last comment roused the room in discussion.

My Auntie Sarah spoke up on this rare occasion, "We willna need to invoke the Clan MacDonald in this room, remembering ye have one of them standing here amongst ye."

Meetings of the Fine were honestly the only occasions I see Auntie Sarah, wee Robbie's mother, and the widow of the second of the brothers MacLeod. Born between Laird Graham and my father, Adrian

MacLeod married a beautiful, auburn-haired MacDonald lass, only to die tragically at sea just after wee Robbie was born.

At first, there was controversy about having a union between our two clans that spent centuries often in brutal conflict. Their marriage made Sarah part of the gentry for Clan MacLeod. She rarely engages in the politics or the operations of the castle, however, she always wants to ensure there is a female voice in the discussions—even if she is outnumbered. I also believe that she knows that her position can benefit her son in the future. I welcome seeing her friendly face across the room.

Whatever the thoughts on the doomed Jacobite cause, Flora MacDonald was a woman who had the strength and fortitude to do what she wanted in support of her beliefs. Flora earned her reputation on Skye as the woman who helped Bonnie Prince Charlie, dressed as her lady's maid Betty Burke, escape Scotland after the debacle on Culloden moor.

Without saying the words themselves, the objections Fergus and James made were simple and clear—*we dinnae want to give a woman too much power in Clan MacLeod!*

The laird took this one again, subtly ignoring the Clan MacDonald reference, which was as much legend as truth, and just another slight on a woman taking on a leadership role. Instead, he focused on the second complaint—the risk of an unmarried woman leading Clan MacLeod.

"She could indeed. But this is precisely why sending my brother, Alexander, to study law in Edinburgh was so important. My brother has advised us on everything we need to protect Clan MacLeod, Dunmara Castle, and our clan lands from outside or any undue influence from marriage. I will let him weigh in on the protections we expect from the law himself," he said, nodding to my father to speak.

"Aye, Laird Graham, we are prepared. We drafted a marriage contract for Alexandra with no name of the betrothed on it. The contract grants my brothers standing here, if living, the right of approval on who Alexandra marries. And even if none of her guardians are alive when she marries, it limits—by Scots law—what her betrothed can gain upon such a match. She will be beholden to this contract that protects her as much as the clan."

As there was a moment of quiet in the room, Father held up the contract before the audience continued, "I have pledged to both of my brothers and my daughter that I will honor her wishes on who she marries, but I will protect this clan and these lands within the bounds of the laws of Scotland. On that matter, I am resolute."

Despite my determination to be independent, and suddenly feeling like a prized mare for sale, I now understand more than ever how a marriage could impact the entire clan. While the room did not seem fully convinced, they went silent on Father's answer with respect to the law and with respect that the brothers were fully prepared for the inevitable question. No one else seemed to speak up, so I stepped forward.

Perhaps I can put an end to the naysayers with my statement of commitment. However, the statement I have crafted in my head this evening is not exactly the same as the one drafted with my father and uncle the night before. It was a risk to adjust in the moment. But it was a risk I needed to take. If I am going to stand on my own in the future, then I need to stand on my own this night.

"Thank ye, my laird." I nodded my head dramatically and then with a hand over my heart, to show my deep love and respect. "Thank ye, uncle."

His words and his support this evening were genuinely touching, and it was worth reminding the room that we are all family. Looking back out at the faces about the room, I said, "My family and my friends. I dinnae take yer objections lightly. Yer raising the right concerns."

Hearing my own voice reverberate off of the stone walls in the room made me even more nervous. I sounded winded, out-of-breath, and not at all emoting the confidence I needed to show in this moment. I paused, closed my eyes, and breathed in deeply to steady myself. That pause was just what I needed as I raised my head once more confidently and with resolve. I know that my next words will be provocative.

"That is… if yer aim is to preserve yourselves in a past that has already left ye behind."

Immediately, the audience moaned. The men who voiced their opposition, and all who agreed with them, felt vindicated at this moment. The brazen act of a woman scolding them from the front of the room was likely more than they could bear. Out of the corner of my eye, I could see Duncan nudge my father in the ribs, as I was clearly diverting from our script. The script they wrote for me was softer and, well… more polite and deferential. While I was antagonizing the vocal objectors before me, they needed to hear the truth and I walked head-first into a different response.

I do not know any other way than to speak from my heart. My own feelings about tonight led me to the words I must say. Despite their understandable fear of what I was about to say to the room, the Council of Brothers did not stop me. I took their silence as permission to continue.

"We are all looking toward an unknown future as a clan—and as Scots. But, as the laird said this verra night, the future is already upon us.

And the future is not waiting for our agreement to what it demands. It requires that we make some changes. Changes to how we work and build a livelihood on the lands we love, the livestock we raise, and how we hold fast to our beloved way of life, yet still pay the taxes required to stay in the good graces of the Crown. If we dinnae adjust here and now, we will put ourselves and our clan in peril. Every one of us—every single man, woman, and child—in Clan MacLeod will become ghosts amongst the ruins of our own lands if we just stay the course and change *nothing*."

I squared my shoulders and proudly said with conviction, "I stand before ye to say this day, to pledge that I will serve the interests of Clan MacLeod and to do that, I will serve ye. The future health and happiness for ye and yer families is at the center of every decision I will make. Laird Graham has taught me well. The decisions we make in the months and years to come will resonate through the generations that follow."

There were some side conversations in the audience, and while I could not immediately tell if it was positive or negative, no one was forcibly removing me from the room.

"I will work with ye and Laird Graham to define what we should continue—and what we need to stop—across all aspects of life on our lands. However, we must accept that we find ourselves in a position where the future before us may have many leaving the beloved MacLeod lands for a new life elsewhere. We will help families look at other alternatives in the cities and even beyond the shores of Scotland if it makes sense. For those that need to make this choice, we will support them with compassion and kinsmanship—as there is a positive side to extending the reach and influence of Clan MacLeod beyond Skye. I will look to yer counsel to make this so. Ye have my commitment—that we will ensure that Clan MacLeod is strong, united, and making a difference on Skye, across Scotland, and even on lands beyond our shores."

The few women in the crowd immediately started applauding, and some men joined them. But it was clear I was going to have to earn the trust of the others in our family. I stepped back in line with the brothers and tried to steady my face and my own emotions.

And that was it. There was no additional debate. No one else stepped forward to protest any further. This conversation was over, at least for now and after a quick vote in my favor, we walked together united into the Great Hall.

Auntie Sarah caught my arm on my way out of the room, and said, "I am so proud of ye, my dear lass."

I hugged her and said, "Och! Thank ye! That was a lot harder than I thought it would be."

"Ye spoke from yer heart, and it made all the difference!" She touched my hand and continued, "Ye have been so supportive of my wee Robbie, and I ken that if you give that same loving care to the clan as ye have that lad, ye will be successful in everything ye do."

+++

The Great Hall was full, and the expectations of the congregation of kinsman were building in anticipation, knowing that there was a meeting of the Fine prior. I am certain the rumors were rampant about what would cause such a gathering.

Laird Graham immediately called the room to order and moved to the roster of notices set for this evening. All items we discussed earlier today. I stood by the laird's side in front of the room to show unity in our judgment, as he requested.

We heard the three tenants' notices. Three more crofters stood before us and declared that they were leaving Skye and MacLeod lands. Of course, the laird, on behalf of the clan, wished them all well and agreed to follow up in the next Great Hall meeting with confirmation of any reallocations of the lands, sheep, and crofts.

To close, the laird said, "As you know we just completed a meeting of the Fine where I announced that my niece, Alexandra Flora MacLeod, is now my heir and will be the chief of Clan MacLeod upon my death."

The room murmured in disbelief, but before anyone could speak out in protest, he said, "This declaration has been accepted."

The matter of succession was no longer a debate, and the room made no other objections. I could only imagine that the notion of a woman as chief would be debated over whisky and ale well into the night and for many days to follow.

+++

My father met me on the side of the hall and whispered in my ear as he took my hands, *"My dear Alexandra. I am so proud of you! Well done, lass! Well done!*

I sighed relief as I fell into his arms for a welcome and much needed hug, *"Och! Bless you!"*

There was a man I did not recognize standing right behind him who shared his congratulations by grabbing one of my hands from my father's and shook it furiously.

"Aye! I agree, well done!"

I removed my hand from the icy grip of this unknown shadow. I said nothing to him and spoke only to my father. "This evening has gone longer than I expected, and I need a moment. If you will excuse me, sir."

With a smile and a wink, he knew exactly what I meant and moved his shadow aside so that I could pass. As much as I wanted to know who this strange man dressed all in black and with the moody countenance was, I needed to leave the Great Hall as quickly as I could. I needed a moment to collect myself and headed straight for the stairs in the back of the room, shaking hands, and exchanging brief pleasantries along the way.

There was one thing and one thing only, driving me straight to my chamber. My bladder was about to burst, and I could barely stand without swaying back and forth. Just as I got to the back stairs that would lead me directly to my bedchamber, another moody figure suddenly blocked my path.

"Och, Christ above! Mary!" I said, bowing my head in resignation at this last obstacle to my relief. *Mean Old Mary MacAskill* always reveals herself at the worst times.

You have to be kidding me! Not tonight! *Mean Old Mary MacAskill* always made enemies of the other lasses on our lands. The reason for such behavior was the sin of *envy*. Mary could always find a reason to dislike another lass who was prettier, smarter, or who just made the unwitting mistake of catching the eye of a lad she wanted for herself. Mary would then torment the other lass relentlessly to the point of tears and resignation. You would think by now that she would know that I am not one to be bullied in such a manner. However, I can only imagine the announcement this evening sent her into a jealous rage. In some ways, I might have relished her jealousy… had I not been singularly focused on returning to my chamber as quickly as possible.

"Ye think yer so clever, Alexandra," she said as the resentment resonated in her tone.

"Are ye implying that I am… not… clever?" I asked, refusing to allow her insult to hurt me. I would not be deterred from my mission. My aim was clear, as I pushed her aside to climb the back stairs.

"Yer arrogance will get in yer way, lass! It always has and it always will! Yer nuthin'!"

"And there you go," I said as I continued climbing each of the stairs to my room. I will not stop to debate my intelligence or my arrogance this night. Not with her. I yelled down to her as I took stair after stair, "I can always count on yer bitter jealousy, Mary. If nothing else, yer predicable! If ye did not hear tonight, I am the heir destined to be the next chief of the clan and yet I am nuthin' but an arrogant woman. A woman protected by my father, and my uncles… not to mention the laws of Scotland. So, tell me again, how ye think I am *nuthin'*."

She was so angry she could not say a coherent word back to me. I could almost feel the waves of envy from her to the top of the stairs as she sighed and sputtered her frustration. I continued forward, not giving her much of a chance to respond.

For a moment, I looked back and said, "Perhaps ye should stick to yer own realm, lass. Missus Gerrard is likely waiting for ye in the kitchen, is she not?"

"Ye ken I dinnae work in the kitchen!" She spat the words through her teeth, her face burning red hot with anger.

"Funny! Aside from this verra moment, the kitchen is the only place I ever see ye!" I said, each word haltingly through my teeth, mimicking her own indignant response.

She had nothing to say back to me and I would not have been interested in hearing it, anyway. I ran as fast as I could to my room and slammed the door behind me. I know the Council of Brothers would be disappointed in my exchange with Mary, but I could argue she asked for it. *Mean Old Mary MacAskill* always does.

I made the chamber pot without a second to spare. I do not know how I avoided an embarrassing catastrophe on the stairs. Once I collected myself, out of breath on the altercation and the run to my room, I sat on the edge of my bed for a moment of peace. I do not know that I could have imagined a day like today. The history, family, and even moments of humor brought a smile to my face.

After checking my face in the mirror, I reluctantly walked back downstairs. I should remain visible in the Great Hall this evening. I am also starving. If nothing else, I can make my way to the kitchen for some bread and butter. Even at the risk of seeing Mary again, the trip would be worth it.

The crowd had thinned out, but there were pockets of people in the corners of the room talking or at the long tables already set out for breakfast in the morning.

Laird Graham retired to his chamber, no doubt telling Lady Margaret all about the objections made, how I abandoned my drafted remarks, and yet still finally secured acceptance from the Fine. But I hope he told her that her prayers worked. My face, my mouth, and my attitude remained in check. Well... *mostly*.

My father and Duncan were in conference with other men in the back of the room. I do not plan to interrupt their talks, so I ignored them and headed straight to the kitchen. I secured buttered bread and ale to take to my room.

Before I could get back to the stairs, Duncan yelled to me, "Lass! A word?" I stopped immediately. I am not sure I want to join the rowdy bunch of men sitting with him, yet I walked over confidently with the declaration this night.

"Uncle?"

From his seat, he poured himself a glass of whisky, and then a second. He handed the spare glass to me. I sat down my kitchen items for a moment to take the glass offered.

"Well done today, Alexandra. Yer a natural speaker." My father smiled up at me with pride. Duncan took another sip from his glass and continued, "But dinnae keep me up all night writing words you dinnae intend to use. I need my beauty sleep!"

He and my father laughed hysterically at this light-hearted admonishment, and I took the joke for what it was. I drank all the whisky in my glass in one gulp and leaned down to place the empty glass on the table in front of Duncan. I held myself in a half-bow for a moment to inspect his face. I took my time and just at the moment he became uncomfortable by my lingering stare, I waved my finger in his face and said with a smirk, "I am afraid ye need more than sleep for that face, uncle!"

He wanted to laugh but was beaten to it by his friend Angus and my father, who doubled over and slapped him repeatedly on the shoulder.

"She's up t' high doh!" exclaimed Angus.

Angus, our distant cousin, fought at Culloden under another clan banner and was released from the prison at Tilbury Fort before being tried. He returned to Scotland and sought work from his most loyal friend, Duncan, who secured him odd jobs across the MacLeod lands, until he earned his own place at the forge.

I just stared at him as my father said in a stronger Scottish accent brought about by drink, "Christ, man! I never ken what yer sayin'!"

Between the whisky and his thick Scottish brogue, I have never understood a single word Angus said either. Duncan is the only person who can understand him, and often translates for the rest of us. I left the men to their raucous laughter and shoulder-slapping-whisky-drinking with a smile as I headed back to my room.

I thought about all the little victories of this day as I finally sank into my soft and warm bed. Before I could begin obsessing over the expectations and challenges ahead, the warm blankets and pillows enveloped me, taking me straight to the sleep that eluded me the night before.

+++

When I was a little girl, people would say, *"Lass, yer the spittin' image of yer Da?"*

With the innate wonder that only a child could muster, I would reply with a huge smile, "My name is like his!" I enjoyed letting people in on our little secret. Alexander. Alexandra. One and the same.

I am the daughter and only child of Alexander MacLeod, and his name has brought me nothing but pride and strength. As a wee lass, I took the question to mean that I looked like him and I do. We are both tall, with dark hair and brooding features. While his eyes are blue-gray and mine are brown, there is no question that Alexander MacLeod is my father. Not remembering my mother, it is hard for me to say who I favor more. Though Father always reminds me that I look like her. He cannot help but comment on that very fact every time he sees me.

My father and I spent much of our lives apart. Ours is a connection forged by blood and the shared grief at the loss of my mother. And yet, despite the separation over the last fourteen years, there has never been a moment that I ever doubted that my father loves me. Miles and circumstance separated us, but not love.

The laird had the foresight that with the changes across Scotland he would need to have the full weight of Scottish law on his side to preserve the MacLeod lands here on the Isle of Skye. This became even more important following the aftermath of the last Jacobite rebellion and the Scottish defeat at the Battle of Culloden in April 1746. By establishing his brother—someone he trusted more than anyone else in the world as his lawyer and advocate—would certainly benefit Clan MacLeod for years to come.

From what I have learned from my uncles and others, my father was also not cut out for working around Dunmara Castle. He was often on the receiving end of his brother's teasing—and rightly so—as he was constantly getting injured.

Duncan insists that the strategic and well-timed injury was how my father got out of doing any significant chores around the castle and surrounding clan lands. While he and Graham were out every day doing back-breaking work, my father was in a hidden corner somewhere reading a book or studying a map.

While university took him from me and from his home, it was, in fact, the best use of his natural talents in service to the clan and to his family. I know and appreciate every day that Father's departure allowed me to have a life that I do not take for granted. It has given me an education and a purpose, all within the safe walls of Dunmara Castle. Now, my father has to leave once again. With his shadow behind him, he told me the news just after we sat for breakfast.

"Today? Ye have to leave *today*?" I asked, heartbroken as I embraced him. My father arrived without warning and now suddenly has to leave me.

"Aye, lass. I have to travel back to support my clients, and I am no longer needed here." Realizing the coldness of his response, he tried to correct himself saying before kissing me on the forehead, "My darling lass, you are protected and cared for here. That is all I could ever hope for. You and Graham will be just fine, and I am so proud of the woman you have become."

Before I could speak, he said, "Alexandra, I want you to meet Allan Calder. I did not get to introduce him last night, but he works for me in Edinburgh."

Master Calder stepped forward and took my hand. Again, the coldness of his touch ran through me. He said, "It is a pleasure, Mistress MacLeod. I ken yer father is most proud of ye."

I released my hand from him as quickly as I could with a weak smile. Despite the formal pleasantries, I can tell that in every way Allan Calder is a slick eel of a man. An eel is the best I can describe him with his pointed nose and black, beady eyes. It is unclear what he put in what remains of his hair to slick it back so, but it gives it an unnatural sheen and darkened the color to pitch. It looks as if his hair had never been washed a day in his life. This darkened hair against a pocked face and pallor that only the dead have seen made him look as cold as his touch. His physical countenance equally matched his personality. More so than any other person I have ever met in my life. As far as I could tell, Allan Calder, was completely devoid of any redeeming qualities.

I also sensed a stiff formality in my father's own voice when he introduced the man. He seemed to do so only because the man was standing there, not because he actually wanted me to know him. Perhaps Father knows the man is a slick eel, as well. Before I could say anything or ask him, we were joined by my uncles, who walked us out to the courtyard for our farewells.

+++

Duncan, Laird Graham, and I said our goodbyes as my father left us. I bit the inside of my bottom lip as hard as I could to stop myself from crying. The minute the horses disappeared through the gate, I ran for Cairn's Point as fast as I could. I could hear Duncan calling to me, but the closer I got to the edge of the cliff, all I could hear was the sound of the wind and the churning sea below.

I know Father has a life and work in Edinburgh, but he just arrived. For the last few days, everything has been heirs, clan lands, whisky, and marriage contracts. We did not even have a chance to really talk with each other. I had so many other stories to tell him—so many things to ask him. This time, saying goodbye broke my heart, and I did not want anyone to see me cry.

"Mother, he has left us again," I said into the sea winds as I fell to the ground and stared out at the horizon. Only the churning waters below offered me any response and comfort.

I was not seated there long before I heard Duncan yell as he rose over the rocky hill, "Lass! Did ye not hear me calling to ye?"

I could not even look at him and turned my head, trying to will the sea wind to dry the tears streaming down my face. He sat down and placed his arm around me. Through halting sobs, I placed my head on his shoulder as he spoke to me.

"I ken it was hard to say farewell to yer father. Yer thinking that he arrived without warning and left just as suddenly," he said as I nodded in agreement, still unable to speak fully.

All I could muster was a pained, *"Why...?"*

I knew Duncan was serious, as he did not even play the game to ask me why my first response was a question.

"We discussed the plan for a while, but with the uncertainty with Lady Margaret's health, and now that of Graham, we had to move forward faster than expected. Alex insisted on being here for ye at this important moment in yer life. But the timing and the travel needed between here and Edinburgh meant he couldna stay at Dunmara for verra long."

I said softly through my tears and sniffles, "Why... *why*... did he not tell me that himself?"

My uncle gave me a small, embroidered linen handkerchief from his coat so that I could wipe my face and nose and said, "Well, if I ken my brother—and I think I do—I believe it was as hard for him to say goodbye to ye as it was fer ye to say to him."

I sniffled some more but thought about what Father felt leaving us all again. We sat quietly for a moment before he spoke again, "Think about it, lass! He actually has the worst part of it as he has to ride for days with that slimy eel of a man, Calder and you get to stay here at Dunmara with me!"

I laughed through my tears immediately and said, "I love ye, Duncan." My uncle could always make me laugh and would always try to. Ever since I was little, he hated to see me cry. But he would not just try to make me laugh, he would comfort me. He is a kind man, a loving uncle, and my friend.

"Aye! That is it!" he said, holding me tight as I tried to recover myself.

I lifted my head from his shoulder and asked, "What do we think about Master Allan Calder?"

This line of questioning is another one of our games. The *why is your first response always a question* game, is directed at me. But *the what do we think about* game is shared. We often ask each other this question if we want to talk about someone. The premise is, *I have an opinion, but I want to hear what you think first!* And mostly *I want to know if your thinking is the same as mine!*

Duncan is more open than I am and makes friends wherever he goes, but he is just as judgmental as I am and is a mighty good gossip. He rivals Missus Gerrard on this account. The fact that we both referred to Allan Calder as an *eel* is not a coincidence. We usually like and dislike the same people.

"I thought he was odd! But I refused to speak to him, as he was of no importance to me," Duncan said.

"I felt the same!" I said, laughing. "Could you tell what was in his hair?"

"The best I could tell is it was some sort of grease. Black as the Earl of Hell's waistcoat, it was! God bless Missus Gerrard if she can get that darkened mess out of the bed linens!"

We both smiled at the thought. But I am certain that Missus Gerrard will fare just fine with the challenge. I asked him, "Why was the man here?"

"Alex said that they were working on some important case, and he had to bring him so that they could keep preparing and not lose any time with his travel back and forth between Edinburgh and Skye. It is about a week, each way."

"Interesting," I thought for a moment about what Father must see in him to not only tolerate the man but to work with him. I know little about the work my father does, but I know he is usually an excellent judge of character, and I can already tell this man might be a miss.

"I have never met someone so... *cold*. At least not someone living."

"Well, ye ken that is what his name means?"

"Allan?"

He shook his head, laughing at me. "No, not Allan. A *calder* means *harsh and cold waters*."

"Ye are joking!" I said, as I spun around to look at him in disbelief.

"'Tis true."

Duncan stood up and brushed his breeches before extending both of his hands to help me up off the ground. I brushed the cold, damp land off my own skirts when I stood and handed his damp handkerchief back to him.

"Have ye ever heard of someone so fittingly named, Duncan?"

"No, lass. I have not."

+++

FIVE
A Lady's Heart

Dunmara Castle
Isle of Skye, Scotland
May 1766

All I could hear was the sound of loud, persistent knocking.

BOOM! BOOM! BOOM!

I could see myself knocking on a large wooden door. I do not know where this door lead to or who was on the other side, but I knew that I needed it open. I needed it open now!

BOOM! BOOM! BOOM!

I kept pounding on the door and shouted, clearly desperate for access, "Please! Let me in! *Please!*"

Just as the door opened in front of me, I awoke with a start. I sat straight up in my bed and realized that the knocking was coming from my own bedchamber door, and it sounded as urgent as it did in my dream. It took me a moment to register before shouting out, "Who is there?"

"Duncan, lass. I need ye to get up and come wi'me."

As I wiped the sleep from my eyes, I opened the door to find my uncle standing on the other side.

"My God! What time is it?" I asked, waking from what was a very deep sleep. I looked toward the window to see the faint orange light of the sun on the horizon."

He did not answer my question. There was no telling how long Duncan had been outside the door but bent over to place his hands on his knees in sheer exhaustion.

"Christ, Alexandra! I am fair puckled! I nearly broke down the door wi' my fists!" He caught his breath, looked at his sore hands, and said, "Lady Margaret is asking for ye, lass."

With his weary tone, I knew in my heart this summons would be the last. We looked at each other with the understanding of what was ahead of us for the rest of the night—the loss of a beloved member of our family.

It took me a moment as I broke the fog of sleep and delayed understanding, but I grabbed his hand in shared sympathy. I had to think about what to do next and said, "Of course, sir. Let me just grab my robe."

We walked in silence together across the cold stone halls of the castle to Lady Margaret's bedchamber where we found Father Bruce waiting for us outside her door.

"Father Bruce," I said, nodding to him in reverence.

He nodded back to each of us on our names as he said them aloud, "Alexandra. Duncan. May God bless ye both." Then he turned to me directly and said, "The lady has taken a bad turn this evening and the laird called for me straight away." Duncan and I bowed our heads again in reverence and sorrow for this solemn moment.

He continued taking my hand in his, "Ye have been called here Alexandra, because Lady Margaret has been asking for ye all evening. She has been adamant. I believe she will not…"

What he did not finish in his statement was his belief, and apparently that of my uncles, was that she could not pass from this life until she speaks with me. The responsibility of this ask was overwhelming, but I will help in any way I can—even if it means helping her leave us.

The door to Lady Margaret's chamber was slightly ajar and I looked past Father Bruce's shoulder as he spoke to me. I could see Laird Graham, leaning over the bed, talking softly to his love. Duncan and Father Bruce turned around and stood together in silent witness for the tender moment. The surrounding room glowed with the fires lit aflame, surely to warm her tired and weary body.

Laird Graham called to me, "Alexandra, is that you, lass? Come in, please."

I stared at Duncan, but it was Father Bruce who granted me the strength I needed to walk into the room. He grabbed my hand and said, "My dearest Alexandra, listen to what she has to say. Ease her heart and her mind. Give her the peace she needs to leave this life. She is fighting so hard." Father Bruce felt my apprehension and guided me closer to the door and whispered, *"I ken it will be difficult, lass. It speaks volumes about who ye are that Lady Margaret is waiting for ye. She has something to say to ye, that ye need to hear."*

I glanced at Duncan on these words, tears welling in my eyes, as he joined Father Bruce with a reassuring nod to walk forward. I then gave them both a weak smile of understanding and crossed the threshold. The heat of the room rushed over me as I walked slowly across the room. Beads of sweat were already forming on my brow by the time I made it to her bedside.

"Alexandra is here, my love."

I touched my uncle's shoulder gently before I sat on the edge of the bed and took her hand in mine.

"I am here, my lady."

My uncle looked at me through weary eyes still shining with the damp remnants of his own tears. He wiped his face as he whispered into her ear again with a wry smile said, *"I will leave you to talk… as women do."*

He kissed her softly on her hollow cheek and turned to walk away. He paused for a moment next to me. Side-by-side, our faces showed the shared grief and loss before us. He walked past me without a word and out the door, where his brother and Father Bruce were waiting for him.

Her eyes fluttered briefly and then opened fully as she stared straight at the ceiling. Her hands were so cold that I was starting to no longer feel the suffocating heat of the room. For many days, she had been slipping away from us and it was hard to tell if she could hear what we said to her, but the squeeze of her hand was a most reassuring sign that indeed, she could.

"Alexandra," she said to me in a broken whisper.

"You sent for me, and I am here," I said, taking her hands in both of mine now, trying to keep hers warm and mine cool.

"I owe," she said, but then stopped and closed her eyes. Suddenly, as if the veil of death lifted from her for a moment, she spoke to me in the clearest voice without weakness or pain. A voice that I had not heard in many days.

"I owe you an apology." Before I could say anything, she continued, "When ye came to us, I was overjoyed. Graham and I sadly did not have bairns of our own and it was a blessing to me—to us both—to see to yer care."

"I am forever grateful that ye did, Lady Margaret. Truly, I am."

"But I was false in this task."

Her words to me were absolute. I looked at her, but before I could protest the statement, she continued, "I didna fully let ye into my heart. I led with a lady's heart, but not a mother's heart. A heart focused on obligation and duty. A heart that protected but did not truly defend. A heart that educated but did not truly teach. A heart that cared but did not truly love."

Each point resonated throughout my body. I grasped her hands tighter in my own. *"Lady Margaret…"* I said as I choked on my own tears. I just bowed my head to my chest, not knowing what to say to her in this moment. She was saying everything I had felt for many years, but could not understand or articulate myself. I wanted to receive every word and to reassure her, but she was actually reassuring me in her last moments. I was overwhelmed by my own emotion at her words. She had been a blessing, but a distant blessing in my life. I never understood why… until now.

"I kept you at arm's length, because I told myself that I did not want to replace yer own mother. She was my dearest friend, and she loved ye with all of her heart. But I ken… now… that I was telling myself… and ye… *a lie*. I tried to protect my own heart. I could not bear to love ye should ye leave me and return to yer father. But lass, I cannae leave this world with ye thinking that I didna love ye." As I sat there, my eyes overflowing with tears at her side and unable to speak, she continued, clutching my hand tighter, "I dinnae think I have ever said the words, but second only to Graham, ye have been the greatest love of my life."

I could not speak through my tears and tried my best to breathe through the weight of the heavy air in the room. All I could do was fall on her chest again and sob. I held onto her and thought about the last fourteen years and what this woman has meant to me and my life. To say goodbye to my second mother was tearing my heart apart. Finally, I caught my breath.

I collected myself and spoke decisively, "Lady Margaret MacLeod, yer the only mother I have ever truly known in my life. And fer everything ye have done for me, fer everything you have given me, I will love ye always."

Lady Margaret was quiet for a moment and then said softly, "I ken how fleeting life is, Alexandra. Ye must tell people that ye love them when ye have them."

When I lifted my head, I saw she was asleep again. Her breath rattled and her face was pale. She used all the strength she had left to show me the last of her heart. I knew in this moment that we would never speak again in this life.

I kissed her softly on the forehead and squeezed her hand and repeated, *"I will love ye always. Thank ye for yer words and thank ye for showing me yer heart. Please go from this world in peace."*

I let go of her hand and walked out of the room with tears still streaming from the last goodbye. Between the sweat and tears, the minute the door opened, and the cool air hit me, I collapsed straight across the threshold into the arms of my uncle.

+++

I opened my eyes to see Duncan's face, a little too close to my own. Startled, I pulled my head back quickly and forcefully hit the stone wall behind me. If I did not have a headache before, I certainly did now!

Putting his hand behind my throbbing head, he laughed and said, "Christ above! Are ye trying to split yer skull, lass?"

"What happened?" I asked as I pulled my hand up to replace his on the back of my head.

"You walked out of the chamber and fainted dead away into my arms."

The fog in my brain lifted a little, and I said to him, "It was so hot in the room, Duncan! So hot! I couldna breathe!"

He handed me a glass of water. "Drink this. It will help."

I drank the water he gave me and choked on its cool purity. I said, laughing, "No whisky, then?"

"Erm, I might have had all the whisky fer myself here waiting for ye." I gave him a disappointed look and slight nod of my head, to which he replied defensively, "Ye were in there a long time, lass!"

I took a few more sips of water and leaned gently back against the stone wall behind me. Despite my head still aching from the last blow, the coolness of the stone and the water actually made it feel better.

I looked him in the eye and said, "I always thought that Lady Margaret loved me, but from afar. As connected as I felt to her, there was always a distance between us that I could not explain. Do ye ken what I mean?"

"Aye," he said, thinking about the last fourteen years since I have been under the care of my aunt and uncle.

I wiped my eyes with the sleeves of my robe as I told him everything she said to me in the room. When I was done sharing the last words she spoke to me, I turned to him as he handed me a clean handkerchief.

"Ye never have a handkerchief, lass."

"What she said meant something else to me. She said that she *led with a lady's heart and not a mother's heart*. There is a difference, is there not?" He said nothing at first, but I kept staring at him—willing agreement out of him.

"'Tis," he finally said as he nodded in a point of understanding that he had to process and comprehend the words himself. I wondered if it was anything they had ever discussed together as a family.

"She wanted me to ken that she did indeed love me, and…" I paused on the weight of the words, to say them myself, "… second to Laird Graham, I was her greatest love."

My tears were flowing again, but I paused for a moment and thought aloud, "I took in the words she shared and realized that she was admitting to keeping herself at a distance. A safe distance to protect her own heart."

I grabbed Duncan's hand and looked him straight in the eyes and said, "I do the *same* thing."

"That ye do, lass. That ye do. And we can talk more about that when the whisky is more accessible. Fer now, I need to tell ye that Lady Margaret passed shortly after talking to ye."

He saw me lean in and absorbed my sobs on his shoulder. The grief and sadness were final this time and I could feel by the way he held me tight that he was grieving with me.

"Father Bruce was true, lass! She needed to speak to ye to leave us, to leave this world. Ye brought her the comfort and peace she needed. I ken it was difficult. It is hard to lose someone ye love. Come now! I will walk ye back to your bedchamber."

Once we arrived at my door, he raised my face up and looked at me. "Try to sleep. Ye will work with Laird Graham and Father Bruce to prepare fer the funeral in the days ahead. As the MacLeod heir, ye now take on the responsibilities and title of Lady MacLeod as the most senior woman in the clan. Do ye understand?"

After a moment of thinking about his words, I finally nodded my head and said, wearily, "Aye, I do."

+++

There is something about going to bed after a night of crying. I used to think as a child that crying on your pillow simply meant that *tears get in your ears*. But as I have grown, it is more than that. It means a shallow and restless sleep, resulting in the same emotional exhaustion you went to bed with the previous day, and you will most certainly wake with a pounding head and puffy eyes. Of course, my incident with the stone wall lingered and did not help. A bump the size of an egg is still throbbing on the back of my skull.

I do not even know the hour, but I made my way quietly to the kitchen in the dark for some cold water. I found two spoons and dipped them in the water bucket and placed them on my swollen eyes, and laid out prone on the bench in front of the fire.

"What the devil, is this?!" said Missus Gerrard while laughing at me laying on the bench with cold spoons cupping my eyes.

I did not move, but said, "I imagine it looks silly, madam! But it feels so good on my weary eyes and pounding head."

"Aye, but aside from looking like yer serving porridge from yer face, I need those spoons clean for breakfast. Ye will need to hand them back, lass."

"Here ye go!" I said, as I reluctantly handed the healing spoons over to her. We laughed together, and we certainly both needed a laugh today. But we were quickly reminded of our grief.

She touched my face gently and said sadly, yet with the same motherly tone of Lady Margaret, "I am so sorry fer yer loss. Ye have a task ahead of ye, Lady MacLeod."

"I do, and I am ready. Thank ye for the spoons."

+++

The process the heart goes through—letting people in and letting them go—is a universal aspect of the human experience. The service for Lady Margaret was held in the small chapel at Dunmara, aptly named St. Margaret's Chapel. It is believed that the naming was in honor of the small chapel at the heart of Edinburgh Castle. We restricted the ceremony to family, members of the Fine, and a few of the closest to the family—like Knox and Maggie Gerrard.

With the end of the service, Father Bruce spoke one last line as a reassuring family friend, "Those that love deeply, feel loss deeply and ye must embrace your grief in honor of the Lady Margaret MacLeod. Please bow your heads and join me in the Lord's Prayer."

We all recited the prayer together.

> *"Our Father who art in heaven,*
> *hallowed be thy name.*
> *Thy kingdom come,*

Thy will be done

on earth as it is in heaven.

Give us this day our daily bread,

and forgive us our trespasses,

as we forgive those who trespass against us,

and lead us not into temptation,

but deliver us from evil.

For thine is the kingdom and the power, and the glory,

forever and ever.

Amen."

We stood as a family at her grave in the chapel for our last goodbye. With our silent, personal prayers, we left the laird alone for one final private moment with his lady. I walked with Duncan as we led the assembly back to the castle in solemn, mournful silence.

+++

I thought all day about the loss of Lady Margaret. The one thing that I focused on was that I was so fortunate to have two mothers in my life. But now I have now lost two mothers. I feel the sadness of that loss deep in my heart. You may be conscious of love and grateful for that love every day. But sometimes it is only when you have to say goodbye do you realize the depth of that love. You also learn how the pain of the eternal farewell is unlike any other in life.

Lady Margaret taught me to read. She lead my instruction on the Greek and Roman classics and some French along with Latin from other educators brought to Dunmara Castle. We shared a love of the prose of William Shakespeare and John Donne and read them together often. She showed me every day in the living of her own life with dignity and Christian virtue, with her subtle instruction and guidance on what it means to be the Lady MacLeod. I whispered small prayers of gratitude for the woman and her instruction. Despite the sadness I felt at her loss, I had to focus on the blessing of having her in my life and my hope of continuing to honor her in my own service to the clan.

Missus Gerrard had the Great Hall set for the mourners with plenty of food and drink. From what I could tell, it was not only a grand remembrance of a noble woman, but it was also a way for her to channel her own grief in honor of her dearest friend.

Laird Graham and Duncan stood at the front of the room talking to everyone here, paying their respects. When I walked in, Duncan motioned for me to join them in the receiving line.

Once he could break free for a moment, the laird got the attention of the room by moving to the front. His remarks were simple.

"We are here this night in honor of my beloved wife, Lady Margaret MacLeod. Thank you, Missus Gerrard, for the feast and the drink. I, my brother, and my niece join you all in the celebration of her life and in honor of her devoted service to Clan MacLeod."

I know it had to be difficult for him, but his voice never faltered. The room raised their glasses and in vocal agreement acknowledged the life and memory of Lady Margaret MacLeod.

+++

"I am so sorry fer yer loss, Alex!" my old friend Grant MacAskill said as he hugged me tight. "Or should I call ye Lady MacLeod?"

"Thank ye, friend," I said with a weary smile and hugged him back. "I take over her responsibilities now, but I have no use for such

73

formalities. We are here to honor and respect only one Lady MacLeod tonight."

"Aye."

"I did not expect to see ye until June. But I thank ye for being here."

"I am trying to earn my permanent place in the forge. When I heard Auld MacClure was leaving for North Carolina, I thought it might benefit me to arrive early and make my intentions known."

"That is a clever move," I said, smiling at him. I would love for my dearest friend to be working here permanently.

Grant MacAskill is two years older than me and has been coming to Dunmara Castle each summer since he was eight years old. Quite by accident, I met him the summer after my mother died. I tripped in front of him in the courtyard and even at his young age, he politely picked me up and asked if I was hurt. We became friends instantly. He was such a wee lad, but I soon learned that his own mother also died when he was young.

Grant would often join me at Cairn's Point, where we would sit together, stare at the sea, and talk about our shared grief. We would also talk about the happenings at Dunmara and our hopes for the future. We often sought each other out to share our thoughts and our secrets.

I sent Grant letters about the news of the castle often, but his work on his own father's lands and training as a blacksmith's apprentice meant he was not always as responsive as I would like. When a letter did arrive, I read it over and over until the folds in the parchment frayed, and the ink faded.

"How is the laird?"

"As well as he can be having just lost the love of his life," I said, looking for my uncle in the Great Hall. At some point, he must have found a moment to slip out of the room and continue his grieving in private. Duncan, Auntie Sarah, and I remained to represent our family this night.

I could not talk to Sarah before now, but suspect out of all of us, she knows more about how Laird Graham was feeling. I told myself to make sure I talk to her before she leaves. Grant must have read my mind as I looked at her and said, "Go talk to yer auntie, lass."

"Aye, thank ye," I said and walked away before turning back to my friend and raising my glass to him.

I walked over to her but was soon intercepted on my trip by my young cousin. "Well, hello there, my wee Robbie," I said as I moved my glass to my left hand so that my right could go straight into his tangled, auburn curls.

"Are ye well, lad?"

"Aye, but I am sad. Ma says that is normal."

"'Tis Robbie. It is normal to feel sad when someone we love leaves us," I said, trying to show more resolve in comforting another than I actually felt myself. We walked together toward his mother, and I continued, "We have those feelings because we love that person, and that love will never go away. We will always love Lady Margaret, aye?"

"Aye, always," he said just before he ran from me straight into the arms of his mother.

"How are ye, Alexandra?" Sarah asked as I approached behind Robbie. She hugged me tight, and I hugged her back.

"I will say the same as Robbie just did to me… I am sad."

She nodded in agreement but did not say a word.

"May I ask ye?"

"Of course, lass," she said as she sipped from her own glass as wee Robbie now set about wandering off on his own pursuits again.

"How can I support the laird with such a loss?"

Before she could respond, I continued, "I do not always ken the hearts of men and I want to support him as I should, but I do not want to intrude on his own personal grief at the same time. That is not my place."

"Aye," she said and took a sip of her glass again. She put her hand on mine and smiled and said, "When my beloved Adrian died, ye all came to support me and wee Robbie. Ye did the best you could to help me in my house, fer my care, and fer that of my precious bairn. Ye helped me keep going with all aspects of living when I was not sure how to manage on my own. We never spoke of it, it just happened." She paused for a moment to sip from her glass before she continued, "I never doubted for a second that you grieved *fer* me—that ye grieved *with* me—especially the MacLeod brothers. But when it came to talking about my husband's passing, ye let me come to ye with my sadness and loss, on *my* terms."

"Aye," I said, nodding to her and thinking about how we helped her.

"Dinnae smother Graham with love and sentiment. Just be there. Be there for him as ye are every day, because ye love him."

"I understand," I said, nodding my head that there was a difference in supporting someone who is grieving and talking openly about that loss and the state of grief. While shared, our grief is not the same.

She continued as tears formed in her eyes, "Aye, ye may take on more tasks to ease his burdens as Lady MacLeod, but let him come to ye with his feelings and memories when he is ready. A person in mourning doesna need the perfect act of sympathy or enlightened words of comfort. They just need to ken that ye are *there*. He kens full well that his family loves and supports him in his grief."

"Thank ye," I said as I hugged her, tears forming in my eyes again.

She pulled away to look at me and moved my wayward curls away from my face and stroked my cheek, and said, "Ye will also be a comfort to the laird by honoring the woman who raised ye and by being the lady ye are meant to be."

Robbie came back to tell his mother that he was still hungry, and she smiled and escorted him back to the food table. I nodded to her in appreciation for her wise counsel.

A typical Scots funeral can be quite the spectacle fueled by plenty of whisky, ale, and food. All of which Missus Gerrard provided in abundance. Since this funeral was for Lady Margaret, it seemed a tad subdued out of respect for her own countenance and position.

However, despite the reserved decorum at the start, by the end of the evening and long after Laird Graham and I retired to our chambers, the lamentations for the departed were still being sung in the Great Hall at Castle Dunmara. I am certain that they were also heard across all of the MacLeod clan lands on Skye.

SIX
The Lads Of Summer

Dunmara Castle
Isle of Skye, Scotland
June 1766

After the last Great Hall and Lady Margaret's funeral, Laird Graham and I set about preparing for the annual shearing. Along with Auld Knox and Missus Gerrard, we needed to be ready to accept an influx of the summer lads returning to Castle Dunmara.

I resumed my role as niece of the laird, took my orders daily from him and Missus Gerrard and for now, tried to ignore the expectation for me to help define the future of our clan. I know the ask will catch up with me at some point, but I also needed and relished a moment of normalcy. The noise of the courtyard and hall below roused me from sleep earlier than usual. I dressed and walked out of the castle to find a heightened state of affairs as lads started arriving for the summer.

The shearing was the primary reason for the infusion of young men around the castle in June and July. Our sheep are central to our clan lands, as they are adaptable to the Scottish hills and climate on Skye. This is due to the fantastic insulating and waterproofing quality of their wool coats, but they require an annual shearing once a year as part of their overall care.

We usually start in June with year-old sheep being shorn for the first time. By that time, they will have grown an early *rise*—a thick layer of new wool between the skin and the old wool. Then we tend to the older males. We finish the summer with the ewes who have been nursing their lambs. Nursing impacts their wool growth but also provides a natural process to pace the work throughout the summer.

But this time of year was also about bringing up lads in key apprenticeships across the clan lands and castle. Whether in the stables, the forge, farming, or fishing, lads of all ages come here to live and work each summer to help their families and to prepare for their future.

The lasses around the castle were buzzing about the *lads of summer*. This is an important time for the clan, and summer work assignments can help the older lads to secure a permanent position in the clan's employ, finally take a wife, and settle down.

This morning, I am looking for my dear friend, Grant. But what caught my eye first was the gorgeous head of red hair belonging to my sweet cousin, standing alone in the archway before the courtyard.

"Och! Good morning, my wee Robbie," I said as I walked to him and immediately placed my hands in his soft auburn curls and hugged him tight around his shoulders. He did not move away from me as we had the same shared focus on the lads arriving in the courtyard of Dunmara Castle.

"Have ye seen my friend Grant, lad?"

"No cousin," Robbie whispered. His tone was solemn, dulled by his longing to be part of the spectacle of arrivals he was watching from the doorway. He turned to look at me with a sorrow I had often felt but had rarely seen, and I immediately felt the lad's longing to be somewhere else. Robbie wants to help with the horses more than anything. My heart broke for him. He not only felt excluded from the other boys his age, but he was also being kept from the horses he loved dearly.

"Aye," I said as I ran my hands through his hair once more. He just looked up at me again with the sad eyes of a lad confined to a world he did not want to be in. A world he inherited all because of a foolish choice that led to an unfortunate injury.

I put my arms around his shoulders as we stood in the doorway together and I tried to keep my tears at bay for his sorrow. It was then that I realized that if I was going to talk to the clan about the changes needed for the future, then perhaps it was time that I encouraged a bit of grace to those who actually represent the future.

That starts today with wee Robbie MacLeod.

I left the lad to seek a moment with Auld Knox, who seemed as equally focused on avoiding me as I was in talking to him. The courtyard between the stables and the forge was overflowing with horses from the incoming lads and those headed out to the further reaches of the lands. I knew he was busy, but I finally cornered him overseeing the instruction of two young lads in the essential art of mucking the stalls *his way*.

Knox Gerrard, husband to Missus Gerrard, has been at Dunmara Castle as long as I can remember. Like his wife, he serves an essential role and is one reason the castle runs so well. Knox is rough around the edges, but is truly good at what he does. He earned his position as stable master after he moved here from Ireland as a young man and is expanding his leadership on the castle grounds by taking over the estate factor role. He and his wife are beloved and trusted members of our family.

There are two things I admire most about Auld Knox above and beyond his impressive leadership and stable operations. The first is the love he has for his wife and the second is his sense of humor. Every summer there is always some brave lad that asks him, *"How did ye get a name like Knox?"*

And each year, he comes up with a new answer.

"The faeries gave it to me!"

"Ye'd have to ask that of me Ma and Pa... but they are dead."

"It is short for obnoxious... much like this question... get t'work, laddie!"

"What brings you to the stables? D' ye need a horse, lass?" he asked me while keeping both of his eyes focused on the mucking operations before him. Only occasionally yelling to the lads when they were not doing it his way.

"No, sir," I said as I moved into his line of sight.

"Did Maggie send you then?"

"Missus Gerrard doesna ken I am here. I thought I might have a word with ye about wee Robbie." He gave me a sideways look, but let me continue, "The lad loves the horses, and he kens the stables. His weariness after the accident has left him and his blindness is confined to one eye. That is not something that should prevent him from doing whatever ye require here, sir."

He looked at me fully now and his silence meant that I kept talking. "In fact, I believe his deep *desire* to be here makes the lad an asset to ye.

He would gladly brush every horse and muck out every stall, if ye would let him!"

I believe Knox only hesitated in his response because his absence from the stables is how Robbie took the horse to begin with. It was an accident of timing—one that I know he has regretted since that very day. He wished he could have stopped the boy from doing something so foolish.

"Are you asking me this on direction of the laird?"

"No, sir. Laird Graham doesna ken I am here. But be assured that I will let him ken of my ask. Aside from my belief in the lad, I do have the responsibility of thinking about the future... with yer help, of course."

The silence from the man was more than I could bear, and I made my last argument, "Ye and I both ken that there is no future for Robbie as a permanent castle messenger. He is caring for his mother and will one day care for a family of his own. Why would we not give him the opportunity to learn and grow in an area where he has so much passion?"

We stood silently for a moment. He corrected one of the young lads in the stalls about preserving the clean hay.

"I want to harness his love and dedication to this clan, his family. What say you, sir? Can we work the lad into your stables this summer?"

Knox looked at me with a scowl, yet I took some pride because he was still listening to me. "He cannae help it! He runs down when there are horses in the courtyard. And I ken that the stables or the forge offer the best opportunities fer Robbie's future. He has to learn a trade. He has to have a path forward."

Knox remained silent for a moment before saying in jest, "You are an absolute pain in my arse, Alexandra MacLeod!" Both of us could barely hide our smiles while he admonished me further. "Ye would make a good advocate, like yer father!"

"That may verra well be true, but can we help the lad?"

"Aye, we can."

"Och! Thank ye, sir! Ye have made me so happy!" I exclaimed as I wrapped my arms around him and kissed his cheek multiple times. Knox reluctantly accepted my joyous response.

"I have one condition, lass," he said as he unwrapped my arms from his neck, "Ye will have to clear this with Maggie, *and* the laird."

"I will sir, I will not leave ye to this decision alone and agree that I should have started with them before coming to ye. I just left the poor lad and wanted to help him straight away. I ken Missus Gerrard and Laird Graham will forgive my trying to solve this issue backwards from the way I should have."

Knox gave me a sly smile. "Good luck with that! Ye may want to spend some time with Father Bruce and Christ Himself in the kirk over there before ye have that conversation!"

We laughed together, but the man had a point. I may need divine intervention on this score. I hope that wee Robbie could serve them both to start. I would wait until after the arrivals and lunch rush to talk to Missus Gerrard and my uncle.

+++

I was watching the scene of the courtyard below as I sat above the activity near the stone wall. Finally, my friend saw me before I saw him.

"Alex!" he yelled up at me as he climbed the hill.

"Grant! The activity has picked up today!" I said as I ran to and hugged my dearest friend in the world.

"I meant to say it the other day, but it seems ye are much taller this year," he said, hugging me back and patting the top of my head. He is still taller than me.

"Och, ye ken I hate it, Grant!"

"Dinnae hate it! It is a sign of yer strength, and it matches yer personality."

"Ye almost encouraged me for half a minute and then had to make fun," I said as I glanced at him from the side in slight annoyance at his statement. Like Duncan, Grant likes to make a sport out of teasing me to the point of anger or frustration.

"Ye should expect that being part of this line of MacLeod's, ye would be tall like yer father and uncles. Was yer mother tall?"

"I dinnae ken! If ye can believe, I never asked!" I thought to myself that I would have to ask Duncan when I saw him next.

Grant was a distant cousin on my mother's side. She was also a MacAskill. He and his older brother, Gordon, were part of the summer shearing since they were young boys. Gordon fell in love and married a young lass on the Isle of Harris three years ago and has not been part of the shearing since.

Grant has brown hair that turns many shades of copper in the summer sun, but his eyes captivate you the minute you meet him. One eye is green, and the other is blue. He hates it when people stare into his eyes as the unaware make the innocent mistake of looking back and forth from one to the other.

I made the same mistake many times myself. I had to train my eyes to only look at the space between. Now, I do not even notice the color difference. We all have things that make us different and sometimes insecure. Grant's eyes are just part of who he is. They are the magnificent eyes of my friend.

While we have never talked about it, I have always known that just as I was not looking for a husband, Grant was not looking for a wife. I knew the truth, but we never really talked about his secret—his interest in other men. That secret is a chasm between us and what has otherwise been an open and honest friendship.

I leaned against the stone wall and said, playing our old game, "What do we think of the summer lads this year?" I asked him in part because of my impending role and mostly as a point of connective gossip. Like Missus Gerrard and Duncan, Grant is more than willing to share what he knows when he can.

"Well, that depends. Am I talking to ye, Alex? Or am I talking to the Lady MacLeod?"

"Stop it!" I said quickly with a purse of my lips in disappointment. I was also trying to reconcile who I was in this new world of succession and heirs. "Ye are *always* talking to *me*, friend."

"Then sit with me here on the stones, and I will tell ye what I ken," Grant said as he grabbed my arm and hoisted me onto to the old stone wall, where I had a perfect view looking down on the courtyard. Sitting beside me now, we both watched the bustling activity below us.

"See that lad there?" he said as he pointed to a young man carrying a large barrel of water on his shoulders, as if he were carrying a cloud.

"That is no *lad*, Grant!" I said in response, almost laughing as I spoke the words. "That is a *man*, and a giant of a man at that! His shoulders are so big that his arms dinnae touch his sides."

"That *man* is William MacCrimmon."

"No! It cannae be!" I said in disbelief as I looked closer and indeed saw a familiar face from summers past. "That is *Lach*? *Really*?"

I did not know him well, but William MacCrimmon's middle name is Lachlan. Years ago, the lads started calling him *Lach* as there are always a good number of *Williams* at Dunmara each summer. Along with the expected group of *Roberts*, both names represent how Scottish parents honor of the legacies of William Wallace and Robert the Bruce, respectively. The lads try to address some by their middle name or another nickname to avoid confusion.

"He has reclaimed his name and goes by William or Will now. He said that as one of the oldest summer lads here, someone else could have another name. I dinnae think he liked being called Lach."

"He is taller and bigger than you, Grant!" I said, in admiration of his stature and apparent strength. William MacCrimmon had similar Norse features many in the clan do. He was a tall man with dark, wavy hair. Here, working hard in the stables, his curls usually found a permanent spot anchored to the sweat upon his brow.

"Aye! Will hit multiple growth spurts over the last few years and is now the biggest man on MacLeod lands." Grant suddenly jumped off the stone wall, spread his arms wide, and declared, "Dunmara Castle now has its verra own *Gillies MacBane*!"

"*Who?*"

"Gillies MacBane!" he said again, like I should know who he was talking about. I shrugged my shoulders and looked at him like he was speaking another language. MacBane sounded like a Highland clan name, but I cannot place it. Perhaps my knowledge of Scottish history is lacking.

"I'm sorry! Who is *Gillies MacBane?*"

If I could say anything about Grant MacAskill, the only thing he loves more than sharing gossip or a story is telling the tale dramatically. And to be honest, it was one of the traits I loved most about him. He instantly brings you into the history, characters, and intrigue with his well-timed and dramatic storytelling.

"You dinnae ken the story of Gillies MacBane?" he asked with the excitement of a potentially having a new tale to tell. I had not heard of the man, but even if I had, I would not stop Grant from telling me all about him.

"Imagine it... Culloden Moor... the battle pipes bellowing somewhere beyond in the mist and fog." I just smiled and laughed at the drama of it all as he continued, "Gillies MacBane of Kinchyle was at Culloden with a hundred of his kinsmen serving under the MacIntosh banner. He was a giant of a man, lass! Depending on the version of the legend, the man himself was anywhere from six feet, four inches to six feet, seven inches tall!"

As tall as we both were, the thought of a man of six feet, seven inches, had to be an intimidating sight indeed. Especially if you found yourself across from him and his broadsword on a battlefield.

"The Redcoats broke through a barrier that allowed them to attack the Highlanders from the side. MacBane bravely put himself in the gap in the wall and single-handedly killed over thirteen English soldiers himself. He became a legend of *The '45'*. There are even poems about him. Let me see if I can remember the words."

After looking up to the sky for recollection, he said, "I dinnae ken where it came from, though it is rumored to have been a lament written by his anguished widow!"

"With thy back to the wall, and thy breast to the targe,

Full flashed thy claymore in the face of their charge,

The blood of the boldest that barren turf stain

But alas! Thine is reddest there, Gillies MacBane.

Hewn down, but still battling, thou sunks't on the ground,

Thy plaid was one gore, and thy breast was one wound,

Thirteen of thy foes by thy right hand lay slain,

Oh! Would they were thousands for Gillies MacBane."

I clapped my hands at the story and Grant's delivery of the widow's lament. "Well done! Well done! That is a great story!"

I looked back down at William MacCrimmon and agreed, "I believe ye are right, friend! Dunmara Castle does indeed have our verra own Gillies MacBane."

+++

"Will!" Grant yelled down to the courtyard and waved for William to join us at the stone wall. As the lad walked up, Grant patted him on his broad shoulder and said, "Ye remember, Alexandra?"

"Aye, great to see you again, Lady Alexandra," he said, smiling at me and almost bowing his head. "Congratulations on the announcement and yer future role. I am here to serve ye and the clan, as ye need."

What seemed like an incredibly formal response was endearing at the same time. He seemed genuine in his offer to serve, and it was delivered in such a respectful and mature manner.

"Thank ye, verra much, William! It will honor me to have yer support here at Dunmara." I said my words with the same respect he was affording me at this moment. We know that there are still some men on our lands that are not happy with the laird's choice that I succeed him, and I will need all the support I can get.

Up close, William MacCrimmon was even larger than he appeared amongst the lads in the courtyard. I always thought Grant was tall, but William was taller and broader. Once he leaned up against the stone wall, he brushed his curls out of his eyes, and I could see that they were a bright blue and rimmed with thick black lashes. His hands and arms exposed by the sleeves he had rolled up to his elbow moved slowly and deliberately. This showed that he had a gentle nature underneath—one unexpected for a man of his size and strength.

Just then, Grant said, "Och, Alex! Here comes yer not-so-secret admirer!"

Making his way up the hill to join us was wee Robbie. He explained the relationship to William as the boy approached, "Ye ken, Robbie is Alexandra's cousin. He absolutely *adores* her—and she him. Fell off an untamed horse and hit his head, he did. Poor, lad!"

Once Robbie was before me, I grabbed him by his shoulders before he could speak and turned him around to face the others. "Aye Robbie! Ye remember, my friend Grant. And this is our kinsman, William."

The boy nodded to each man, and they nodded back. But he could not contain his excitement and turned back around to me quickly and took both of my hands in his own.

"Master Knox is gonnae let me work in the stables this summer! Can ye believe it?"

How could you not smile back at him and revel in such pure joy? I touched his lovely auburn hair and brought him close for a quick hug around his neck. He hugged me back in what I sensed was a mixture of both happiness and relief. This was such a contrast to the despondent lad

I encountered this morning staring longingly at the horses in the courtyard.

"That is such wonderful news!" I said, realizing that I had better get to Missus Gerrard and Laird Graham before the lad did. "Look here, William will be in the stables with ye, and Grant will be in the forge nearby. Ye can count on them both, understand?"

"Aye," he said as the other lads patted him on top of his head, and each congratulated him on his new summer assignment. Robbie left the three of us walking on air back down the hill.

William asked me, "I saw ye talking with Auld Knox this morning. Was that yer doing?"

"Aye! I might have had a word with Auld Knox this morning. We should not confine the poor lad to the castle all summer. Robbie suffered from his fall from the horse. He spent almost a year in poor form and suffered with sick headaches that would often keep him in bed for days on end. In the beginning, the poor lad couldna even stand without falling over. He has improved considerably but completely lost the vision in his right eye."

"Bless him!" William exclaimed, looking back at the boy bouncing his way back down the hill to his newfound happiness. "I heard the story of him taking the horse and falling, but never heard about his suffering… and fer so long!"

Grant nodded and said, "It was a miracle the lad lived!"

They both were sympathetic to what wee Robbie endured. I continued, "He has been working under the instruction of Missus Gerrard and as castle messenger for the laird himself. But he wants nothing more than to be in the stables. It was the least I could do for him."

"That was verra kind of you, Alex," Grant said. With outstretched arms, he bowed deeply before us and declared, "This, my friends, is the first official act of the *Lady Alexandra MacLeod!*"

"Well, this Lady MacLeod expects ye both to look out for wee Robbie!" I said as I discharged my orders to them both.

"Aye, my lady," they said in unison.

When we all stopped laughing at this dramatic spectacle, Grant continued, "What do we think of the other lads?"

This time, the shared game was asked of William. I anxiously awaited his response. William reflected on his words, and then said slowly, "I believe it is a good lot. Everyone is younger this year, but it is unusual for us to still be here, Grant. We are now the elders of the summer lads being over twenty years, no?"

"Aye, we are aging out!"

+++

I laughed with Grant and William and agreed that I may have aged out as well. As men over the age of eighteen, it is rare that they would return to the castle for the summer unless they were hoping for permanent positions. I know why Grant is unmarried, but I know nothing about William's story. I know Grant is hoping for a permanent spot in the forge this year so he can stay at the castle and can only assume that William may have the same ambition for the stables.

Now all three of us were seated on the wall lined up together as we stared down, watching all the activity in the courtyard below us.

William continued his assessment of the summer lads. "Grant, we do have the *Wesley* situation."

Looking at each of them seated on my left and right, I asked, "What situation?"

Grant laughed and said as he bent his head back, "Och, Alex! Yer gonnae *love* this one!" He jumped off the stone wall and prepared to tell another story, one that I think he regretted not telling earlier. William remained with me on the wall for the full spectacle. We smiled at each other, knowing that we were in for one of Grant's amazing stories.

Grant put his finger to his lips and looked at the sky as he pondered where to start. "Wesley MacLeod is a distant cousin. I am not sure if he has been to Dunmara before. If he has, no one can seem to remember him. Erm, sadly, he is a forgettable sort of lad."

William nodded in agreement on this point, and said, "Aye, that the lad is, but he has been to Dunmara before." Neither Grant nor I questioned his direct assertion on the fact.

"How old do ye think he is, Will?"

"I dinnae ken. Eighteen? Nineteen?"

"Aye, probably eighteen. But it doesna matter. Within hours of setting foot on the castle grounds, the lad set fire to the stables."

"*No!* Ye ken I was just there for wee Robbie, and Auld Knox didna say a word!"

Grant continued, "It was a few days ago. From what I heard, somehow in an awkward exchange for his horse when he arrived, the lad bowed formally to Auld Knox. You ken how the man revels in intimidating the lads."

"Aye, I do. He has made quite a sport of it over the years," I said, thinking about all the poor souls that came before this Wesley. "Some play Shinty, but Auld Knox makes his own sport."

William, who was serving in the stables again this summer, nodded in agreement on this point. Knox Gerrard has built an incredible team of stable hands by weeding out those that did not work at the level he requires *or* with the level of respect he demands. Master Knox is not someone you want on your bad side, and I could not think of anything more dire than potentially burning down his beloved stables. I cannot wait to hear the rest of this story.

"Knox started laughing so hard at his *reverence*, the poor lad backed into a lantern post. Startled and burned by the hot metal of the lantern, he jerked violently and knocked it clean off its hook onto the hay below."

"He didna!" I exclaimed and put my hands to my mouth, panicked at the thought of such a thing happening and the damage it could have caused.

"The stable hands quickly drenched the flames, as they always have water on hand fer the horses, but Wesley will probably never live the moment down."

William picked up the story here and added, "Wesley MacLeod has become the object of ridicule amongst the other lads on the clan lands. Everyone now calls him... *Sir Wes of the Stable Ashes.*"

We all laughed together at this, and Grant said, "It may be cruel, but ye have to admit it is funny. Though the poor lad is miserable fer it."

This moniker made its rounds throughout the castle. In one day, the mistake at the stables set Wesley apart from the rest and, like it or not, he will serve as the best laugh these summer lads have had in a long while.

+++

SEVEN
Sir Wes Of The Stable Ashes

Wesley MacLeod was alone at the end of a long table in the Great Hall. His build and features must have favored more of his mother's family as compared to other MacLeod men. He had light hair and green eyes, and even though he was seated, I could tell he was not very tall. At least not by the usual MacLeod standards.

Wesley moved from the object of relentless ridicule to poor outcast in the matter of days and the teasing by the other men on the castle grounds became nothing short of brutal. They even went as far as to announce his arrival wherever he went, with all the regal splendor of nobility. I am not sure King George III gets such a grand reception at Court.

I felt sorry for the lad. I explained to the laird that while we could expect some natural teasing between lads on our lands and we would not want to engage in every dispute, it might be worth shutting this one down. Wesley MacLeod was getting hit from all sides and was on the verge of being an outcast at the very start of the summer. We could show the clan that, as leaders, we would not allow that level of isolation and humiliation for a kinsman. Thankfully, my uncle agreed with me.

+++

"May I join ye? Wesley, is it?" I asked, sitting down with my ale pot before Wesley MacLeod could answer. The man next to me silently moved over and gave me room on the bench.

"I guess ye can do as ye like," he said, looking at the men around him for help where there was none. They were too focused on their own plates to be worried about him.

"My name is Alexandra. I am the niece of Laird MacLeod," I said, nodding to the head table at the front of the room where my uncles currently sat.

Unimpressed by this, and not even bothering to look above his plate, he said, "Then why are ye sittin' here and not with yer family?"

The lad was eating like he had not eaten in days, but I suspect he is actually trying to get his supper and leave this room and the company of his tormentors as quickly as possible. Anything to limit his time as the outcast sitting amongst his own clan.

Taken aback by his indifference and wondering why I am helping someone who does not seem to want it, I said, "Well, I wanted to show ye some kindness and to welcome ye to Dunmara Castle. If kindness is not needed, I *can* sit elsewhere."

I sipped my ale with a look of disapproval, almost daring him to look up at me. While waiting for some response, I glanced over to the head table again and had a short visual exchange with Duncan. He looked concerned that I was not seated by his side. I nodded my head slightly to him, hoping that it would silently convey I that was safe and would be back at my seat in short order.

"No… I apologize. Stay. I am Wesley MacLeod."

"Aye, I ken! Ye made quite a first impression on everyone, Wesley McLeod! Or should I call ye by yer new name, *Sir Wes of the Stable Ashes?*"

I felt bad for teasing him, as I could clearly see his pained reaction when I said the words. But, I have a point to make if he will permit me.

"Call me what ye wish. I reckon it is a name I will *never* live down. *Christ above!* This is going to be a *long* summer!"

"Well, that is why I am here," I said, as he still never looked up from his plate. Annoyed now, I leaned in across the table. "I think there may be a way to redeem yerself, *Sir Wes*… if ye are willing to take the chance, that is."

I tried to break the gaze he had with his own plate and waited patiently until he finally looked me in the eye for the first time and he said with both interest and suspicion, "How is that?"

"Och! Ye can see me now, aye?" I said as I pointed to myself. I did not wait for a response from him and instead leaned in more across the table. I continued with all seriousness, "I think ye should march up to the head table and introduce yerself to the laird, and actually use the name given to ye from birth *and* the one you inherited on arrival, *Sir Wes of the Stable Ashes.*"

He stared at me with an open mouth half-full of food. But before he could object fully, I continued with my plan. "Ye can tell him how thankful ye are that the stables of Dunmara did not burn to the ground on yer innocent mistake and how ye are here to serve him and the clan faithfully this summer. It is that simple."

Leaning back with my ale pot, I was satisfied with my own clever plan for redemption from, as he noted himself, the relentless teasing that would surely follow him all summer. I was not only a clan chief in the making, but I was a benevolent angel, already having a positive impact on other members of my clan.

Shattering my moment of undue triumph, Wesley just looked at me in the eyes with fear and said through his locked jaw, "*I… could… not!*"

I leaned in again across the table, astonished he did not fully understand how brilliant this plan was and said, "Wesley, the minute ye say the words aloud in the Great Hall, ye will take the joke out of the mouths of everyone in this room. Not to mention yer apology will earn the respect of the laird… and dare I say, Auld Knox. But if ye would prefer to be known forevermore as the lad who bowed in reverence to the stable master and nearly set the stables on fire, ye may do so. Then, aye, I suspect it will be a verra long summer for ye."

He whispered across the table, "*Ye are either a genius or a troublemaker. I dinnae ken ye… so maybe it is a bit of both.*"

"Maybe it *is* a bit of both, but I didna have to help ye. I *chose* to."

He finished his meal, took one last drink from his ale pot, and wiped his mouth on his sleeve, "This plan might work, but if ye are sending me into greater ridicule than I have already suffered, we will have words."

"I have faith in ye! Go forth!" I said, motioning him with my head and ale pot in the direction of the head table.

He stood up with an annoyed look. But the lad marched straight for the head table as instructed. The entire room fell silent, table by table, as he passed them. I must admit, I did not think it would be this easy to convince Wesley MacLeod to reclaim his name before the entire clan and said under my breath, "*Go on, lad.*"

He looked back briefly mid-way when he realized the room was going quiet with each step forward, but he turned back to the front of the room and kept walking. I watched Laird Graham and Duncan at the head table stop eating in anticipation of the approaching visitor.

"Erm," Wesley said as he cleared his throat. When he saw he had the attention of everyone at the head table, he said loudly for the now silent room to hear, "Laird MacLeod, my name is Wesley Alasdair MacLeod— the only son of Donald MacLeod." He paused for a moment and looked around before continuing, "… and as of three days ago, I am also kent by the name, *Sir Wes… of the… Stable Ashes.*"

Wesley bowed his head to the laird in embarrassment as the entire room roared with laughter. I could not help but laugh myself and bit my lip to stop straight away. This lad showed more confidence than I expected. Unbeknownst to him, however, I briefed Laird Graham this morning on the incident at the stables and my plan to restore his name. The poor lad does not know yet that he is now in the safe hands of a benevolent clan chief.

Wesley turned red in the face immediately as the target of the ridicule that he had endured for days. But he raised himself up slowly. Once he did, he squared his shoulders and stood tall in resistance to the raucous howling still going on around him.

Laird Graham played his role perfectly. He paused just long enough to make the poor lad sweat a little before putting his hand up. The minute he did, the room fell silent.

The lad continued, even more confidently, and with the hint of a smile at this sign of support, "My laird, I want to express my gratitude to be here at Dunmara Castle for the summer and acknowledge the kind welcome I received from the minute I stepped foot within the castle grounds." Bowing his head as his eyes went back to his feet, he said, "I am deeply sorry to have started the fire at the stables—it was an unfortunate accident. I can assure ye, sir!" Looking back slightly to the side of the room where Knox was seated, he said, "I understand the potential harm this caused Master Knox, the horses, and the structure itself."

From my seat, I could see Knox purse his lips and cock his head in acknowledgement of the lad's words just before taking a large gulp of ale. I could not read his mind, but wanted to think he too sat in appreciation for the lad's apology.

"I hope to be of service to ye this summer and to right this wrong, sir. But, ultimately, to make my father proud."

Laird Graham stared at him blankly for what seemed like an eternity before speaking to him in his booming voice that resonated throughout the Great Hall.

"Wesley MacLeod, I dinnae remember granting any new titles at Dunmara Castle over the last few days," he said with a slight smirk. "Alexandra, I dinnae believe I granted any new titles this week, have I?"

"No, sir! I didna transcribe any such declarations, my laird."

The laird stood up from his seat, raising his glass, "Wesley MacLeod, ye are most welcome here at Dunmara Castle as our kinsman. I believe ye will serve us well this summer and make yer father *and* yer mother proud."

Wesley nodded his head with the specific sign of respect to his mother, as the laird drank from his cup and placed it down with his own nod to the lad. This was the signal Wesley was dismissed and supper could resume. The audience in the Great Hall erupted with applause as he returned to his seat. On the way, some men stood up from their seats and slapped him on his back in respect of his daring move, and some of the young women gave him flirtatious looks based on their newfound respect for this potential prospect.

You could see on his face that Wesley knew in that very moment he had been absolved of a summer of embarrassment, just as I said he would. Before sitting down, he grabbed his ale pot, raised it to me, now seated across the room at the head table where I belonged. I nodded back in kind.

I could see his mouth form the words, "The summer may not be lost, after all."

+++

My plan went well, and I was proud of it. While I could not articulate it fully, I also felt the first twinge of power. I told a man what to do and not only did he do as I asked, but it worked to his benefit.

"I must say, that went even better than I expected," I said to the laird, shoving my bread into the butter on the table. "All due to your mercy and humor, of course!"

As I spoke, I realized that both of my uncles were staring at me.

Laird Graham said directly in response, "I want ye to be wary of the lads living here this summer, Alexandra. A lass yer age should have been married by now."

"Ye did right by the lad, Alexandra," Duncan said, helping his brother and leaning in with a mischievous smile. "It was a sight to see, was it not?" We clinked our ale pots together and laughed in agreement. It was a sight, indeed!

"We might have to spend more time and effort on understanding this lot. This is not something we are used to as yer uncles. It is one of the consequences of naming ye as heir. Yer new station may be… let us just say… of interest to some of them. We want ye to mind yerself around the lads."

I ate the rest of my supper in silence, slowly surveying the room. My uncles were right. I may need to be more cautious in the future. As much as I wanted to help Wesley, I shamelessly put myself in his way by doing so. That could be seen by the lad as an act of *flirtation* and not *leadership*. I am not looking to be married to anyone—especially not one of these summer lads.

+++

EIGHT
Watching The Dust Settle

Just as my uncles predicted, I found myself the focus of unwanted attention. A lot of unwanted attention, in fact! I could not turn a corner without some summer lad wishing me good health, paying me a compliment on my dress, or randomly asking for directions. While there was an element that was flattering, the attention soon became overwhelming. I could not let my guard down.

One day, as I walked toward the kitchen, I ran into Wesley MacLeod in the corridor. It was odd that he was there and not out at the shearing where he should be. Before I could ask him, he must have read the confusion on my face and said, "I was looking fer ye, Alexandra!"

"Me?" I asked, unsure of what reason he could possibly need to look for me.

"I wanted to thank ye again for helping me out with the clan. Yer plan was brilliant, lass! The lads have not teased me once since that day, and the summer season is almost over."

"Well, I am glad to hear it," I said. Wesley moved closer to me. I chose in the moment not to cede my ground to him. That was a mistake. He looked at me with an odd look and forcibly took my arm by the elbow and tried to kiss me. I turned my head immediately and his wet mouth landed on my cheek.

"Mind yerself!" I yelled at him loudly as I pushed him away.

His hand took my elbow again, but harder this time. He was actually hurting me and had the audacity to try to kiss me again. I pulled my arm from him and slapped him with considerable force across the face. He stood there with a shocked look on his face.

"Dinnae *ever* place yer hands on me again, do ye hear me?! Ye have no right! No right at all!" I said through my teeth as I wiped his unwelcome kiss off my cheek. Walking away, I said back to him, "We will never discuss this again and ye will stay away from me the rest of yer time at Dunmara."

I was angry with him, but mostly with myself. I should have made him keep walking with me to the kitchen within sight of Missus Gerrard and any others if he wanted to speak with me. I failed to protect myself and my own honor and for that, I was ashamed.

I left him standing in the corridor, holding his cheek, and unable to speak. He clearly misjudged my intentions when I helped him in the Great Hall. I let my guard down to my own peril. What is worse is that I knew better. There was no excuse for me, a young, unmarried woman, to be in a corridor alone with a man. Thankfully, no one was here to witness my total lapse in judgment.

+++

Days and weeks passed from the moment of unexpected shame with Wesley, and I tried to forget the embarrassment it caused me. The lad did just as I asked, and I did not see him again.

"Alexandra!" I heard the booming voice of the laird behind me as I walked into the courtyard.

"Aye! Good morning, sir!"

"Walk with me, lass."

I took the Laird Graham's arm as we walked the grounds together, surveying the morning's bustling activity at Castle Dunmara. I smiled, thinking about how grateful I was to live in such a beautiful place.

I told him all that I had learned over the last several days in the treatment and dying of the wool, along with the waulking process to set the cloth. I especially found the ancient recipes using natural vegetation from the Islands for dyes to be nothing short of remarkable.

"I learned that the beautiful blue wool in the dress made for me to wear in the Great Hall was a dye made from blaeberry."

"Aye, it is good for you to learn all the roles on our lands so that you can understand the needs of the people you serve and respect the hard work that keeps this clan thriving."

We talked about the how the shearing was going both at the castle and the shielings further afield. All seemed well on land, and the fishermen seemed to do so well at sea that we were selling some of the catch in the village so that nothing would go to waste.

"I may send ye out with Duncan this week to observe the last of the shearing first-hand. Ye have learned part of the process, with the women, but it will be good for ye to ken the shepherds and learn the shearing process that gives ye the wool to dye. Then ye should spend some time with the weavers."

"I would be happy to," I said, though I suspect I would be about as successful shearing sheep as my father was. However, I know that what the laird was saying is true. Understanding and respecting all on our lands, the responsibilities they bear, and the work they do to contribute to Clan MacLeod is the mark of a good leader. I need to understand the entire process, even if I cannot do it all well myself.

As our talk continued, Laird Graham mentioned he seemed to be genuinely pleased with how the summer lads were progressing across the shearing, fishing, and other apprenticeships. Permanent positions have been secured. The odd skirmish between a few lads has happened, but he said this was to be expected with a *bunch of young bucks* converging at once on castle grounds.

After a brief moment of quiet, I said, "I wanted to thank ye fer supporting my decision on wee Robbie."

"Ye did right by the lad. He is doing well, aye?"

"I believe so. He is still splitting his time evenly between the castle and the stables. Missus Gerrard and Auld Knox came to an agreement on the time spent in each of his jobs. But I have to tell ye, I have never seen the lad so happy."

"I agree. He is all smiles when I see him, as well."

"I planned to spend time with Missus Gerrard today, to ensure she is equally happy with the arrangement and to see if she needs anything. She kens she expects to lose the lad to the stables at some point."

"That would be a good idea, lass," he said with a wink. "The last thing either of us needs is for Maggie to be unhappy."

"Aye," I agreed with a smile. It was always a good idea to stay in the good graces of both of the Gerrards. "In fact, I will leave you to the rest of yer walk and take care of that now, sir."

"See me later today, to plan the next Great Hall. We have an interesting list of topics this month," he yelled to me as I walked away.

I respond with a slight nod and wave but wondered to myself what he meant by *interesting*.

+++

I walked into the kitchen from the back courtyard to talk with Missus Gerrard, only to find *Mean Old Mary MacAskill* lurking about. For a lass that insists she does not work in the kitchen, she certainly spends a lot of time in it.

"Och! Christ above!" I said under my breath as I realized Mary was here, and Missus Gerrard was not.

"What is for supper tonight, Mary?" I asked, trying to sound as positive as I could in the awkward moment, knowing that it would absolutely send her into a rage. And it did—which I found most satisfying.

"You *ken* I *dinnae* work in the kitchen!" she said, seething with contempt at the repeated insinuation that she was a kitchen maid. I do not know why she seems so put out by the prospect, as the kitchen is a fine place to work. I just nodded my head at her. Again, with the rare exception, this is truly the only place I ever see the miserable lass. Increasingly curious, as I know she was supposed to be preparing the wool for dying. We had been in the same group of young women all week preparing, dipping, and setting dyes. This is now the second person who keeps appearing where they are not supposed to be on castle grounds.

"Where is Missus Gerrard?" I asked her dismissively.

Before she could answer, Missus Gerrard barreled into the room carrying fresh loaves of bread from the bakehouse.

"What are ye doing here, Mary? Do ye not have work to do blending the dyes?"

"Aye, missus," Mary said as she walked toward the door. But not before giving me an angry glance. I just smiled and eagerly waved to her with a huge grin that she was finally leaving.

"Why is Mary *always* here?"

"Och! Lord! At first, I thought it was her way of avoiding doing her own work, but it turns out that she is just here to give sweet Jenny a hard time."

"Why Jenny? Is Mary just praying on yet another kind and quiet lass for her own amusement?"

"Aye! Some sort of love triangle as best I can make out."

Not missing a chance to gossip, I took a freshly cut slice of the warm bread from her hands and said, "Tell me!"

"One of the summer lads from the shearing," she said, continuing to slice the loaves and placing the beautiful, warm bread in a large basket. I watched her and thought that I wanted to fill each of my pockets with the beautiful bread to take to my room.

Jenny, the kitchen maid, was bonnie, fair-haired with bright blue eyes. She stood out against many MacLeod women, who, like me, were much taller and had darker hair and eyes. I did not know her well, but I knew she was quiet and seemed kind-hearted.

Mary MacAskill, as another point of contrast, has red hair and green eyes. She could be seen just as bonnie, but her sour countenance made her physical appearance almost irrelevant. You could not choose two more opposites for a love triangle. This lad has some things to figure out about himself and what he wants for his life.

"Erm, some younger lad. Wes something. Ye ken, the lad who almost burned the stables down."

I laughed so hard that I nearly fell off the bench. Choking on my bread and butter, I cleared my throat and asked, "*Wesley MacLeod!?*"

"That is, it! Not exactly the lad you would picture in a love triangle, but to each his own! Ye never ken who ye will fall in love with!"

"My guess is that love has nothing to do with it, madam!"

She nodded in agreement. I would not dare tell Missus Gerrard or anyone else what happened in the corridor weeks ago. But I wondered if this love triangle was the real reason Wesley was lurking outside the kitchen where he should not have been.

I could not wait to share the latest gossip and castle intrigue with Grant and Duncan. Though if history was anything to go by, I am likely the last to learn this information. I changed the subject for a moment and asked, "How has everything been with wee Robbie, splitting his time between yer needs and that of the stables?"

"It is fine. Knox and I came to an agreement, but I have never seen the lad so happy."

"I said the exact thing to Laird Graham this morning!"

"He has never let me down when he works inside these castle walls, but I told ye before that ken I will lose him to Knox and the stables in the end. Before the end of summer, I expect."

I smiled at the thought and believed her instincts were right. We all wanted the same thing for the boy—for him to be happy. I would let them decide when that change took place. They did not need my direction or counsel here. I will report back to the laird on this account, and I believe he will also leave it to the Gerrards to decide.

"I ken how much work goes into feeding and caring for this lot when the Great Hall is overflowing during the summer. Do ye need anything?"

"We are running fine. We increased the lasses in the bakehouse and here in the kitchen, but also simplified our suppers to feed the larger numbers, as ye may have noticed."

What Missus Gerrard thinks is simple is exactly the hearty fare and warm comfort any would want at the end of a long day of work. "Aye!" I nodded and said, "But a fortunate bounty of cod this summer has helped keep things fresh. Well done!"

"Ye are right on that point, lass! We have also been shipping out food supplies to the shielings across MacLeod lands to hold them," she said. "The laird saw to them being given some provisions as they cannae always make it to the castle fer meals. Fresh bread, smoked fish, and ale have been most welcome."

"Well, I ken that they all appreciate everything ye have done. As do I, missus!"

"Aye, some of the summer lads have even come to me to thank me personally."

"That is kind!"

"Starting with William MacCrimmon!"

"William MacCrimmon?"

"Aye, that lad was raised right to show such appreciation for the hard work done in the kitchens and bakehouses."

"Really?" I asked casually, but still interested to hear the complete story. This was not William's first year at Dunmara Castle, but apparently, on his first day this summer, he walked straight into the kitchen to thank Missus Gerrard for the hearty supper and immediately won her heart. She would not confess when I asked her, but I would bet that she provides William a little extra food to keep up his strength during the day in the stables.

This may, in fact, be another reason—aside from his maturity and size—that he seems to separate himself from the others. This is something Grant pointed out to me in one of our talks and I have noticed now more myself. Perhaps part of that separation is that William does not want the other lads to know that he has a direct line to the kitchen. If I know Missus Gerrard, she has no problem showing favor to an appreciative and respectful lad.

"I am not so sure Knox is as impressed with the lad as I am, however. The man refused to tell me the story. He always says that he is not going to add to my tales of castle intrigue."

We both laughed at the truth hidden within the humor of her husband's response. She continued, "Apparently the offense was fighting, though I dinnae ken who the lad fought with. Knox told William to stay away from the stables today to cool his head."

"That is surprising to me! William doesna seem to be the type to fight another for no reason." Missus Gerrard nodded in agreement, as it did not seem to be in the character of the man who showed genuine gratitude for her cooking. I cannot think about him attacking another and I want to know more about what would drive him to do such a thing. Despite his imposing size and strength, my impression had always been that William MacCrimmon was a *gentle* giant. He has a kind heart and surely would not want to risk securing his permanent position at the stables with Master Knox.

I took one more piece of bread and walked away from the kitchen, wondering if this might be the *interesting* item the laird mentioned earlier.

+++

I joined Laird Graham in his chamber to discuss tomorrow's agenda for the Great Hall. I transcribed our meeting as always and set about the task as he read the list to me:

Great Hall of Dunmara Castle—25 July 1766

— **Announcement**: *Master Alistair Murray and his wife, Anne are vacating Belmont croft and headed to Glasgow at the end of this month.*

— **Announcement**: *Decision on the potential purchase of 100 head of blackface sheep from Clan MacLennan.*

— **Announcement**: *The assignment of a new parish educator, James Harmon. We expect Master Harmon to arrive at Dunmara Castle by the 15th of August.*

And finally, the last item.

— **Dispute Resolution**: *Stable Master Knox Gerrard requests the resolution and punishment for the brawl between William MacCrimmon and Wesley MacLeod on castle grounds.*

I could barely write the words of the last item as they were said. The fight must have been terrible if Knox was bringing the two lads before Laird Graham for resolution. Surely, he could resolve and reprimand the lads on his own.

"Alexandra, that last item on the dispute involves ye, and I have asked Duncan to join us today for his advice and counsel."

I responded immediately, nearly spitting the words in shock, "How could their dispute involve *me*?!"

At that very moment, Duncan walked in the room and headed straight for the whisky as he said, "Why is your first response always a question, lass?"

I did not even let his insistence on playing this game stop me. "Well, to start, uncle, I never even heard of the fight until Missus Gerrard mentioned it this morning when I saw her in the kitchen. And I have nothing to do with either of these lads that would necessitate disagreement... let alone a brawl!"

Now, I was not only bewildered but incensed. *How in the world could I be part of a dispute between William and Wesley?*

"I hear ye. Duncan met with the lads and will share what he learned with both of us. Ye will hear what I do, and ye will help me in the final decision on what to do... when we get to it."

My face went red hot at the thought of my last seeing Wesley in the dark corridor leading to the kitchen, but I kept that information to myself for the moment. It had nothing to do with William, so it may be best to see what the actual story is before telling my uncles any more than I should. I can only imagine that they would be as disappointed in me, as I am in myself, for what happened.

We discussed each item on the list and I noted the laird's remarks or decisions to guide him in the next Great Hall. I argued we should not replace the crofters and instead look intently at the sheep from Clan MacLennan. If we could spare someone to inspect them and import them during shearing, that would be a bonus to our output this year. I explained that shepherds in the lands could manage many more heads of sheep under their watch. In doing so, we would almost be ahead on the books financially between additional fish, meat, and wool production than having another family on the clan lands to house and feed. Both of my uncles acknowledged my recommendation, applauded my research, and agreed.

Duncan asked his brother to assign him the task and he would work with Knox, as estate factor, to select a shepherd who could be spared to ride out to inspect the sheep along with him.

We agreed to reestablish one of the small rooms off the back of St. Margaret's chapel for school and would ask Missus Gerrard to prepare a small chamber within the castle for the new educator. It has been some time since we had an educator on our lands. The man is unmarried and English, so both of my uncles believed it would be best to keep him close both for observation and potentially for his own protection.

"Sir, I would like yer permission to work with Master Harmon on the plan for the new school term and that includes allowing young lasses to be educated on our lands." Both of my uncles looked at me, but before either could respond, I continued, "I believe we can lead here, as a clan. Ye asked me to look to the future and I ken what my education has meant for me. Every lass on the MacLeod lands should know how to read and write. And not to mention…"

"Ye have my permission, Alexandra. However, surely ye ken that Scotland and England have verra different views on educating lasses. Ye dinnae ken if the man will be as open to yer ideas as ye hope."

"Then I will have to help him see the benefits of such a mindset, sir," I said, recognizing the slightest hint of naivety behind the conviction of my words. Duncan shook his head and turned back to the whisky bottle.

"When Master Harmon arrives, I will set my expectations with him to work with ye on a recommendation for this, lass. Ye both will come to an agreement and present it to me fer approval, understood?"

"Aye! I thank ye, sir!" I said in gratitude for an uncle that saw to the benefit of the education of young girls on our lands. He was right, of course. I do not know what this James Harmon may be like or how agreeable or disagreeable he may be to my grand plans.

"Now for our last topic," he said solemnly and sitting up in his chair. "Duncan, please tell us what happened with the lads being brought before me and what ye learned when ye met with each of them."

Duncan placed a glass of whisky in front of each of us and said, "Here, ye both might need this, and this report is not for yer notes, Alex." He motioned for me to put down my quill and pick up my glass instead. He took a sip of his own glass and said, slowly, "Here is what I ken... Auld Knox walked into the stables yesterday to find William MacCrimmon beating Wesley MacLeod senseless."

I interrupted him, "But Wesley should have been at the shearing, why...?" Wesley is once again not where he should be. *Is the lad working at all this summer or just lurking about the castle grounds?*

"*Always!* Always a question, lass," Duncan said wearily, and with a look that told me to remain silent. If I did, then we might hear the truth of what happened and the answers to my questions.

"Sorry, please continue, uncle," I said, standing now and backing away to the far side of the room, clutching my glass.

"Knox broke up the fight immediately. He asked Wesley why he was at the stables when he should not be and got no answer." Sipping once again, he said, "From the look of the lad, likely because he could not speak if he wanted to! Getting no clear answer from Wesley, he then

114

demanded that William, under his own charge in the stables, explain himself. William admitted straight away that he told the lad to meet him there, knowing the other stable hands would be out working horses and Knox would be with them, supervising. The admission of the planning of a meeting for a fight just added to Knox's anger. He told both lads that he would bring the matter to ye to settle in the Great Hall and they kent in that moment that they were in trouble."

"For Knox to bring it to me, the lads *are* in trouble."

I returned to my seat and looked at both of my uncles. We agree on this point—the lads are in a lot of trouble to answer to Laird Graham in front of the clan.

"Knox sent a battered and bloodied Wesley back to where he was supposed to be. He told William to leave his sight immediately and to take a day to cool his temper," Duncan said bringing his glass to his lips. "Since the matter was to be resolved in the Great Hall, I spent time with each lad today to find out more about the *why* behind such a brutal altercation and the need for this grievance at all."

What my uncle said matched a part of the story Missus Gerrard shared with me earlier this morning. Wesley had already proven to be someone I could not trust, but I could not imagine what would make William beat him senseless. Laird Graham and I listened intently, wanting to know the same thing—*why?*

"Wesley MacLeod has been telling tales to the other summer lads of... bedding the heir of Clan MacLeod."

It took me a moment to realize this meant *me* and the whisky Duncan provided was not enough to dull my senses for a such a shocking revelation. I stood up immediately in protest to both my uncles and screamed, "No! *No!* That is *not* true! I *have never...!*"

115

Laird Graham sat stoically with his hands folded in front of his mouth, taking in the sordid tale. Duncan placed his hand gently on my shoulder as he guided me back down into my chair. I sat down, shaking at the thought of such a vicious rumor. *A vicious lie* that could have the entire clan thinking that I was no longer a maid. I placed my head in my hands and started to cry.

Duncan, as expected, handed me his handkerchief quickly as the sobs got louder. He said, "We ken that. We do."

Laird Graham agreed, "Aye! We do, lass."

Despite the reassurances from both of my uncles, I felt nothing but shame and embarrassment that my name was being used so throughout the clan.

I sniffled and wiped my face with my hands and Duncan's handkerchief as he continued, "I spoke to MacCrimmon first. He told me the entire story from his side. I believe he was speaking the truth. He said that he did not believe the stories. He stated that Wesley had been telling the stories to make himself sound more important than he actually was and with no regard fer who those tales might hurt. Alexandra, William and yer friend Grant confronted Wesley and told him to tell the truth, or they would bring the matter to the Great Hall before Laird Graham and the clan *themselves.*"

"Honorable lads, no?" Laird Graham asked, as both uncles sipped from their glasses and nodded at the thought. I nodded as well, as I choked back my own tears, thinking of them both trying to protect me and my honor. I was grateful for my friends—old and new—in this moment.

"Aye! The lad was given time to think about it and was told to come to the stables the next day to give his answer. MacCrimmon only used

116

the timing to ensure they could have a conversation without Auld Knox there. They were not trying to be disrespectful; they were trying to avoid any detection to settle this themselves. The lads genuinely hoped they could end this scandal on their own. When Wesley arrived, as instructed to the stables, he refused to admit his lies. He said some fairly awful things to MacCrimmon... essentially asking the lad if he was jealous because he wanted ye fer himself."

I doubled over in shock. I wanted to punch Wesley MacLeod in the face myself. Clearly, a slap was not enough to keep this horrible man in line, and this was an act of revenge for my rejection of him earlier this month. But all I could manage in this moment were hot tears. I cried and was so angry that I was crying, that I just sobbed more. My uncles gave me a moment to recover from my emotional outburst and then I finally raised my head up in defiance.

"This is *my* honor and virtue we are talking about!" I said as the tears finally stopped, and I used Duncan's handkerchief to dry my face and wipe my nose. "I tried to help Wesley MacLeod regain his own name in the clan and, in return, he is trying to destroy my own! I would punch the lad myself if he were standing here before me now!" I was furious to have wasted my kindness on someone that clearly did not deserve any bit of it. My uncles nodded in agreement with this sentiment. "And this lad's scandalous lies just give additional fodder to the objections of my being named heir and successor."

Duncan continued the story and tried to stop my feelings of defeat. "Defending your honor, Alexandra, William beat Wesley. Handily, I might add. The lad is a sight! His entire face is bloodied and blue. His eyes are swollen, his nose is broken, and he also has a few bruised ribs. He cannae speak or breathe without pain."

I had barely a moment to think about William defending me, but the thought of Wesley's injuries seemed some vindication. Duncan turned and said, "I will also share with ye that MacCrimmon showed complete remorse fer not bringing this matter before the Great Hall as he and MacAskill threatened and instead resorted to physical violence. He didna intend to cause any additional shame to ye, my laird, Alexandra, or the clan. The lad reacted in the moment as he saw it as a matter of honor. I will say, however, he wasna apologetic for hurting Wesley. Honestly, I tell ye that I dinnae blame him on that."

Laird Graham just nodded on this statement and asked, "And what was Wesley's account of the matter?"

"When I met with the lad, let me just say, he was apologetic when confronted by the uncle of the object of his lies," he said with a twinkle in his eyes, and a sly smile as he sipped slowly from his now refilled glass. The look on his face made me suspect that a few of Wesley's bruised ribs may not have been caused by William MacCrimmon.

"He quickly confessed to the rumors he spread for his own gain but offered no suitable apology. I was disappointed that he tried to diminish the lies he told as harmless and expected talk amongst lads. He placed blame squarely on William for the fight and for, as he said, *affecting his personal health*. The lad has absolutely no remorse and asked me directly what I was going to do to punish William. He has no understanding that his lies hurt Alexandra, or that he brought this beating on himself. Wesley is a proud and arrogant lad! Had I not been on the mission to uncover the truth, on yer direction my laird, I woulda finished what MacCrimmon started."

We all were quiet for a moment on these last words. Laird Graham finally spoke. "Thank ye fer getting the truth from the lads. I am so sorry,

Alexandra. Lady Margaret was concerned something like this would happen once ye, as an unmarried woman, were named heir and successor. And as usual, my beloved wife was correct. Duncan, I have an opinion on my course of action, but ye talked to both lads. What do ye recommend Alexandra and I do?"

Duncan paused for a moment, sipped from his glass, and then said, "First, I should inform Knox what I uncovered in talking to them both, so that he willna take any further action on MacCrimmon."

"He is quite cross to bring the fight to the Great Hall for resolution. But I will ask that ye *not* give Auld Knox warning and let him react to the revelation in the room. He will do the right thing by the lad. I am certain of it."

"Aye, I understand yer thinking and will say nothing. Then I suggest we have Wesley confess his lies before the entire clan, apologize to Alexandra, to ye, and to William—preferably on his knees—if it suits ye. And at yer pleasure, ye should banish the lad from MacLeod lands, never to return, under penalty of death."

Shocked at this suggestion, I stared at both of my uncles with my eyes and mouth wide open. Duncan finished his glass, and the laird replied immediately, without emotion, "That is usually a punishment reserved for theft against the clan or an act of murder or rape, Duncan."

"Aye, brother, but what has the lad tried to *steal* from Alexandra, but the thing most precious—her honor and virtue? Ye asked me, and I believe that Wesley MacLeod deserves nothing less than banishment."

I admired my uncle's impassioned defense and wondered if the laird would be so bold to banish Wesley. Not sharing his decision, Laird Graham said, "It is settled then. I will handle tomorrow. Brother, ye will stand with up front with us as ye sought the truth of the matter, and the lads should expect that ye have informed yer laird."

Then he turned to me and said with the calm direction of a father, and not just the Laird MacLeod said, "Alexandra, I have an ask of ye."

"Aye, sir."

"I need ye to not cry when the story is repeated in the Great Hall. What ye are feeling here in this moment with just us will be magnified tenfold when ye see the lads involved standing before ye, ye hear the confession in front of the entire clan, and ye hear their reaction to it." I nodded in agreement as he continued, "I ask this not to diminish yer pain but ask that ye not give Wesley the satisfaction, ye ken? Yer tears are yer own and he doesna deserve to see them. I want him to feel nothing tomorrow but his *own* pain and the just punishment he brought upon himself with such malicious lies, his own arrogance, and his lack of remorse."

He was right. I also could not let the clan see weakness, even though Wesley deeply hurt me. The focus should not be on me or on the fight with William, but on the lies and the punishment Wesley brought upon himself.

While harsh, I believe my uncles were doing this to not only set Wesley MacLeod right, but the lad's punishment would also serve as a powerful lesson for anyone else that may want to hurt me or my reputation in the future. I could not get in their way on that score and very much appreciated their belief in me.

As for Duncan, I could tell by looking at him he also meant what he said. Banishment or not, he would not need William's help to carry out his own penalty on Wesley MacLeod, given the opportunity.

"I understand and will do as ye ask, sir."

+++

NINE
The Brave And The Banished

The Great Hall at Dunmara was assembled, and we went through the topics for the month. We slowly announced each one, and the laird spoke about the decision for each, using the notes from our meeting.

We wished the Murray family well and announced that we would not be seeking a new tenant at Belmont croft until we completed the summer shearing and could evaluate any moves across the lands. Duncan will be sent to inspect the MacLennan sheep, and if suitable, will distribute equitably across the lands. Some crofters seemed quite eager at the prospect of adding to their herds.

We will welcome the new educator with open arms despite him being English. A topic that got the room talking in hushed whispers at such an assignment. Old wounds run deep in Scotland. From what I could hear, some seemed shocked at this man's openness to take an such an assignment knowing the history between our people and countries.

Others seemed skeptical that he would last long on remote Skye, even protected within the castle walls. Laird Graham declared we would respect Master Harmon's assignment and his willingness to be here with us—knowing what he was walking into—before passing judgment on the man as a suitable educator.

The room finally went silent in agreement on the fair ask to give the man a chance. They did not know what I asked of my uncle, and we would not broach the idea of expanding education on the clan lands to lasses until he approved the recommendation and plan Master Harmon and I must draft together.

Finally, Laird Graham called up Auld Knox, William, and Wesley for the last item on our list this evening. All three were standing in the very back of the Great Hall waiting to be summoned. As they walked forward, this provided the first chance for me to set eyes on this trio. I looked to the side of the room and, for the first time, saw the face of my friend, Grant, who moved forward on this topic and nodded his head at me with sympathy for what was coming. I suspect he was also there to help defend William if called to do so.

Duncan was right. Wesley's face was swollen and blue. He had two black eyes, one that he could barely open. His broken nose was still bloody. He carried a torn cloth and had to place it under his nose several times. His movement to the front of the room was slow and deliberate, presumably by his bruised ribs. If you did not know the reason he stood before us this night, you would feel sorry for the lad for such a beating and have empathy for the physical pain he must be feeling.

William did not have a scratch on him except for a small white cloth wrapped around his right hand that covered his swollen knuckles that were the same colors of red and blue as Wesley's face. Standing next to each other, the height difference between both lads was astonishing. I knew William was incredibly tall, but I do not think Wesley could have landed a punch on William's chin if he stood on a bench. I bit my bottom lip so that I would not smile at the thought.

"What have ye brought before us in this Great Hall, Master Knox?"

"My laird, it pains me to bring this matter to ye, but I walked into the stables yesterday to find the lads standing here before ye—William MacCrimmon and Wesley MacLeod—fighting. Ye ken verra well, sir, that I have no patience for brawlin', especially in my stables."

Both of my uncles nodded to him instantly in agreement on this point. Knox continued, "I cannae tell ye the reason for the fight, as I got no suitable answer from either of the lads, but I immediately broke them apart and told them I would bring their dispute to resolution and punishment before ye."

Knox Gerrard was as angry as I have ever seen him—his face was bright red, and his voice was shaking. He stepped to the side of the room and let the men stand before us alone. As a man of honor and principle, I worried how he might react when he hears *why* the lads were fighting. With that simple thought, I realized the brilliance of the laird asking Duncan to hold off on telling the story in advance. He wants the stable master to receive the shock we did with the story and see for himself the very different reactions and intentions of the lads standing before us.

"William MacCrimmon, what say ye about this brawl in the stables?" the laird him asked calmly. The room was quiet and still waiting for his response. I sat up again in my chair, bracing for what was coming and hoping that every tear I had would not find a way to the surface, as my uncle requested.

Showing the same respect and remorse Duncan described, William lifted his head and said, "Master Knox is correct. I punched Wesley…"

"Ye punched him several times from the look of it, lad."

The room erupted in laughter, and I bit my lip to keep from laughing myself. Even in serious matters, Laird Graham could always find a little humor. It was a trait I admired and one that made him so beloved amongst the clan. In this moment, it might not only be a lesson in leadership but also help keep my tears at bay. As much anger and resentment as I have against Wesley MacLeod, there is some satisfaction in seeing how uncomfortable he was standing in yet another moment of ridicule before his own kinsmen.

"Aye," said William, nodding slightly to the bruised and battered lad standing next to him. He could not argue the point. William continued with his head held high and looking directly at Laird Graham again, "I say to ye honestly, my laird, I ken I am here at Dunmara Castle—to serve ye and Clan MacLeod—under yer grace. I take no pride in brawlin' with another kinsman on these lands, but this dispute, sir, was a matter of… *honor*." He squared his shoulders back and said, full of conviction, to the shock of the room, "And I would do it *again*."

I am not sure my uncles expected that last line as he had shown remorse to Duncan, but it was the perfect opportunity for the laird to ask, "Wesley, if this was a question of honor between men, whose honor was William defending? His own or that of another?"

Wesley understood from his discussion with Duncan that the laird surely knew the answer to this question. He looked doubly pained to have to provide his confession in the Great Hall, but he did, ever so slowly, through his physical pain. As each breath was a torment, he finally said, "William… was defending… the honor of …yer niece, Alexandra, sir."

The entire Hall erupted. Those that did not know the gossip asked, and those that knew shared. The laird put his hand up to silence the room and regain control of this conversation. "Tell me lad, why yer kinsman would need to defend the honor of my niece?"

I could tell that as my uncle's tone grew colder, his patience was growing shorter. However, Wesley did not back down and said, "I… was spreading… lies and rumors about her, sir."

I will give him credit for admitting the lie, but if I knew my uncle, he was going to make the lad confess the whole truth of it all before him and everyone in this room.

"And what were these untrue rumors ye knowingly spread about Alexandra, Wesley?"

Wesley shut his eyes knowing he had no choice but to confess his sins to the lads he lied to, me, his laird, and the entire clan. I straightened myself in my chair, ready to receive his words and the expected reaction of the room. I also braced myself to fight any notion of a tear or other emotion on my face. I bit my bottom lip again to keep myself calm.

He could not speak and for the first time, the laird, raised his voice, "I asked ye lad *what* untrue rumors ye were…"

Wesley opened the one eye that he could and before the laird could finish his question, the lad yelled out, "That I had been… bedding… Alexandra in secret, sir!"

I looked at Auld Knox, who seemed to sway with the announcement, realizing that William had indeed beaten Wesley in defense of my honor and Wesley deserved every blow. I could see Missus Gerrard grab his

126

elbow to keep him from charging the lad himself as his face turned from bright red to nearly purple with anger.

The Great Hall grew loud with protestations once again. I sat as stoically as I could before the room. My heart was warmed by the faces of those I loved defending me and the strength and support of the uncles on each side of me. Somehow, the truth of the confession also brought me some peace. Surely by admitting it was a lie, I was absolved of both it and the shame it carried.

Raising his hands to silence the room once again, the laird said, "So, ye are here to confess that the story ye told is not only untrue, but I have to assume spread with some malicious intent, lad?"

For the first time, the reaction of the clan and the questioning before them all gave Wesley MacLeod a huge dose of well-earned humility as he said, "It was a lie. I apologize to ye, yer brother Duncan, and especially Lady Alexandra."

The hall erupted again, seemingly uncertain how genuine this apology was and his attempt at trying to be formal by using my title.

He then directed his one good eye to me and confessed, "I tried to kiss Alexandra once outside the kitchen." I knew better than to acknowledge this remark, as it was said with the last ounce of spite he could muster. Even he knew it would not help him, but he did it anyway.

"What did she do, lad?" Laird Graham asked. I had not shared the story with my uncles and regret it being shared now. Luckily, they did not look at me. I am uncertain I could remain stoic if they did.

"She slapped me in the face," he said, and I bit my lip again. I could see William MacCrimmon doing the same as the room erupted with laughter. We looked at each other briefly. In embarrassment, I looked away quickly to Grant, still standing to the side. He just looked at me with sympathy and then a slight, reassuring smile. I took that as approval for my act of violence and the fact that Wesley MacLeod was doing very little to help himself tonight.

"Nearly broke my jaw, she did!"

The laird raised his hand again to silence the room. The revelation of the unwelcome kiss might have helped me more here than if I had actually shared the story with my uncles last night.

"I spread the false rumors out of anger and spite for the rejection I felt." He looked down at the floor for a moment and raised his head once more to finish his confession. "I first used the story to make another lass jealous. I didna realize how cruel it was to ye, Alexandra. Erm, Lady MacLeod. But the rumor spread quickly, and I kept it alive. I was just looking out fer myself and fer that I am verra sorry."

But just when you think he was going to redeem himself in this moment of shame, he continued, "But false words amongst lads didna warrant the vicious beating I received from William MacCrimmon, sir! Look at me!"

On those last words, I could see William's bandaged right hand form a fist. I could not see them, but suspected Duncan and Knox were doing the same. He did not get the apology he wanted with the lad on his knees, but the confession was complete. True to form, Wesley MacLeod's insolence justified the judgment coming his way.

The room rumbled for a moment that the lad was trying to equate a beating he deserved with the lies he told. He wanted William to be as culpable as he was and there was no chance my uncle would agree to that. Most of the clan saw the false equivalence of his statement. The room became silent in anticipation. I thought he had decided last night with Duncan's recommendation, but he seems to have settled on it here and now. He started with William.

"William MacCrimmon, ye said this altercation was a matter of honor. Do ye confirm that the honor ye were defending was Alexandra's?"

I turned to my uncle for the first time, but he did not look at me. This was an unexpected confirmation, as Wesley just made the situation clear. But there must be a reason for him to ask William to confirm before the clan. Perhaps it is one more indictment against Wesley and one more point of honor for William.

"Aye, sir, it was. I ken that what the lad was saying was a falsehood and cruel to Lady Alexandra," William said plainly, as the room went more silent than before. I could not look at him, but I knew his eyes were on me. In fact, there were too many eyes on me, so I just looked down at my hands gripping my chair.

"William MacCrimmon, ye are absolved of any transgression against this clan. My brother, my niece, and yer laird, thank ye for being a man of honor."

William stood up taller on these words of support and he looked at me with a slight smile. This time, our eyes met briefly, and I lost my confidence and looked at Grant again standing behind him. They *both* bravely defended my honor.

"Master Knox, I ken ye will restore William to his position at the stables immediately and without reproach."

Auld Knox stepped forward, bowed his head, and said, "Aye, my laird. William, lad, 'tis done." William nodded his head in appreciation. I suspect Auld Knox will be even kinder to William, knowing the truth of the story of the brawl now.

"Wesley... MacLeod..." the laird said the lad's name slowly, letting it linger in the now silent room before setting about his punishment. I knew in this moment that my uncle was not only defending me, but he was also teaching me how to be a clan chief. I had to take myself out of the situation before us and learn from him at this moment. The ideals of honor and justice were being reinforced in front of me. Once day, I may have to do something similar.

Laird Graham stood up from his chair on this point, and the room went deathly silent. With his booming voice he said, "Ye have admitted to yer kinsmen in this Great Hall and to yer laird, that ye created and spread lies that questioned the honor and virtue of my niece and heir, Lady Alexandra MacLeod. This is an insult to her as a woman, but as she will be the next chief of Clan MacLeod, this is also a mistake on yer part. My understanding of this situation then is that ye are not only careless and cruel, but ye are also not verra intelligent."

Some in the room laughed, but quickly stopped as he continued, "Tomorrow morning at first light, my brother Duncan will escort ye to the edge of our lands. Wesley MacLeod, ye are *banished* and will never step foot on MacLeod lands again."

The room gasped and Wesley protested, "My parents *live* on these lands!"

"Ye will *never* step foot on MacLeod lands, or I will let William MacCrimmon finish what he started. And if he cannae, then my brother Duncan will. Do ye understand, lad?"

With tears in his eyes at his own banishment before the clan, he finally said softly, *"I do."*

"The dispute between William MacCrimmon and Wesley Macleod is resolved. The record of this Great Hall will reflect the decision and punishment handed down this day." I nodded on the task he gave me to record this decision in the ledger and followed my uncles out of the room. The clan has not seen a banishment like this in many years and as far as I can remember, this must be the first banishment Laird Graham had ever ordered himself.

As soon as I could, I climbed the stairs to my bedchamber. I needed to release all the emotion I had pushed down this evening. I could not speak to anyone now. Missus Gerrard came to my room immediately and sat with me while I cried all the tears I had swallowed tonight.

"Knox is beside himself, lass. He didna ken. He wouldna brought something forward to embarrass ye if he had known the truth of it."

"I ken! I do! Please tell him I do!" I said, trying to stop my own tears. I wish I had Duncan's handkerchief and instead wiped my tears with one of my sleeves.

I did not blame Knox for this situation. In fact, I appreciated him bringing the matter to the Great Hall. If he had not, I could have continued to be a point of gossip for several more days. Over time, it could have been even more difficult to overcome the lies with truth.

"Ye will need to be present downstairs—even for a short bit. The room has thinned, but ye cannae hide out here, lass. Ye have to be visible as Lady MacLeod and ye cannae show any shame."

She helped me clean my face and walked with me downstairs. I walked with her until we saw Grant and she graciously left me in the care of my old friend. Grant gave me a look of sympathy without saying a word.

"I have to get something to eat from the kitchen or I will faint dead away. Will ye meet me at Cairn's Point in a bit?"

"Aye."

"Why did ye not tell me about the rumors and the brawl, Grant? Who can I count on to tell me the gossip of Dunmara Castle, if not ye? I had to suffer the ridicule in front of the entire clan!" My tears running hot now with anger and frustration.

"I could not tell ye, lass! Not something that awful... that personal... and it all happened so fast." He continued by confirming the truth of the story William told Duncan, "Will didna ken what to do. He came to me in confidence when he heard the dreadful rumors Wes was spreading. Everyone kens we are friends, lass! So, no one else dared tell me what the lad was saying. We confronted Wes in the stables, together. Ye woulda thought that he would have been rattled by the pair of us towering over him, but he was as self-righteous and unrepentant as ye saw this night. How Will did not beat him in that moment, I will never ken!"

"We told him we would bring the matter of his disrespect and lies before the laird ourselves. We gave him the night to think about his answer. What was said tonight was true. Wes was told to meet Will at that verra spot in the stables the next day or we would go forward with our plan. Auld Knox contained the story of the fight verra well and sent Will away immediately. I couldna find him to hear what happened. Not until we *all* heard the truth of it tonight!"

My face showed the pain of what I just heard and the reminder of the embarrassment I suffered before the clan. Following his words, I said with regret and sadness, *"Until we all heard the truth of it tonight."*

"I promise ye, Alex! I woulda come to ye immediately. I just didna want to hurt ye if Will and I could handle Wes ourselves." He bowed his head and said earnestly, "And we truly thought we could."

As annoyed and as hurt as I was, I believed my friend. He would have tried to spare me the embarrassment of Wesley's lies if he could. He and William were of the same mind to stop the story from spreading any further and setting Wesley on the right path. Wesley just did not cooperate with them.

I stomped around the cliff, saying to myself as much as to Grant, "My uncles warned me to be wary of these summer lads. I am trying to prove to everyone that I am worthy of being clan chief and my name and reputation were almost destroyed by the verra man that I helped regain his own. Ironic, is it not?"

"'Tis, Alex. But it was masterfully done! I mean, for a kinsman to be banished from clan lands is almost unheard of!"

"I think Duncan woulda finished what William started." Duncan was fiercely protective of both me and his family's honor. He would not let someone like Wesley MacLeod tarnish the reputations of either with outright lies.

"I ken he woulda! Did ye really slap him in the face?"

"Aye! I suppose I thought I could handle Wesley myself like ye and William."

We sat together quietly for a moment, and I said, "If I didna already ken yer preference, Grant, I would beg ye to marry me and remove me from all the rumors and speculation that may haunt me for the rest of my days... simply because of my position. I fear that Wesley MacLeod willna be the last to take advantage of me or try to ruin my name as an unmarried woman."

I said the words with more conviction than I actually felt inside and immediately regretted them. But the thought of warding off the advances of men, potential lies, and future scandal already made me weary.

"Alexandra, I love ye with all of my heart," he said as his voice moved into a whisper. *"I just cannae be the love... ye... deserve."* I looked up to see a tear forming in his eye, and it made me hurt for him. It made me ashamed that I said the words I did. I pushed my own emotions down deeper and deeper to not cry before him.

Two years ago, on another summer visit of the lads, I made the mistake of falling captive to one of Grant's incredible stories. As he finished, I was so moved, I leaned in to kiss him. Not in the aggressive way that Wesley tried to kiss me in the kitchen corridor, but it was an unwelcome kiss all the same. It was the most embarrassing moment of my life when he pulled away from me. He did so apologetically, but his rejection still hurt. We sat together quietly, and he could not form the words to tell me the truth of his heart. All I could feel was how he was silently breaking my own.

I only learned the truth when he explained things to me last year, after I witnessed a flirtatious exchange he had with another summer lad. He was flush with excitement about his new friend. While I did not understand his preference completely, I knew that I still loved Grant. The words I said tonight resurrected the silent wedge that exists between us, and I was truly sorry for it.

"Christ, Alex," he said as he bowed his head in resignation. With as much grace as I could muster, and realizing my error, I reached out and touched his hand. I refused to show any emotion. "I may never live and love in the open, but I would not condemn ye to a world of shadows and lies with me, lass. Ye are too important to me and too important to the clan for that!"

With a tone of reassurance, I squeezed his hand in mine and said softly, "Yer friendship is so precious to me, Grant. I dinna regret it. I just spoke out of foolishness tonight because of my frustration on the events of the last few days. I apologize, friend."

I smiled at him genuinely, and with a kiss on his cheek, I stood up and walked away as he yelled back at me, "Alex! Dinnae leave!"

Rejection, even if you understand it and expect it, still stings. *I will not cry.* I did not turn back to him. As I landed at the bottom of the rocky hill, I turned the corner and ran straight into the solid chest of William MacCrimmon. I looked up at him and knew that he could see tears forming in my eyes. He then saw Grant standing behind me on the hill.

"Are ye alright, Lady Alexandra?" William said as he placed a protective hand on my shoulder and directed me back on the path home. He was a kind soul and I know he genuinely meant the question he asked. He wanted to ensure I was safe.

"Aye, thank you, William. I shouldna be here and I just want to go back to the castle."

William exchanged quick glances with Grant standing behind me, and while unsure of what he had just walked into, he asked, "Do ye need an escort back, lass?"

"I can find myself to the back stairs. The moon is fine tonight and will light my way now that I am on solid ground." I raised my head and swallowed my tears. "Thank ye fer the offer."

I started walking forward on the path William redirected me on and stopped. I turned back to him and said, "William, I must thank ye for defending my honor and virtue with Wesley—and in front of my uncles and the Great Hall, no less! It was a brave and honorable thing to do."

He looked at me with a slight smile and a nod in receipt of this appreciation and said, "To have such a mouth on him, the lad really should learn to be a better fighter. I fear he has many beatings ahead of him."

William was right. This was likely not the last beating Wesley MacLeod would bring upon himself. I just nodded and smiled back at him in agreement, then turned to run down the hill and up the back stairs to my room as quickly as I could. After what I had endured in the Great Hall this night, it was not wise to be out on the cliff in the company of Grant and William alone. Friends and defenders or not.

I made it to my room and stood leaning against the door behind me. I was weary from the emotion of the entire day. A day filled with embarrassment and heartbreak. I am aware enough to know that tonight just opened old wounds, but suddenly they hurt more this time. I told myself years ago that I *never* wanted to feel this way again. Yet here I am, and it was of my own doing.

+++

The next evening, I was late for supper, but walked quietly to my seat at the head table and sat down next to Laird Graham. I thought about not coming down at all, but felt like I needed to be there. I could not leave him alone and I could not have anyone in this clan think I was so shattered by the events of the last few days, that I could not leave my room for the shame of it.

My uncle glanced at me but did not say a word. My red eyes and puffy face were an incredible clue that I had spent the night crying. At some point, the laird placed his hand on mine and offered me a tender smile. He said softly, *"I am glad to see you here, lass. Ye cannae hide from things like this. Ye have to confront them head on."*

I gave him a soft smile and nod of my head in understanding. He was right, of course. He offered me another lesson in being a leader. I sat in silence, staring at the plate in front of me. Despite Missus Gerrard's effort this night, nothing on it looked appealing. Instead, I filled my glass once again with wine and leaned back in my chair, looking at the people before me. I was present but detached from the room and everyone in it. Kinsman or not, I wanted to be anywhere but here. In fact, I wanted to be under my covers or in front of my fire—alone.

I hoped that my glass would be enough to get me through the evening. Unfortunately, a supper made of wine and self-pity does not make for a good evening—*or* a good morning.

TEN
Upon The Laird's Orders

I stood before Laird Graham in his chamber as he handed me the small and worn leather-bound book of Shakespeare's first one hundred sonnets. This was the book that Lady Margaret and I used to read together. I was so touched by the gesture, but I could not speak the words of gratitude I should. He gave me the book that served both as a foundation for my studies and my connection with my aunt.

With this book of sonnets in hand, I turned directly to the page bearing the bard's prose in Sonnet 71, and read it to myself. These are not exactly the words to share with my uncle or amongst my kinsmen at Lady Margaret's funeral, but were the first I thought of immediately after her death and hoped that they would bring me some comfort now.

> *No longer mourn for me when I am dead*
> *Than you shall hear the surly sullen bell*
> *Give warning to the world, that I am fled*
> *From this vile world, with vilest worms to dwell*

138

Nay, if you read this line, remember not
The hand that writ it; for I love you so
That I in your sweet thoughts would be forgot
If thinking on me then should make you woe.

O, if, I say, you look upon this verse
When I perhaps compounded am with clay,
Do not so much as my poor name rehearse.
But let your love even with my life decay,

Lest the wise world should look into your moan
And mock you with me after I am gone.

Sonnet 71, William Shakespeare

I was overcome with emotion at the thought of him giving me this gift and the words I read to myself. I told my uncle that I would treasure this book, along with the silver MacLeod broach Lady Margaret gave me, forever. These items will serve not only as a personal connection to the woman who raised me, but as an inspiration for the woman I must now be.

+++

The days passed, creating a space between our grief and the continuing operations of the castle and the unending activity of the lands. Between the shearing and the fishing, we were soon lulled back into the day-to-day of castle life and the focus of our responsibilities this summer.

I was standing with Father Bruce in front of the chapel yard, showing him the lovely book of sonnets Lady Margaret left for me, when wee Robbie came to join us.

"I am sorry to interrupt ye," the boy said politely and breathlessly on his arrival.

Father Bruce nodded and said with a wink to the boy, "A man must do his duty, Robbie." Like the rest of us, he said his words as his hands reached the top of the young lad's head. The *tamin' of the locks* overtakes everyone—even Father Bruce.

"Duncan has returned, and the laird is asking for ye, cousin," Robbie said to me, quietly ignoring the hands in his hair.

Before I could speak, I had to take a moment to place my own hands in the lad's wooly auburn hair that was calling to me once Father Bruce retreated. The wee lad had to muster all of his strength to ignore us both.

I asked, "Father Bruce, is there any sin of having such an unruly and gorgeous head of hair?"

Robbie gave me a look of shock at the question and Father Bruce immediately began telling us the story of the Israelite Samson from the Book of Judges. "While not a sin," he said, "Samson was a man beholden to his hair and the strength and power it gave him."

Before he could get to the Delilah part of the story, which I should have anticipated, I interjected and said, "Aye, Robbie, the laird is waiting. I will follow ye to his chamber."

"Thank you, Father!" I yelled back on my way to the castle with wee Robbie.

This summons meant that Duncan had news from his travels. He has been gone for several days escorting Wesley to the edge of the MacLeod lands and then stopping to inspect the MacLennan sheep. The laird has been so thoughtful about keeping me informed of any clan matters and I know he would make Duncan wait until I could be there to hear what he has to say on his travels.

140

Duncan had news, indeed! First, it turns out Wesley took *Mean Old Mary MacAskill* with him to the borderlands, and they set out together—destination unknown. Duncan commented that the entire trip was in complete silence, as Wesley and Mary refused to speak to him.

They both did as they were told, but did not acknowledge any of Duncan's directions or answer any of his questions. He said that he did not know if that was in pure protest or if they were so intimidated by him and their impending fate that they could not muster the words. Considering who we are talking about, I suspect it was more of an act of spite than any act of fear. They are both incredibly belligerent souls.

Duncan reminded Wesley at the border that he was never to set foot on MacLeod lands again and that Mary, by choosing to accompany Wesley on this journey, accepted the same banishment. Duncan said that she bristled slightly at this, and for the first time spoke, saying that was not fair. But he told them he would make her decision known to Laird Graham and it would be recorded and announced in the next meeting of the Great Hall.

He said they silently accepted their banishment and rode off on his horse together. They did not look back at him as he said under his breath, *"Good riddance to ye both!"*

Laird Graham supported his brother on this declaration and agreed that Mary took on the same fate by going with Wesley. A fact that I suspect will cause great grief within her own family. He asked me to record this decision for the next Great Hall in our ledger, and I did so.

I had not seen Mary for several days but thought nothing of it other than perhaps the slight relief of that fact. I am in shock. Missus Gerrard said nothing to me. Perhaps she did not know, as Mary was not her responsibility. Upon hearing this news, I said to my uncles, "Then I am verra sad fer the lass. As much as I dislike Mary, and ye both ken, I do. I worry she has placed her trust in the wrong person."

"Aye," Duncan said, "she has indeed. But if I ken anything of this lass, then so has he!" We all laughed and nodded in agreement on thinking that perhaps these two miserable souls might actually deserve each other.

"On the way back, I inspected the MacLennan sheep put up for offer… they were fine and healthy blackface sheep. We should buy them, and I recommend distributing equally on the lands so as not to overwhelm the shearing operations already underway."

"What say ye on this, Alexandra?"

"I have no issue with this recommendation, but, Duncan, have any of these sheep been shorn already?"

"Excellent question, lass," the laird said, reassuring me in my questioning as a *chief-in-training*.

"Aye, lass. Not all. Nearly a third—twenty-eight of the one hundred—had already been shorn. All hoggs and rams, of course. Not any ewes. So, we get no wool from them this season."

I continued to them both, "I have no question of Duncan's assessment here. If there were a question about health, and we still wanted to purchase, I might isolate them to one shepherd for further observation and not mix them with our own."

Duncan replied in support, "I can swear for the health of the entire group after inspection. MacLennan needs the money, and he has lost many more crofters than we have to the cities and colonies. They cannae maintain their herds at this rate and need to make up their losses on rents."

"Then it is done. Duncan, with Alexandra's approval, I will ask ye and Knox to complete the purchase and assign the heads upon arrival."

I said, "I approve the purchase and allocation as Duncan and Knox see fit. We will optimize allocation for shearing, but if we need to reallocate heads after the season, we can. Crofters need to know that reallocation of new heads may happen once the season passes, and we have to ensure they are prepared ahead of lambing."

Duncan looked at me with an approving smile, nodded, and said, "Well done, lass. Consider it done, *Laird and Lady MacLeod.*"

As strange as it was in the moment, I appreciated the sign of respect he offered me. This discussion with my uncles was the first time I felt worthy of my position and valued for my point of view. I smiled at them both for teaching me while also treating my opinion with regard.

As Duncan and I were confirming the distribution of sheep, and his approval of my direction at the clan map, the Laird Graham opened a letter with a black wax seal that I did not recognize as usual correspondence. It was likely delivered as part of a parcel Duncan brought in from Dunmara village on his return to the castle. He read the letter and then handed it slowly to Duncan without looking at him. Upon reading the parchment, Duncan's face went ashen. He placed the letter to his chest and shut his eyes.

"What is it?" I asked.

Neither Duncan nor Laird Graham answered my question, and a sense of silent and cold dread took over the room. Duncan handed the mysterious note to me and turned his back from the room to face the window.

I took the letter and repeated my ask, for which there was no answer, *"What is it?"*

I looked down at the parchment with the broken, ornate black seal and the fine black ink script and read the note.

20 July 1766

Laird Graham MacLeod of MacLeod
Dunmara Castle, Isle of Skye, Scotland

Sir,

It is with regret that I inform you with this letter that your brother, Alexander MacLeod, died this day in Edinburgh City.

His physician, Doctor Edmund Tyndall, determined his death was caused by apoplexy and that the man passed peacefully in his sleep.

Master MacLeod's household and staff are at your service and that of his daughter, Alexandra. We all await your instruction.

With my deepest sympathy,
A. Calder, Esq.

I lost my ability to breathe. Having recently lost Lady Margaret, I did not know how I could bear the loss of my father. But my heart was not the only one breaking in this moment. I do not know how my uncles could bear losing another brother too soon.

"It is not *true*," I said softly, but shaking my head as much as the paper in my hand and the tears flowed freely. *It could not be true!*

The laird bowed his head in resignation and Duncan remained faced toward the window. I understood enough about their relationship, and as the youngest of the brothers, that this news would hurt Duncan deeply. It had to be hard for him to hand me this paper, knowing it would do the same to me. I stood up and went to him, forcing him by the shoulder to turn around and look at me instead of the view of the sea outside of the laird's window. If anyone could tell me the truth, it would be Duncan.

"Tell me it is *not true!*" I pleaded through my tears.

The minute his crying eyes met mine, I knew this letter spoke the truth. My father was dead.

+++

"*Duncan*," I said in a soft whisper of shared grief and my attempt at consoling the inconsolable. I fell upon his shoulder and he on mine. He was broken. I could feel it. He tried to comfort me and I him, but we were both in shock, holding tight onto each other as if our own lives depended on it.

When I could breathe again, I let go of Duncan and turned to the laird and said, "*How?* We just lost Lady Margaret… *how* can we bear another death in this family?"

Laird Graham remained quiet until now. He spoke his direction to us with almost no emotion. He was resolute in saying, "I ask ye both to please return to this chamber this evening after supper and we will plan our next steps. Fer now, I ask that ye not tell anyone else of this news until that plan is agreed. Do ye understand?"

Duncan and I just nodded in agreement and then left the chamber together. I could imagine that Laird Graham did not want to be emotional in front of us. But I also realized that the implications of my father's death could be another concern for the Fine and perhaps the entire clan, about my future as successor. I could tell he was concerned and needed a moment to think.

Either way, it would do us all good to take a moment to collect ourselves and our own emotions. Duncan walked swiftly out of the room ahead of me, and I ran down the stairs and out the door, directly into the moody and misty fog hovering over the sea-front promontory of Cairn's Point.

Staring out to the sea and breathing in the briny spray rising in the air from the waves crashing below was the first memory I ever had. No matter where you were on the MacLeod lands, you could not escape the smell of the sea surrounding us. As I grew older, this smell, along with my perch above this western point of the Isle, brought me comfort and peace when I needed it most. Casting my eyes down on the water again, I could not help but smile briefly through my tears. I breathed in and allowed the sound of the waves ease the pain of loss lingering in the deepest part of my soul.

My father was an imposing figure in my life—even in his absence. He was a man of education and strength, borne out of his position within the clan. But he was always so gentle with me. I know he loved me, and I think in part because he saw the face of my mother in my own.

As a wee lass, whenever I cried, I remember him wiping the tears from my face gently and telling me why tears are salty. He loved telling me the story, and I loved hearing it.

"Och! My darling, Alexandra. Come now," he said, wiping each tear from my face and taking my mind away from whatever caused me pain. "Do ye ken why yer tears taste salty, lass?"

"No," I said, looking up at him with a misty, wide-eyed reverence. As the years passed, I knew the answer to this question, but my response was always the same. I let his explanation be the reassurance I needed in the moment. No matter how old you are, the loving words from a parent can always soothe your wounded soul. I willingly let him fulfill a father's duty—that of comforting his child from any pain.

"We live here at Dunmara Castle by the grace and mercy of the Lord above us, the rich lands around us, and especially the salty sea below us. We respect it, reap food from it, and travel by it. We are drawn to its power, and it lives within each of us. We cannae help to return to the sea when called. Do ye understand, lass?"

I remember nodding my head in agreement each time as my tears dried up on his words and the calm tone of his voice lessened whatever the hurt was on my body or in my heart. As I grew older, I believe this even more than I did in those childhood moments because I know the role the sea has had in my own life. My mother drowned in the sea below me and it remains both my peace and my torment. I know my father, who mourned her throughout his life, felt the same.

He would say, "Yer dear mother loved sitting here on the headland cliff of Cairn's Point. Like ye, she would come here to think, to pray, or even to cry when she needed."

Soon, I caught the rhythm of the water softly lulling me into its familiar trance. I stared out at the sea and whispered to him and to myself, *"Ye were so right, Father. We all return to the sea, and this is the most peaceful spot. I hope that ye and my mother are here together."*

For most of my life, my heart ached for the loss of my mother and now, it aches for the loss of my father. I cannot think of his spirit only in Edinburgh. He should be here. He should be here with *her*. I succumbed to the pain I felt in my heart and sobbed once again. Today, I became an orphan in this world and I feel like I will never be whole again.

+++

Just weeks ago, we all stood in this chamber talking of heirs, guardians, and inheritances. Now, we stand in stunned silence at the reality of an unexpected and deeply felt loss.

To hear of Father's death, so soon after losing Lady Margaret, is almost more than we can all bear. Duncan has taken it especially hard and shed his tears in front of me. It only added to my grief. I reached out and held his hand, and he held mine. It broke my heart, but I admired him for showing his feelings so openly.

Laird Graham spoke to us both, "Please sit."

Duncan responded harshly this command and said, "I will sit when I have a whisky in my hand, brother."

My guess by looking at him and his glassy eyes was that whisky had fueled Duncan most of the day. He moved immediately to the glasses and the bottle. I cannot say that I disagreed with his focus in this moment and appreciated him all the more when, after filling three glasses, we sat to reconvene this new family council.

The laird spoke to us first as family, "We raise our glass in tribute to the soul and life of our departed brother... and father, Alexander Ewan MacLeod."

We all nodded in agreement and drank our first sip from the glasses Duncan poured us. "I appreciate ye keeping the news of Alexander's death within this chamber fer now. I needed to think more about the plan for ye, Alexandra, and fer our dear brother before sharing broadly. We all ken that there are new risks with his loss at this time."

Duncan and I both nodded in agreement for the wisdom and restraint the laird was showing in feeling his own emotion and thinking of the clan first.

"Brother, I must ask ye to go to Edinburgh. With the time that has passed, it is unlikely that we can bring his body home," he said as he bit his lip on the last word. I had not even thought about it, but he was correct. All of us took another silent sip at the notion. There was no way we could bring my father home, and I was sad thinking that he was by now buried somewhere in Edinburgh. I bowed my head in sorrow at the thought and tried not to cry again.

"Ye will wrap up his affairs, settle Alexandra's inheritance, sell what ye can, and then return to Dunmara. Do ye understand?"

"Aye, I do," said Duncan stoically.

I spoke up immediately in protest and asked, "Why cannae I settle my own inheritance and see where my father lived and is buried? My laird, I deserve that right! I should be able to accompany Duncan to Edinburgh."

Duncan spoke first and said solemnly, "The lass deserves to know the last of her father. I can escort her to Edinburgh and back."

It took him a moment, before the laird said, "I can agree to that, but I am going to ask that William MacCrimmon accompany ye both on this journey."

"*Why*? He is not our family!"

I do not want or need William MacCrimmon being part of our family business, especially one laced with such personal grief. Before the laird could answer me, Duncan educated me on his brother's thinking.

"Lass, word of ye being named heir and the next chief of Clan MacLeod has spread. That makes ye a target. Not to mention the roads between here and Edinburgh can be treacherous any day, especially for a woman. We need the added protection. MacCrimmon is our kinsman and has already proven that he is a suitable and honorable defender." He

149

did not give me a chance to respond and turned to say, "And with yer permission, brother, I would like to take Angus with us, as well. He can serve as our advance man surveying the roads and securing lodgings ahead of our traveling party, so there is no disruption in our travels."

"Aye, excellent idea! I support this plan. Robbie," the laird yelled, as wee Robbie walked into the chamber instantly. I could not bear to look at the boy and turned toward my back to him. "Send for William MacCrimmon and Angus MacLeod immediately! They are to join me and Duncan here in this chamber. Be quick about it, lad!"

Robbie was already running down the stone stairs before the he could affirm the ask.

"Stay here, Duncan. I want all the men to hear my expectations fer this journey and I will give ye the coin ye will need."

Duncan nodded and picked up a quill and parchment, "With yer permission, I will write yer letter now to Alexander's household staff, led by a Missus Douglas, I believe. And then to Mistress Hay in his office. This is so that they are prepared to expect us in the coming week. We can send them ahead with Angus to get in the hands of a messenger to get them on the post coach at Fort William before our arrival."

"Aye, I will sign and seal what ye draft. Should we not respond to the sender of this notice, Master Calder?"

"No," Duncan said immediately, and I silently agreed. "The first we saw of this man was when Alex was here last and I tell ye brother, despite the respect shown in this letter, I dinnae trust the man. I dinnae think our brother did either. I ask to move forward without notice to Master Calder."

"Ye ken more than I do, and I trust ye."

Duncan continued, "We will need to have Auld Knox prepare the horses for a departure tomorrow. Alexandra, I will have him prepare a horse for ye as well. It will be a new horse, as ye will need a larger one that can go the distance and across the Highland terrain."

I nodded in silent agreement to this plan, but also numb to a conversation that seemed to be happening around me and not with me. I have never ridden across the country, new horse or not. I finally found my voice and asked, "Will ye need me for this meeting, my laird?"

"No, Alexandra. It is essential that I set these men upon their task." Before I could object, he continued, "I want to be clear on my expectations of their care for ye on this journey, *and* be clear on the consequences if they dinnae do as I command."

I was disappointed at first that he did not want me to join the meeting but somehow also understood that even if I did not like it, sometimes men need to come to an understanding. There is also only one clan chief at a time, and these men will not be riding under my command, but his. As much as it hurt to admit it, he was right in his ask for me to step aside.

I nodded in acceptance of his instruction but then asked, "When will we tell the Fine and the clan?"

"After I talk to the lads tonight, we will tell Auld Knox and Missus Gerrard so that ye are all prepared to leave tomorrow morning at first light. I will tell the rest of the clan in the next Great Hall once you are gone and far from Dunmara. To that point, Duncan, please have Maggie and Knox here to receive my instruction immediately following our meeting with William and Angus."

"Aye, consider it done," Duncan said as he drank the last of his glass and placed it down on the desk next to his half-written letter and headed for the door. As Robbie was away on his task, he would have to summon the Gerrards himself.

"Before ye leave, Duncan. I would like to put Father's name on the cairn with my mother's. Will ye grant me that ask, my laird?"

"Aye, consider it done, lass," he said. I could tell that my ask touched him as he showed the first sign of emotion in his voice. The ancient stone cairn has memorialized many throughout the ages, but has only one name carved on it and that is my mother's. My father should be with her.

Duncan nodded to me in sympathy as he walked out of the chamber. I stood up to walk out the door. I knew I was dismissed. Laird Graham could tell I felt excluded, and that I wanted to resist being put in the care of a bunch of men—especially men with unknown expectations. I am certain it showed on my face and in my slow walk to the chamber door.

"We cannae give anyone advance notice of this trip or the reason fer it, Alexandra." I turned to look back at him as he said, "Alexander's death could give the objectors another argument against yer becoming clan chief. Ye need to hasten yerself to Edinburgh, lass. Ye will be in excellent hands... *safe* hands."

I just said as I picked up the ledger from the back table, "I understand, sir. I will record this and Mary's departure, along with the decision on the MacLennan sheep for ye before I leave."

"Thank you, lass. Ye do me a great service."

On the walk back to my room, I noticed the last rays of sunshine streaming through the windows. The warm threads of light reminded that I had plenty of time to watch the sun retire once more into the sea at Cairn's Point before I would be forced to leave my beloved home. I exchanged the ledger for my cloak on my bed and ran down the stairs once more.

+++

ELEVEN
Dunmara Farewell

Dunmara Castle
Isle of Skye, Scotland
July 1766

I sat upon the edge of Cairn's Point staring at the sea below to say farewell to the only home I have ever known. The sea once again matched my inner turmoil with its own rhythmic churn. Tonight it sounded as troubled as I was. I do not know how long I had been here absorbing the last light of the day and the lull of the crashing waves on the rocks below before I heard another voice call to me across the wind.

"Alexandra!" William shouted as he rose over the hilltop of Cairn's Point. "I thought I would find ye here!"

Startled out of the trance the water and wind had on me, I replied, "Did ye?"

"Well, this is yer place, no?"

"How would ye ...?" I asked as my voice trailed off haltingly in the middle of the question. I sounded defensive when that was not my intention. Everyone at Dunmara Castle has seen me atop this cliff more than once.

Before I could try to set my words right, he said, suddenly looking a little embarrassed that he had made this observation himself, "Erm, well... ye come here often."

"Aye," I said softly in resignation. I do come here often, and I will miss it when we leave tomorrow. No longer having this place as a refuge and a comfort when I need it will be difficult for me.

William retreated slightly on his observations about where I spent my time, as I suspect he had started thinking that he should have said nothing to me about it. "When I was in the stables behind, I often saw ye sittin' up here. It just seemed to be... yer place."

Letting go of the argument and questioning his honest observations, I said, "It truly is, William." I looked back out dreamingly to the ocean rising and falling before me and the last of the red-hot evening sun dancing across the endless water, like fire. This is my place, indeed.

I spoke again, albeit awkwardly, "There is a line in *King Lear* where Shakespeare describes it perfectly. It is not the meaning of the line in the play itself, but I often think of the words when I am here."

He looked at me sideways slightly with a smirk and asked sarcastically, "Ye are gonnae quote Shakespeare now?"

"Surely ye have heard of the play, Will," I said with sarcasm, suddenly realizing that I was using a more familiar tone, starting with his name. I hoped he did not notice. "Mock me all you want, but the words in the play always come to mind when I come here."

"Please, tell me. I didna mean any offense."

"Well now, let me see if I can remember all the lines," I said, looking back out to the sea for inspiration. I tried to channel my friend Grant and his effortless delivery of a story or a verse. I sat upright and spoke the words Shakespeare wrote with the full dramatic effect they deserved.

"There is a cliff, whose high and bending head
Looks fearfully in the confined deep.
Bring me but to the very brim of it,
And I'll repair the misery thou dost bear"

I smiled with pride that I remembered the words. But, not to be outdone, William responded quickly.

"I believe Gloucester's line continues," William said confidently, continuing from my last line without hesitation.

"And I'll repair the misery thou dost bear
With something rich about me.
From that place
I shall no leading need."

King Lear, Act 4 Scene 1, William Shakespeare

"Ye *had to* finish it!" I said, laughing slightly on the display of one-upmanship and a little more than impressed with William MacCrimmon's knowledge of *King Lear* to recite the lines from memory.

"I couldna help myself!" he said. I just stared at him. Then, with a slightly apologetic attempt to justify finishing the quote, he looked at me and lifted his shoulders and hands in resignation to say, "It was incomplete!"

He smiled, but I could not tell if he was smiling at me or reveling in his own sense of accomplishment. Either way, I sensed that I would have to brush up on my sonnets and plays to match William MacCrimmon should another Shakespearean challenge present itself on our travels to Edinburgh.

We sat quietly for a moment before he continued, trying to break the awkward silence between us. "Why do ye focus on that verse? Gloucester tried to finish himself at the cliff, did he not?"

What he asked was fair, but I connected to the part I said aloud, and it was about finding peace at the cliff. Whatever *peace* means to you. I did not think about the actual plot of the play. For me, just as the Bard says, being at the very brim overlooking the water repairs my misery and brings me peace. It always has. After a moment of shared silence, I ignored his question and changed the subject.

"Do ye see Castle Rock, just there?" I said as I pointed to the rock island before us. So many of the formations around the isle were pointed and jagged shards and stacks. Castle Rock was a distinct formation for both its distance away from the shore and its smooth, weathered shape that looked exactly like an ancient castle floating in the sea.

"Aye, I heard from one of the summer lads many years ago. It is supposed to be haunted by a woman who fell into the sea," he said, immediately realizing that this might make me think of my mother and it did. It was well known that my mother drowned in the waters below us. A young mother lost in such a tragic accident leaving her young daughter and her grieving husband behind was mourned across MacLeod lands for many years.

To be fair to William, however, the old tale of the *Mournful Maiden of Castle Rock* was told for generations before my own mother's death. The story, shared far and wide on Skye, was about a young woman who lost her love in a shipwreck and swam out to Castle Rock, believing her beloved was there waiting for her. Instead, the lass drowned in pursuit of her love, and her spirit waits for him there still. It is said if you go close to the rock, you can hear her crying and calling out to her beloved over the wind and waves.

I do not remember if the lass perished on the way there or way back and, depending on who was telling the story, her drowning was also either intentional or accidental. My observation has been that women leaned more on the intentional side to show the depth of the maiden's lament. She knew her love was gone, but the love she felt was so deep that her spirit would remain on the rock until their souls could be reunited.

"Ye were right… what ye said before. Cairn's Point has always been a special place fer me. I love the peace I get from the sea below—even when it is angry and churning—it has a comforting rhythm within its raw power. I come to sit here when I need to think, or pray, or even just to cry."

I looked back at the towering cairn behind us and said, "But I also come here to talk to my mother. I feel closest to her here." I felt emotional about the loss of my mother, and now my father, along with the thought of leaving my home. He nodded in understanding but did not say a word. So, I changed the subject as quickly as I could.

I leaned in as if I were letting William in on a secret. "When I was a young lass, I used to imagine that I was the Queen of Castle Rock. And one day, I would swim back out to take my rightful place on the throne."

I laughed slightly at my words and the wistful imagination of a child. I looked down at the ground in sudden embarrassment of my confession and said, "But that is what all wee lasses dream of, right? Being a princess or a queen?"

"I suppose so for a lass," he said as he leaned in toward me as if he was sharing his own secret. "Whereas lads would just think, *I would hate to freeze my arse off on that ice-cold rock!*"

We laughed together on this point, and I nodded in understanding, "That is a verra practical—and undoubtedly *male*—perspective, William."

We sat silently for a moment until he said, "I am glad we had this time together, Alexandra. I admire that ye speak yer mind so freely. I ken it was probably a shock to ye that the laird chose me to accompany ye, Duncan, and Angus to Edinburgh."

"I wouldna say *shock*," I said, uncertain how to finish the statement as I honestly still do not know how to process the insistence that he travel with us. But I am also unaware of the expectations my uncle set for the men in their meeting this evening.

I thought about asking William outright what was asked of them, but I knew that question would put him in a terrible position between the laird he serves now and the lady he may serve one day in the future. I could get the information from Duncan at some point any way. Traveling with my uncle Duncan would have been fine. We know each other and have a way of speaking to each other as a family that is less formal. He will be the buffer and translator between me and Angus, who will do his duty to his friend more so than me. But to add William MacCrimmon to the group of travelers, makes an already emotional pilgrimage now an awkward one.

"I am verra sorry for the reason ye have to go to Edinburgh, but this is an instance where my size and fighting ability can come in handy. Yer position is important, and I am proud to be of service to ye, Laird MacLeod, and the clan."

"I appreciate your willingness to help us and ye should do as yer laird commands. Do ye not see your size and fighting ability as an asset?"

"No. I mean, aye! Erm…"

I could tell somehow that he was more frustrated with his response than the question itself. So, I tried to help him. "I must assume, then, that ye mean ye dinnae want to be *defined* by these traits alone. I mean, ye can quote passages from *King Lear,* for Christ's sake!"

"Och! Exactly! That is what I meant, but couldna find the right words. I will do anything I can to protect those that I love or to protect those that cannae protect themselves, but that is not all of me. I have more to offer than my size and brute force. I promised yer uncles this verra evening that I pledge to keep ye safe on this journey, Alexandra. I am honored to escort ye to Edinburgh and back."

"I appreciate that, William… though I hate this task may keep you from your own family. Would you not be going back home now that the summer is almost over?"

"Aye, but I have no home. My parents are dead, and I have no brothers or sisters. I am alone."

His statement struck my heart as I had the same realization myself on this very cliff. I am also alone.

"I believe this is where I am supposed to be. This is what I am supposed to do at this moment. I also received a permanent position in the stables with Master Knox."

"I had no idea! That is good news!" I said in celebration for him earning permanent placement in the stables, that will also earn him room and board along with modest annual pay. He seemed quite proud of himself as he sat up taller and squared his broad shoulders. "Ye ken that Auld Knox is verra particular, so you should be proud of earning a role in the stables here. Well then, sir, I suppose that means that Dunmara Castle is now yer *home*."

"I had not thought of it that way. It feels good to have a *home*. Now I have more than one reason to return to Skye after our journey."

I did not ask him what the other reasons were, but could only assume it had something to do with the previous meeting with my uncles. I will wait for Duncan's confirmation, but I expect there is a financial incentive for these men to complete the task they have been given. We sat silently for a minute. I wanted to know more about his family, but something about his soft tone at the mention of them told me that now was not the time to ask.

William stood up and reached his hands out for mine to help me up off the ground and said, "We should go back to the castle, Alexandra, now that night falls upon us. Duncan said we will start at first light tomorrow and that hour *always* comes too soon!"

"Indeed, I suppose we should go."

Once my hands touched his, he exclaimed, "Och! Yer hands are freezing, lass!"

"I have been here for a while."

As we walked down the hill to Dunmara Castle, he kept my hand in his until we reached the bottom of the steep and rocky hill and were on more level ground. While we still did not know each other well and I had apprehensions on our travel ahead, I was comforted by both how warm his hand was and how it engulfed my own. Much like I observed when he joined me and Grant at the stone wall, his hands were strong but gentle… and thankfully at this moment, *warm*.

I turned my head back for a moment and whispered *"Goodbye,"* under my breath into the howling sea wind while watching the orange sun finally descend quietly into the sea.

I hope my mother and father heard me.

+++

Shortly after I arrived in my room, I ran to the fire to counter the cold damp of Cairn's Point. I was met by Missus Gerrard who was already here to help me pack for the long ride to Edinburgh.

"I am so, so sorry, lass," she said as she hugged me tight and stroked my tangled and windswept hair. "To lose yer own father so soon after Lady Margaret..." She could not finish her words and brought her handkerchief to her nose. We both stood in silent grief at the losses we have endured in such a short amount of time. After a moment of shared mourning and reverence, she immediately went into action. A young kitchen maid delivered two water caldrons and she immediately placed on the hooks above the fire. The moment reminded me of the latest castle intrigue.

"Did ye hear about Mary, then?"

"Aye! Can ye believe it, Alexandra?" she said, genuinely shocked at the notion. "The lass was never all that smart to begin with, but her lack of judgment has given her poor mother fits with this decision."

"I fear she will regret this banishment for the rest of her life," I said, somehow feeling more sympathy for *Mean Old Mary MacAskill* than I ever had, and probably more than she deserved.

"If she doesna already, lass!" said Missus Gerrard.

I nodded to her in agreement on this point. *If she doesna already.*

"Ye have to be ready to leave at first light," Missus Gerrard said as she began pulling clothes suitable for riding in all manner of unpredictable Scottish weather. We also packed a few personal things in a small bag, most notably my lip oil that fights the cold air, a hair comb and pins, and Lady Margaret's book of Shakespeare's sonnets. We said very few words until we were finished packing.

"I will wake ye in the morning," she said, tidying the last items in the travel bag and prepping the wash basin with the hot water from the cauldron. "It is best to wash tonight as first light will come early, and it will be cold. Give me these clothes and yer shift and I will wash for ye now, so they are dry fer ye tomorrow."

I just nodded at her in understanding. I will want to sleep as much as I can, and it is best not to ride out in the morning air with a wet head of hair when you have the roaring fire to help you dry it the night before. I exchanged all of my clothes for a linen wrap so I could wash.

"I will miss you verra much, my sweet lass!" she said, hugging me tight and stroking my hair again. I could tell she was trying to stop her own tears, as I was. "I am so sorry that you have leave us and for this reason."

She pulled back and with her hands on my face and brushing my curls back she continued, "While the laird may be cross at me telling another, I told Auld Knox to make certain that wee Robbie has yer horse ready fer ye tomorrow morning."

With this simple act of kindness, I could no longer hold back the tears that started flowing immediately at the thought of leaving the lad. To see my wee Robbie once again before our exodus from our clan lands and home is a blessing. She continued stroking my unruly hair as I cried on her shoulder, and said softly to me, "I cannae let ye leave Dunmara without saying goodbye to the sweet lad, m'dear. And ye ken he would be brokenhearted if ye left him with nae a word."

She lifted my head and looked me in my tear-filled eyes as she continued with her instruction, "The lad willna ken why yer leavin' until he hears it in the Great Hall wi' the rest of the clan, so be quiet about that. But say what ye need to him, lass."

"Thank ye! He may not understand, and may ask me questions I cannae answer, but I would regret not saying goodbye to him," I said in even greater appreciation of the kind gesture of love and family that Missus Gerrard was offering me. "I do not want to go to Edinburgh. This is my home. I insisted on going to support Father, but suddenly I feel afraid."

"Aye, dinnae, m' dear lass. Ye will be in good hands with yer uncle and the lads. Ye will be back home before ye ken it!"

The first farewell in the courtyard of the day was the hardest. My wee Robbie had no idea why I was leaving with Duncan, William, and Angus on this early morning, but stood proudly holding the reins of a strong and sturdy horse in the courtyard. We did not even speak at first and just hugged each other tight. We both tried to hold back our tears. I had both of my hands in his glorious auburn hair and kissed the top of his head many times over. After a season of eternal loss, it is remarkable that even a temporary farewell to someone you love can tear your heart out just the same.

164

"My wee Robbie. Ye must be here for yer mother and Laird Graham, do ye understand?"

"Aye," he said, staring down at the ground, "but I dinnae ken why ye have to leave."

"Ye will, lad," I said, as I changed the subject quickly and moved my hand to his shoulder. "I thank you for preparing such a grand horse for me. What is his name?"

"Munro," Robbie said softly. "But he is a Highland pony, cousin."

I am not sure I know the differences between ponies and horses, but suspect it has something to do with height, not just breed. I stroked the nose and gorgeous neck of the bay-colored pony with the black mane and tail before me and said, "Aye, Munro is magnificent! Tell me everything I need to ken, lad."

That was exactly what I needed to shake the pain of our goodbye and the reason for it, as Robbie immediately changed his focus and began telling me all about the mighty Munro.

"Alex, he is a large pony, powerful, but gentle at the same time," he said, patting Munro's neck himself. "He will be able to help ye across the Highlands. We tacked up Munro with his normal saddle and blankets. Ye may have to get used to it, as he is a bit wider than the horses ye normally ride." The lad leaned and said with a whisper, "Dinnae tell Master Knox, but I put a few extra carrots, and some sugar lumps, fer the journey in yer saddlebag. Ye will graze and water on yer stops, of course, but a treat can also be fine fer motivating the lad."

Clearly my Munro is getting only the finest treatment out of the stables at Dunmara Castle this morning. I just smiled at Robbie with pride as he continued, "It doesna matter how far ye are going, please show him some appreciation at the end of yer ride. He loves that. Isn't that right, Munro?" he asked the pony promptly nodded his head to the lad. "I have never seen a lad so motivated by positive words and a kind touch. I ken you will be fast friends, and he will do as ye command with a little love and affection."

Munro, with his ears back now, nodded his head to me on these words and I stroked his nose and neck again as he leaned into my shoulder. "Aye, my Munro, we will be fast friends!"

Master Knox stood behind Robbie with his own smile at the lad's advice to me. We nodded to each other in silent agreement that wee Robbie was in the right place, and I suspect that is the very moment Missus Gerrard and Laird Graham officially lost their errand boy and castle messenger to the stables. My heart was filled with pride.

Knox said to Robbie while patting him on the shoulder, "Well done, lad!" He then turned to me affectionately, and said in a tone I have rarely heard from him, "Come home safe to us, Lady Alexandra."

"I intend to, sir," I said as they helped me mount Munro. The saddle was wider than I was used to, but I tucked my skirts under my thighs as best I could. This was going to take some getting used to.

Angus waved to us all and set out on a gallop in advance of this group. The laird came to me and before he could say anything, I said softly, "I updated the record for the next Great Hall and left it in your chamber, sir."

"I thank ye fer that. Be safe, my dear lass. I want ye to heed Duncan's instructions and guidance on this journey and come back to us soon."

We were surrounded in the courtyard by Laird Graham, Missus Gerrard, Auld Knox, and Father Bruce and yet I only remember wee Robbie's face—proud but pained. I could not look at any of them in the eyes or I would surely start crying. Instead, I fussed needlessly with my saddle bag, reins, and my skirts.

Duncan and I acknowledged the laird again with a bow of our heads as we set out together. William followed behind us, did the same. I could hear the faint words of Father Bruce's prayers for our safe journey as we left the courtyard.

+++

TWELVE
On The Road

My tears started flowing the minute we left the gates of Dunmara Castle. Duncan gave me a short look of concern but said nothing. In fact, we rode for many miles in total silence other than the sounds of the hooves of our horses and my occasional sniffles.

I had been to Dunmara village and all parts of Skye, but somehow leaving the castle grounds today hurt my heart. Whatever the reason for a separation, it is still a loss. On top of the grief for the loss of Father and Lady Margaret before him, I already missed home, uncertain of what lies ahead and when I will be able to return. My tears dried quickly between the cool morning air and the warmth of the rising sun. I leaned forward and patted Munro's neck for reassurance and encouragement. He responded with a nod of his head that he understood what I was feeling. Perhaps he could feel all of my apprehension and emotion as we started out on our first journey together.

I said a silent prayer that God would keep us all safe and was suddenly confident that this unlikely band of travelers would see me across Scotland to my father's home and back again. I expect the next few weeks will tell me everything I need to know about this lot. And it may tell them more than they want to know about me.

As we rode, I was always kept between William and Duncan for protection, and I did not talk to either one for many miles. My silence was in part due to inability to speak without emotion. We have quite a journey ahead of us. I am determined to keep up the pace and I must try my best not to cry in front of these men again.

Our first stop overnight was in a small country tavern in the middle of nowhere, and William asked for the reins to Munro immediately as I dismounted. It appears he is not just serving as physical protection on our journey, but also serving as our own stable hand.

"Please wait, William," I asked before he took Munro away. I had wee Robbie's words in my ears and knew I had one more task before I could retire this evening.

"Och, my darlin' Munro," I said as I stroked his nose and under his chin while handing him a carrot from the bag. "Thank ye for delivering me here safely! Ye have been a fine escort, sir. My verra own Scottish knight."

Munro nodded his head in receipt of my words of appreciation and leaned his head into my hands. William took him with the other horses to the stables. I feel horrible having been riding all day. I want to find my room, clean up, and then have supper so that I can sleep. As the men have told me, first light always comes too early.

169

I walked up to Duncan as he was in mid-conversation with Angus. From the small bit I overheard on my approach, Angus secured a room for me in the tavern, but the men could only be housed above the stables. I stopped for a moment and asked, innocently to my uncle, "That does not seem fair after a long day of riding. Surely ye wouldn't want to be in the stables, Duncan!"

"No one *wants* to sleep in the stables, lass. But it is not unusual to come across a tavern with no rooms for the night. The good news is that we have a room for ye, and we will all welcome the warm fire, hearty supper, and some drink before sleep." He saw the look of concern on my face and said, "I hate to tell ye, lass, that ye may have a night in a stable yerself before we make it to Edinburgh."

He and Angus laughed as they saw the look of shock on my face at the thought of spending a cold night surrounded by hay and horses. He took the opportunity to tease me more and said, "Come to think of it! Ye may ken how to sleep in the woods and catch, kill, and cook yer own supper before ye get back to Dunmara Castle. Consider this a journey of personal growth for ye, not just a journey across Scotland!"

"Why do ye hate me so, uncle?" I asked with a smile at his teasing, but a little afraid that his words, while harsh, may very well prove true. I realize how sheltered and protected I have been because of my family, my position, and my home at Dunmara. This may be a journey of personal growth, after all.

Duncan patted me on my shoulder as William handed me my bag and said, "Angus, take her in out of the night air so she can go to her bedchamber."

Angus nodded and motioned me to follow him as he said, "Aye!"

I am certain this is the very first time I understood what Angus said, and I followed him into the warmth of the tavern willingly.

"Meet us for supper downstairs when yer ready, lass!" Duncan yelled to me.

+++

The room at the top of the stairs was large, but sparsely furnished. It had a bed in the corner, covered in many wool blankets—some cleaner than others. There was a small table with two chairs in front of a dwindling fire. In the corner was a small chest with a wash basin and clean linens. The pitcher in the basin was already filled with cool water.

On the wall above it hung a mirror that had been cracked so many times, it looked like it would fall into a hundred pieces on the floor at any moment. In fact, I would guess that the slamming of the door to the room is the primary reason for its current state. In it, I could see many distorted versions of myself and decided that after the emotion of the morning and the long ride, I had little desire to clean up too much before supper. A tavern supper with my current companions did not need a grand entrance from the Lady MacLeod and I am just too tired to care.

I washed my hands and tried to remove the traces of mud from my face and hair as much as I could. I figured that even with the minimal effort, it would still be enough to set me apart from my travel companions this evening.

I tended the fire to ensure it would warm my room more during supper and so I could hopefully sleep soundly tonight in advance of another early start and long day of riding. There was a cauldron of water nearby that, in addition to the basin, would be perfect for me. It was not home, but the room had what I needed for one night.

I joined the men at a table in front of the warm fireplace. Duncan, proving he did not hate me after all, had a pot of ale waiting for me. As soon as I arrived, the barmaid brought us all plates of a hearty beef and potato stew and warm bread. I set about the bread and butter immediately and no one said a word to each other through supper. We were all road weary and clearly hungry. All I could think is that we still have so much further to go. Not to mention, as much as I love my Munro already, I do not know how my thighs and my back will survive his wide saddle.

Finally, Duncan spoke his instructions for the table. "Since ye are in the tavern, Alexandra, I will need to place someone outside yer door throughout the night for protection. We will manage in shifts. I will have William take first watch, then Angus, and I will see you first thing in the morning. Be ready to leave at first light, lass."

I protested immediately, "Ye all are already in the stables and now each of ye will not get a full night's sleep? I dinnae like this plan at all!"

"Lass, I ken yer heart is in the right place, but ye cannae have all of us up there enjoying yer fire with ye."

That was not exactly my thinking. But I felt guilty being the only one to have a bed and a full night's sleep.

"No matter how genuine yer thinking is to care fer us, we could already be in the sights of people looking for ye on this journey. People will also start to take notice of our traveling party, if they havena already," he said, surveying the room himself as he walked away from us to refill his glass.

Angus and William nodded in agreement on this point, and I felt nervous at the prospect of such a thing. I looked suspiciously around the room at the few travelers with us and wondered if they were paying any

172

attention to us at all. They all seemed to agree that protection in this moment was necessary, and I had to trust my uncle on this point. Laird Graham told me to listen to Duncan and take his direction. I cannot argue what I do not know—and I certainly know nothing of traveling across Scotland.

+++

Angus followed Duncan, likely in search of the same whisky bottle my uncle was. William and I were left at the table together. We sat in awkward silence for a moment until he finally said, "Ye let me ken when yer ready to go to yer room, and I will escort ye there."

"Perhaps one more drink?"

"Aye, and there *is* some bread left," he said, offering me the basket, and then filling my ale pot one more time from the pitcher in the middle of the table. Angus delivered him a glass of whisky from the bar as I reached across the table for the small white bowl and what remained of the fresh, creamy butter.

"It would be a shame to leave this goodness behind," I said as I buttered the last of the bread. I handed a piece to William and asked him, "Do ye miss yer home or is there some sense of independence now that ye have yer post at the castle stables?"

He sipped his whisky and thought about his answer while looking at his buttered bread. I already noticed that William MacCrimmon is generally a man of few words, but not because he is simple. He proved that was not the case with his knowledge of Shakespeare's *King Lear*. Instead, he is thoughtful and careful in his choice of words. I wondered for a moment if that was because he was talking to me—because I am a woman or Lady MacLeod. Either way, he was clearly tempering his words.

"It may be a little of both."

I nodded and whether he felt comfortable sharing, or the whisky loosened his tongue, he continued, "I miss my ma more than my da. She was the one that taught me about Shakespeare. She always told me that she named me William after him. But I have to admit the truth to ye. I ken only *King Lear* and *Macbeth*. Nothing else. Those were the only texts she had and even then, her books were tattered and worn." I smiled at him as he continued with a laugh, "I dinnae ken if she had all the pages for the plays, but they made sense to me. I was fortunate that I had a mother that could read, and she read them to me over and over to the point I could act them out like Grant, I kent the lines so well. Well, maybe *not* as good as Grant!"

I laughed with him and nodded in agreement and said, "Grant does like to act out his stories."

After a moment he continued, "Ma helped me learn my letters and then to read from these texts, but I ken that the language is verra different from our own. I like Shakespeare but it has taken me some time to read other writings and feel like I could understand them. I believe I can learn more about Shakespeare and maybe other writers from ye. Ye are much more educated than I am."

"Aye," I said, remembering how Lady Margaret shared the gift of Shakespeare with me in my own learning, but how unique it is in language. "I must say that I love Shakespeare's sonnets the most. I read them more so than the plays. Laird Graham gave me Lady Margaret's book of sonnets after her death. But it just has the first one hundred, though. We would read them together often. I am happy to share my favorites, if ye like."

He smiled and nodded to me briefly. I have so many questions to ask him, but before I could, he spoke again, with his head bowed. The shift in his tone was sudden and solemn. I just let him continue telling me what he wanted to—what he needed to.

"Da was a mean drunk, ye ken? He was a piper for Clan MacLeod. When the ban on pipes went into effect after Culloden, he tried to get other work, but the man was not suited to tending fields or sheep. And when he did find work, he resented it. He lost himself and drank every coin he ever earned. He was always angry when he returned home after a night at the tavern. He would come home every evening and start in again. The yelling. The hitting. I spent much of my childhood hiding under the kitchen table and crying as my dear ma took the brunt of his anger."

I looked at him with sympathy for this, as I could not imagine such a life or what violence he may have witnessed in his own home as a young lad. In some way, it seemed that he was relieved to be able to share his story, as painful as it was.

"Did he beat you as well?" I asked without thinking. His reaction to my question told me the answer, and I quickly tried to correct myself for such an intrusion.

"I am *so sorry*, William," I said, nearly choking on my ale and placing the pot on the table. "Ye do not have to say anymore. Please, dinnae answer my last question! It was rude of me to ask it."

He nodded to me but continued despite my retraction, "He did. But as I grew in size, it became harder for him, so he focused his rage even more on my poor ma."

"Bless her! That had to break your heart to see such anger and violence in yer own home as a wee lad."

"Aye! In some way, I was used to it, and I thought everyone lived like that. But my summers at Dunmara Castle showed me that was not true."

"Really? How?"

"First, it just felt different being there. I looked forward to walking through the castle gates every June. The life of the castle felt warm and inviting. I had a purpose. I was housed. I was fed. And I was happy. I wanted to be there... and looked forward to it most of the year. I believe my ma was grateful to send me away, if for no other reason than to help me escape my own father."

I smiled weakly for a moment at the notion of feeling *safe* at Dunmara Castle. That was part of my worry about leaving today. I was leaving a place that made me feel safe in exchange for an uncertain life on the road and the uncertain destination of Edinburgh.

"It was clear to me that Laird MacLeod loved Lady MacLeod. And from what I could see, she seemed to feel the same."

"Aye, she did," I said, as I smiled, thinking about the love between my aunt and uncle. I bit my lip at the memory of her words to me on the night she died.

"Ye never ken what happens in someone else's house, but to me, when I saw them in the Great Hall, they always looked at each other with such love... such *respect*."

"I appreciate that ye said *respect*. They definitely had love, but it was the strong mutual respect for each other and their contribution to the success of the clan that bonded them. It was an incredible partnership to witness, and I am so fortunate to have been part of their lives for so long."

"By the time I was eighteen, I had already grown taller and bigger than Da. I returned home from Dunmara and one night he set about punishing Ma for something—likely not having a warm supper waiting for him when he returned from the tavern when the poor woman had no way to ken when he would show up, if at all. He started to hit her and after the second blow, I caught his arm with mine in mid-air and pushed him to the ground."

"What did he *do?*"

"He called me every horrible name you could think of calling a person—let alone yer own son! But at some point, I could not even hear him anymore," William said, reliving the distant memory and focused his eyes once again on the bottom of his glass. "Consumed by my own rage, I lifted the man off the floor by the neck as he gasped for air."

My eyes widened at the thought of such a scene. We sat quietly for a moment. He took a sip of his drink and his eyes looked at me finally with shame and pain. His eyes made me sad as I felt both his regret and relief at sharing his story.

"I told the man in that moment to never return to our house or I would kill him, and we never saw him again. I dinnae ken if he is alive or dead. I just have to assume that he is, dead I mean."

"Ye did what ye had to do to protect yer mother!"

"Aye, but I will always live with the shame of disrespecting my own father. Ma died less than a year later, and I have been on my own ever since."

I could see the struggle he was having in protecting and defending someone you love by going against someone you were taught to respect and obey. I wondered more about where he went in the time away from Dunmara with no family to go back to, but I did not ask such a question.

"I said it yesterday, but will say again, yer home is *now* at Dunmara. Ye are a valuable member of Clan MacLeod, and we are proud to have ye, as our kinsman, serving yer laird, and working on our lands."

I wanted to touch his arm out of sympathy for everything he said, but I did not. He looked back at me with a smile and said in a happier tone and with complete relief, "I was *so grateful* that Auld Knox offered me the post in the stables. I dinnae ken where I would go if he had not."

I could feel his genuine gratitude for his new role and home. But it was time to conclude the evening. First light would come early for us all, especially for those on watch outside my door. I did not see Duncan anywhere in the room, and said, "Ye are on first watch then."

"Aye, give me a moment and then I will escort ye upstairs," he said. I understood that he likely needed to relieve himself of drink and he would also want to check the horses, as that also appears to be his responsibility on this trip.

"Dinnae rush. I will wait here. My ale pot is still half-full."

After several minutes, William still had not returned. Then, out of the corner of my eye, I saw Duncan and Angus run out the tavern door at a speed I had never seen before. Something was wrong. I stood up, uncertain of what was happening, and ran after them.

"Duncan! What is it?"

"Angus!" Duncan yelled and snapped his fingers, signaling for the man to stop me at the tavern door. Angus turned around and met me at the threshold, blocking my way and just shook his head, indicating that I could not pass him. I could see that a man, in a considerable drunken state, was challenging William in front of the tavern. William kept blocking the man from returning inside with his body and his arms held wide. Duncan stood behind him as additional support in front of the door.

"I am no' takin' her fer m'self!" the man said as he pointed to William, Angus, and Duncan, seemingly trying to reason with all the tall men blocking his way back into the tavern. "We can *all* have a go, aye?"

It was then that I realized the man was talking about me. Angus looked at me apologetically that I had to hear such vulgar talk from the drunken man. Without saying a word, he nodded his head back into the tavern with a stern look that told me plainly to go back inside.

"Why should ye 'ave the only bonnie lass in the tavern?" he asked, now agitated, and trying to stand tall in the face of William. He still could not match William in any way in size or height, but the drunken man tried.

I moved to stand on the other side of the open door when the tavern owner walked past me and Angus.

"Davy, ye drunken eejit! G'home, man!" The tavern owner tried to apologize to William and Duncan, "Davy got ahead of 'imself this night, 'tis all. He is no threat to yer lass—only to 'imself. He seems hellbent on gettin' his skull crushed in."

The man could barely stand, and shouted, "Tha' lass is 'ere wi' three men! Three! *Come 'ere, whore! Come 'ere!*"

With that, William punched the man right on his chin, leveling him to the ground. He did not move. I bet William did not even hit him at full force, but the combination of drink and a shot to the chin was enough to knock *'Davy the eejit'* out cold in the middle of the courtyard.

"Never ye mind, lad," the tavern owner said, patting William reassuringly on his broad shoulder. "One of the stable hands will throw 'im over a horse and take 'im to his wife. Trust me! She will sober 'im up mighty quick!"

Duncan patted the tavern owner on the shoulder and said, "I thank ye, sir!"

William and Duncan, both out of breath, walked back into the tavern together. Duncan shook William's hand and said, "Well done, lad."

"He cornered me on the way back from the stables, sir," William said. "I could see he was drunk and could barely stand. I tried my best to settle the matter out here instead of having him follow me back in and confronting Lady Alexandra directly."

Duncan looked at me standing in the door and said, "Even if there was no advance notice of yer travels, and we hope there was not, ye are a bonnie lass sitting in a country tavern with three men. Ye will be noticed."

I looked around the room at the few remaining others in the tavern and thought about them all being a threat. I looked back at Duncan and the other men staring at me. I could feel my face grow red and my heart race from the entire scene.

"To yer room, Alexandra! Will, first watch," he said, motioning for him to see that I made it there as instructed.

I felt like I was being scolded and sent to bed by my father, but I could tell Duncan was rattled. His words and his protective tone annoyed me earlier, but I could not argue with the man now in light of what we just witnessed. William followed me up the stairs and ensured I made it safely to my warm room. He checked every corner of the room and even looked under the bed to make certain no one was hiding in there. He then tended my fire for me so that it glowed red hot.

"Ye may need to tend the fire tonight, but I will ask Angus and Duncan to check it fer ye when they arrive on watch."

"Thank ye." Before he closed the door, I yelled, "Wait!" I ran to the bed and grabbed a wool blanket and a small pillow off the top, and said, "Please, ye have to take this if yer going to guard my door."

"Thank you verra much. Erm, I am sorry ye had to hear what the drunk man said."

I just smiled at him in appreciation for his concern, but I suspect it may not be the first unpleasant encounter we have on this trip across Scotland.

"Good night," I said, as I hastily shut the door between us.

"Good night."

I thought about the conversation with William and how much I appreciated him telling me the story of his family. He was right. We never know what goes on in someone else's home, but his experience with his father and mother shaped him into the person he is. From everything I have seen of him so far, he is an honorable man.

This morning, I left Dunmara Castle feeling uncertain about the journey ahead. Now, safely in this bed, and warm room, I just feel grateful that I have my uncle and these men protecting me on the way.

THIRTEEN
The Grief Onward

I slept so soundly that I never heard the transfer of duty between William to Angus, and then Angus to Duncan. Even if they all tended my fire, nothing. But just before daylight, I awoke to my uncle shaking my shoulder and standing above me in the same wool blanket I had given William the night before.

With my eyes barely open, I asked, "First light already?"

"Meet us downstairs, lass," he said as he tossed the blanket and then the pillow back on the bed and walked out of the room.

I struggled to get up out of a deep sleep but sat myself up immediately or I would have stayed in bed all day. I knew I only had minutes to get dressed and be ready for a day of travel once again and not only was I cold, but my back and legs were stiff from the previous day's ride.

I met my not-so-merry band of travelers downstairs, and we ate our thick, tasteless porridge together in silence. I could tell that none of them looked rested, and I felt sorry for them having to spend their night split between the front of my door and the loft above the stables. None of them got a full night of sleep between the uncomfortable location and the chill.

"I must thank ye all for keeping me safe, and I am sorry again about yer night." They all just looked at me. I could not tell if they were unused to gratitude in general or simply uninterested in a show of gratitude for something they had no choice but to do. I changed the subject and asked Duncan, "How far will we ride today?"

"Angus will leave us now, and we hope to make it as far as Fort William—if not just past—tonight. That is, if the weather doesna hold us back. It's a dreich day, lass. Ye will need yer cloak."

Angus departed the tavern on Duncan's word with only a quick wave to us and I knew that just made my first mistake of cross-Scotland travel. I had not even looked outside to assess the weather. I knew it felt damp in the tavern, but I just thought that was due to the early morning hour.

It was a miserable, driech day. I had to have my cloak with a hood protect my head from the elements and to repel the water as best it could. We crossed over on the short ferry ride with our horses from Armadale to Mallaig, finally landing on the mainland of Scotland. I tried not to complain, but thankfully, Duncan allowed us to stop in another tavern to dry off and eat mid-day.

The horses all needed to have a break to graze and be watered. I begged my uncle to stay here for the night and start again tomorrow when hopefully the weather would be better. Despite being August, the rain off the coast still had a chill, and it was a miserable, slow ride. Unfortunately, my uncle was not of the same mind.

I tried to tell myself that if the men could make it without complaint, then so could I. But I lost all of my conviction about an hour after we left the warmth of the tavern. I tried not to focus on my own misery at this moment and instead focused on Munro. I talked and cried to him constantly and no one else for many miles.

We finally met up with Angus and I was so happy to learn that we had secured two rooms this night at the tavern just outside of Fort William. The men could share one room and not have to die of fever after another damp and chilly night in the stables.

Duncan warned us that being so near the fort, the tavern would likely be filled with soldiers. We needed to be on our best behavior and not stay out too late that we invite a scene like we did last night. No one wanted to be fighting Redcoats this night.

I could barely lose the chill I carried all day from the rain. I stood in front of the huge fireplace unable to move other than my unending shivers. I could hear the words of Lady Margaret in my ear, *"Have a care, m'dear!"* She would surely be disappointed in me at this moment. I am certain I look a fright. I could not stop shaking and stood before my travel companions caked in mud, my wet curly hair all over the place, and smelling like my dear Munro.

"Sit down, lass," Duncan said to me as he handed me a glass. "The whisky will warm ye from the inside, as the fire warms ye from the outside."

As far as I could tell, the men seemed to be trying to do the same. The barkeep left an entire bottle with my uncle for this very purpose. He looked at me and said with a smile, filling his glass again, "Ye ken *uisge beatha* can cure anything, lass. Even the chill and damp."

Duncan was correct. The roaring fire started drying my wet hair and clothes, and the whisky started thawing my insides. I could finally enjoy supper. Duncan told us all tall tales of traveling across Scotland and how many times he had to sleep in the snow and wind without shelter or without anything to eat. I could not tell if he was exaggerating for the other men or trying to shame me for being so insistent about staying at the last tavern in my weak attempt to avoid the cold rain. Perhaps it was a little of both.

"Will, go fetch us another bottle, lad!" Duncan said to William, handing him the coin to secure the whisky from the tavern owner. With a second bottle, I could tell that we were no longer just warming our insides.

William returned with a new bottle and once Duncan filled the glasses again, he raised his glass in the center of the table and said, "To ye William MacCrimmon, and yer new role in the stables of Dunmara Castle with Auld Knox!"

We all placed our glasses in with his and said together, "*Sláinte!*"

"Ye ken, lad, that yer on this journey because of Laird Graham himself?"

"No sir, I didna," William said, intrigued by Duncan's impending story. "I just assumed my size and fighting ability were assets."

"Aye! Ye made a great impression after the Wesley MacLeod situation and his decision was further supported by Auld Knox when we spoke with him."

I sat up on the bench at the mention of Wesley's name, and Duncan said, waving his glass in my direction dismissively, "Sorry, lass."

I just nodded my head as the Wesley story was well past us and I would not give it any more room in my mind. The matter was closed for me the minute the lad was escorted off our clan lands.

William looked at me in sympathy at our shared memory and said to Duncan, "I had no idea, sir."

Duncan slapped him on his broad shoulders and said, "Well done, lad! Ye want someone like Auld Knox in yer corner."

Angus, eyes barely open, said as he raised his glass to William, "Lang may yer lum reek!"

We all just looked at the man and then started laughing. Duncan slapped Angus on the shoulder and said, "Yer oot yer face, man!"

Once we stopped laughing, we realized that another early start was ahead of us. Duncan reiterated the same protection schedule for the night, and we retired to our warm rooms. William, once again, took the first watch and settled down in the hall before my door—this time with his own wool blanket.

+++

We were not as fortunate on the next evening. True to Duncan's premonition, Angus was unable to secure lodgings. We were somewhere in the remote Highlands. I was going to be forced to sleep in front of a fire under the night sky with my travel companions. A prospect that was not made any more pleasant when Angus arrived to meet us with three dead hares hanging from his saddle. We would have to cook for ourselves as well this night.

We were in luck, however. Angus said that if we could all manage to ride another mile ahead in the dark, we can shelter in an empty croft over the next hill.

Everyone nodded in agreement, as any shelter had to be better than spending a night under the night sky. I suddenly felt nervous about being in close quarters with this bunch. Once we arrived, Duncan seemed intent on keeping me on the other side of the room, away from them.

Thankfully, I was not asked to gut, clean, or cook the hares. I have no ability—or stomach—to do such a thing. I did, however, give up the remaining carrots in my bag for the evening meal that we roasted over the open flame. Duncan promised we could fill the saddle bags in the next village. Munro had enough fresh grass to graze, so would not mind. I told myself that this sweet lad would want me to have the carrots. True or not, I would make it up to my beloved.

We all ate once again in exhausted silence. At the end of the meal, I tried to clean up all the remnants of supper, as best I could. "Thank ye, Angus, for the fine meal." He nodded but said nothing back to me.

William brought us all our wool blankets from the horses to help get through the night. He and Angus moved to the fire on the other side of the croft to discuss the plan for the next day with Duncan. I barely listened to them as I shut my eyes and tried to absorb as much heat from the fire as I could. Then I opened my book of sonnets.

William walked over and sat down next to me on the wall. It was a bold move as Duncan made a silent point of keeping me alone on this side of the croft, away from them all when we arrived. I looked over at Duncan and Angus, but they were so focused on their own conversation that they did not even seem to notice.

"Would ye prefer to read alone?"

"I do not mind reading together, if ye want to hear some sonnets."

He smiled and nodded to me as he stoked my fire once more before he settled himself against the wall with me.

"I have one that I read tonight that is perfect for a weary bunch of travelers. Let me find it again." I turned back a few pages to find Shakespeare's Sonnet 50. I sat up taller and started reading it aloud to him.

"How heavy do I journey on the way,
When what I seek, my weary travel's end,
Doth teach that ease and that repose to say
'Thus far the miles are measured from thy friend!'
The beast that bears me, tired with my woe,
Plods dully on, to bear that weight in me,
As if by some instinct the wretch did know
His rider lov'd not speed, being made from thee:
The bloody spur cannot provoke him on
That sometimes anger thrusts into his hide,
Which heavily he answers with a groan,
More sharp to me than spurring to his side;
For that same groan doth put this in my mind,
My grief lies onward, and my joy behind."

Sonnet 50, William Shakespeare

I teared up at the end but tried to smile through it. The last line fully depicts this journey. The loss of my father and all that comes with finishing the life he had in Edinburgh is pulling us ahead, and the simple joys and comforts of home are behind us.

I know that while this journey is a lot harder than I expected, it is important for me to be here. I am grateful that Laird Graham did not just send Duncan to handle everything on his own and that he allowed me to be here. But this night, sitting against the cold stone wall of a damp abandoned croft house, I feel weary and regret not having a warm room to myself so that I could cry alone.

"Aye, that is a good one, no?" William asked as he seemed to be thinking about the words more.

"It describes the journey we are on perfectly!" I said. "I ken Shakespeare is lamenting leaving someone he loves behind, but the description of his weary horse and then that last line… it gets me every time."

"I understand. Yer grief does lie *onward*. The loss of yer father and finishing his life in the city has to be difficult for ye. I am verra sorry that ye have to be on this mournful journey."

"Thank ye. Ye are verra kind."

He smiled at me but stood up and retreated just as Duncan approached, knowing that my uncle probably would not appreciate us talking on our own on the side of the room. Duncan said nothing, but sat down next to me, taking William's place against the wall.

Duncan handed me a pewter flask and said, "Here, lass."

"Thank ye," I said after a healthy sip of whisky from the container. I looked at it before handing it back. I do not remember seeing it before, but it had his name beautifully engraved on one side and the sprigs of juniper engraved on the other. This flask seemed special. I had only seen leather hide flasks and had one in my saddlebag myself, but I placed fresh water in it when we watered our horses.

"Duncan, I have a question."

While he did not play the game, he gave me a look to the side that said, *'Of course you do!'* I took the opportunity to give a look of annoyance and took the flask back from him. "Why do we not have relationships with other clans that we could be guests on their lands and not have to stay in taverns or empty crofts?"

He smiled and took another sip from the flask. "That is a fair question, and it shows yer thinkin' like a clan chief, lass. Relationships are often infrequent but important to a clan. If they exist, it can be for defensive or political reasons. Usually, such alliances are forged to protect against another clan they each deem an enemy… or an obstacle."

He leaned into my shoulder and continued, "There are also bonds and alliances that are to help strengthen the individual clans themselves, but those can be rare. Clans do not always seek ways to enrich each other and instead compete against each other. Ye ken what Adrian and Sarah were up against connecting MacLeod and MacDonald, but how their marriage brought us all together fer a time."

"Aye," I said, nodding as I took in all of his words.

"Yer first responsibility as chief is to keep your lands intact and yer people safe. In this case, the answer to yer question is simple. Our strongest alliances are on the Isles more so than the Highlands, and even those relationships are fragile at best given an often violent and bloody history."

I nodded in understanding as our history is filled with warring factions and episodes with Clan MacDonald and Clan MacKenzie, often over lands and allegations of personal insults, political infractions, and blind ambitions of gaining more land and property.

"The laird thought it was best not to alert the other clans of yer travels during this time as it could be seen, following Lady Margaret's death, as a point of weakness for Clan MacLeod. We particularly wanted to get ye away from Skye before anyone in Clan MacDonald found out. We are trying to move across Scotland as quickly as we can without detection. This is why I couldna take an afternoon to stay in the tavern, as much as we all wanted to. We have to keep moving."

I nodded in understanding, but did not say anything.

"Ye have been a good travel companion, lass. Ye have kept yer pace on a new horse and have not complained. Not much, anyway!" He said with a laugh as he leaned into my shoulder again. "This trip will be important for ye. Yer learning more about yer own country. Ye should make certain to learn as much as ye can. Being a clan chief on Skye is one thing, but being a clan chief in Scotland is another."

I smiled with him at the jest and thought about his words for a moment because I understood that, as chief of the clan, I would certainly need to know more about Skye *and* Scotland. Surely more so than what I learned in the books Lady Margaret provided for my study. What Duncan was saying was true. I did have a lot to learn away from the protective and sheltered walls of Dunmara Castle. I must take his words to heart and try to learn. Each challenge on this journey holds an important lesson for me as a woman and a leader.

"Another thing to ken is that there are vast glens, lochs, and forests between Skye and Edinburgh that do not have towns, taverns, or castles," he said. "We chose the fastest route to the city, but not the most comfortable. That route would have put many other travelers in our path, and we would have also been trying to secure the same lodgings."

"Aye, I understand," I said, reaching out my hand for the flask.

Duncan handed it back once again, albeit reluctantly, and asked with a smile, "Why do ye not have yer own flask, lass?"

I just shrugged my shoulders and said, "I am certain it has something to do with a lady not having such a thing. But suddenly, I wish I did have my own pewter flask with my name carved on it and not just a leather water flask in my saddlebag."

He did not take the bait on the story behind his beautiful flask of whisky, and instead patted me on the shoulder as he said, "Dinnae fash, we will correct that. Ye should try to sleep tonight if ye can."

"Aye, sleep well," I said as he walked away from me to reaffirm tonight's security plan with Angus and William on the opposite side of the room.

Just when I started to feel safe on this journey, my uncle reminded me once again that I am not. The continued acts of protection made me feel uneasy. I wrapped myself tightly in my wool blanket and got as comfortable as I could, leaning against the cold stone wall of the empty croft.

+++

FOURTEEN
Respite At Prestonfield

I felt someone gently touch my shoulder, waking me from a deep sleep. Despite every night being in a new place and even after this night of leaning against a cold stone wall, exhaustion completely overtook me. I slept deeper than I had in days. My weary bones clearly needed the rest.

"Lady Alexandra," William whispered to me. *"I am so verra sorry to wake ye my lady, but I need yer blanket to tack Munro fer ye."*

William's soft voice and gentle touch woke me into a cold damp that I had not realized until this moment. I was suddenly freezing and shivered as I reluctantly handed over my wool blanket to him, exposing myself even more to the brisk morning air.

He just nodded and smiled at me in sympathy. He pointed toward the fire Duncan was tending on the other side of the room. "Ye will be warmer closer to the fire over there. Yer uncle has it roaring now and this one here is nearly out."

Duncan yelled to me across the room, "Come over, lass! We are so close!"

I cannot imagine much more riding with this lot throughout the four seasons of Scotland, for much longer. I barely made it off the floor and to Duncan before the fire. I am saddle-sore riding for days, my back is cold and stiff, and I am growing weary from this never-ending journey.

Over the last few days, I switched to side-saddle occasionally just to break things up, but it did not help my back, or my thighs recover. No one asked me what I was doing, but they all knew that I was uncomfortable. In fact, I am certain my face showed my pain and discomfort.

I tried not to complain. But some nights ended with me in tears, trying to use the cold water at my disposal to soothe my tender thighs. Even my hands hurt, holding onto the saddle and reins. Duncan mentioned getting me gloves on our journey, but we never found any in the few small villages we came across.

Munro, however, remained my devoted knight and trusted friend on this trip. We spent time together in the morning before we departed and in the evening after the day's ride to connect. He is the only one I confessed my pain and misery to each day, as I did not want my fellow travelers to think that I could not hold my own. I also did not want Munro to think it was his fault. I just was not used to this amount of sustained riding. I like to believe he understood.

Just as wee Robbie said, Munro is motivated by affection and appreciation and serves with a sense of reverence and duty. He reassured me as best he could. I will ensure that Munro, with his valiant heart, returns me home to serve me for the rest of his days.

We finally arrived outside the village of Duddingston, south of the city of Edinburgh, when Angus met us just before our destination at Prestonfield House.

Standing next to his horse in the middle of a glen by two blue and green pools of water and a babbling brook, Angus greeted his friend Duncan first. After the men talked a bit, my uncle relayed the instructions to me and William.

"Just up that hill is Prestonfield House, but it may be good after a long day to let the horses water here before taking them to the stables. They call this the *Wells of the Weary* as many a traveler stops here on the last of the ride into the city."

"We are weary travelers indeed, uncle! And are fortunate to stop at this fine house before the city, but a quick stop here for the horses is only fair," I said as Duncan helped me down off of my Munro.

"Is that not right, my beloved? Only fair, lad!" I said as I patted Munro's neck before William led him to the water with his own horse.

I stretched my arms above my head and bent forward and back to loosen up the stiffness brought on from another long day of riding. Actually, a long week of riding. I shut my eyes and felt the warmth of the sun peeking through the trees on my face. This was a quiet spot where all ye could hear were the sounds of the birds moving from tree to tree above you and the water trickling over the rocks below.

Like my companions, I walked my freshly watered Munro up the small hill to the fine manor house, where Angus and the stable grooms were waiting for us in the courtyard. The stone stables were busy but welcoming. As best I could tell by the quick response, they had both the staff and the space for all of our horses. The grooms were quick to help us with our bags and promised to deliver them to our rooms. William said very little to the men but seemed quite happy not to be on duty this night in the stables. For the first time, he handed his own horse to someone else.

The stables stood to the left of the grand house, and they were impressive. They were unlike any stables I had ever seen before. First, they were built of stone and looked like a fine house on their own. Most stables I had seen were open and made of wood, with the occasional stone wall or two. William seemed impressed as well. He followed the grooms so he could see inside the impressive building for himself.

We could not have timed a better arrival, as everyone seemed to expect us. It only made me think Angus knows a lot more than he lets on sometimes. The group is tired but elated that we were on the outskirts of our destination, the capital city of Edinburgh. My spirit was restored just by standing in front of this beautiful house.

Being welcomed personally by Sir Alexander Dick, who came toward us from his fine house and place of refuge on this journey, was a blessing. I feel like we finally arranged a suitable respite in our lodgings in this fine home, but I could tell Duncan was apprehensive by his noticeable silence on the side of the courtyard.

I guessed that Sir Alexander is in his sixties. Underneath his wig, you could see that his balding head is crowned with white hair around his ears. His eyes were brown and kind. They matched his brown wool coat.

"Och! My dearest Lady MacLeod, you and your kinsman are most welcome here at Prestonfield," he said, taking both of my hands and shaking them vigorously. "Most welcome!"

I could not help but smile at him. His welcome was genuine and warm. After days of tavern innkeepers and abandoned stone crofts on our solemn journey, a welcome like this was needed to lift our spirits. To lift my spirits.

Sir Alexander is not a very tall man—at least not compared to the MacLeod's of Skye standing before him—but his presence was strong and dignified as he represented his name and his title as the Baron of this beautiful house and land. He immediately took my hand under his own arm and escorted me up the stone steps and through the doors.

"Please come with me into the house. The men will sort your horses and bags. After the rains over the past few days here, I can assure you it is warm and dry inside."

Once we crossed into the entryway of this grand house, we went up a few more stone steps and moved into the first room to the left. The fire was roaring and was a welcome sight. I could see Duncan directing Angus and William through the windows. I smiled at the thought of them all helping each other and even more so that I was standing before the warm fire inside.

"Thank ye verra much Sir Alexander," I said, taking the glass of wine he offered me. "This has been a much longer journey to the city from Skye than I expected."

"I can imagine! Come with me."

He took me straight to the main floor, comprised of small rooms off a long hallway to the back of the house. I could see stairs to my left, but those must have led to the family rooms, as Sir Alexander did not mention them. Our rooms were in the back of the long hall and while small, each was already prepared for us with fine linens, water cauldrons, and lit fires. Duncan and I had our own rooms, while Angus and William shared one.

Our accommodations may be a result of some connection from Angus' past—perhaps his own connections to the Jacobite cause. That may be the reason for Duncan's sudden silent and cautious manner upon our arrival. Thankfully, his personal reservations did not stop us from staying here. We were twenty years from Culloden. The doomed cause was long over and yet all of Scotland was still paying the price. At this moment, however, I have no care of politics, religion, or kings. I see before me a welcome host, a fine house, a warm fire, and the prospect of plenty of food and drink within these walls.

"I will leave you all to dust the travels from yer clothes and prepare for a fine supper we have planned in yer honor," Sir Alexander said. "If ye need anything, call for me personally or Missus Finlay, who runs this house for us. The woman is likely running mad for our supper in the kitchens, but she has an excellent staff, and they will see that ye have whatever ye need. Ye just need ask!"

"Thank ye, sir! Ye do not know what a welcome respite Prestonfield is on our long journey across Scotland."

"Think nothing of it," he said, smiling at me. "I would do anything for Alexander MacLeod's daughter. If I may, I would encourage ye all to take a walk across the gardens if ye get a chance before it gets dark and before supper. We are quite proud of our home, and I have a surprise for yer pudding tonight."

"That sounds exciting! I cannae wait!"

I needed to ask nothing of Missus Finlay as she and her staff saw to every need in my room before I ever entered it. I had water already heating by the fire for bathing, fine linens, and fragrant oils that seem to be from Italy. At the risk of getting dirt from the road on the linens, I could not help but fall immediately upon my back, landing on the plush bed.

I smiled, thinking about the fine sleep I was going to have this night in luxury compared to the croft from last night and any tavern we have seen on this journey. Thankfully, I had plenty of time in my room before supper to clean up from a wearisome day on the road. I tried to remember what Lady Margaret taught me. I knew that I need to represent my clan and to respect Sir Alexander and his family, as our hosts.

I walked downstairs and into the dining room clean and fresh in the finest dress I brought—the one I wore on the night I was named MacLeod heir, including the MacLeod broach Lady Margaret gave me. I am not certain why I thought of travelling across the country with such fine clothes and jewelry, other than I thought I might need them. Tonight is the first time I have worn any of it and I feel as grand as this house!

I suspect that all the men who traveled with me this week did not recognize me as I walked in the room looking nothing like the muddy, wind-blown, and rain-soaked lass of the last few days. I took particular care to groom myself properly for such a fine house. My hair was clean and pinned up neatly with curls showing on the side. I prayed that I did not still smell like my Munro—beloved or not.

"Och! My dear! *My dear!*" Sir Alexander said as he rushed across the room to escort me personally from the door of the dining room into the room where all the men were already seated, waiting for me to arrive. "Lady MacLeod, ye are a *vision!*"

I felt all eyes on me as he lavished me with compliments about my beauty all the way to my seat. Duncan kept a smirk on his face at my being such a focus of attention from our host, so I refused to look at him for fear that both of us would start laughing at the spectacle of it all. No disrespect to Sir Alexander, but this kind of attention was just not something I was used to. I looked at William and widened my eyes at him for a moment as I passed by. He smiled at me and laughed over his drink.

"Sit here by me, lass," Sir Alexander said as he pulled the chair out for me. The man seated across from me stood when I reached the table, and only then did my kinsmen follow his lead.

"Thank ye, sir. Ye are too kind," I said to my host, who then moved to sit at the head of the table beside me. While I was unused to this kind of attention, I had been on the road for almost a week with three men who did not stand or pull out a chair for me once. I welcomed the formality, especially considering the night before I was sleeping on the floor against a stone wall.

The room was filled with Italian paintings and artifacts from Sir Alexander's travels. With all the candles and the roaring fire, the light danced on the scenes, making them come to life on the walls. I looked around in awe of the opulence and majesty of the room. Yet, it still felt welcoming as a family home.

"Sir Alexander, thank ye again for yer hospitality here at Prestonfield House," Duncan said. "I can assure ye Clan MacLeod is most grateful."

Barely acknowledging his comment, Sir Alexander snapped out of his trance staring at me, and finally said, "Right, right, supper!" He signaled to his staff with a wave of his hand to begin filling the glasses with wine and bringing in the first course. "Please, dear friends, let me introduce my eldest son, Garrick Cunyngham."

This was the man seated across from me that taught my companions to stand for a lady. He nodded to each of the men in the room. Like his father, he had similar brown eyes. They were kind, but there was something mournful about them, though.

"Cunyngham?" I asked.

Sir Alexander responded immediately, "Aye, my surname is Cunyngham, but changed it to Dick upon taking the baronetcy here at Prestonfield House. It is the family name of my mother, and they hold this title."

"Aye sir, I understand now," I said, smiling at them both. "It is our pleasure to meet ye, Master Cunyngham!"

"We are most pleased to welcome ye and yer party here," he said respectfully to us all.

"Garrick, this is the lovely Lady Alexandra MacLeod from Skye. You ken her father was our friend, Alexander."

"Aye," the man said, acknowledging the connection. "I am verra sorry for your loss, Lady MacLeod." I nodded to him for his kindness and respect for my father.

"This is her uncle Duncan MacLeod. Ye already know Angus, of course, and rounding out their travelling party is their kinsman, William MacLeod."

I immediately spoke up and said, "Sir Alexander, if I may, William is our kinsman indeed, but his surname is MacCrimmon, a sept of Clan MacLeod."

"Aye. My apologies to ye lad, as I had nothing but MacLeod's on my mind!" he said, laughing and pouring himself another glass of wine.

"Think nothing of it, sir. It happens all the time." I just smiled at William, and he smiled back. I wondered to myself if he had actually been called a MacLeod before or if he was just trying to make his host feel more comfortable after his error. Either way, it was kind and respectful of him.

We talked of our travels and the unpredictable nature of Scottish weather at any time of year. We talked of Sir Alexander's travels to Italy and the inspiration behind the landscapes painted on the walls of the dining room. We talked of food and the beauty and bounty of the Isles. We also talked of our destination as Sir Alexander told me about all the places I should see in Edinburgh since I had never been.

Sir Alexander stopped and said suddenly, "Aye, Lady MacLeod! I should have said this before! Dear friends, *dear friends*, please let us have a moment and raise our glasses in honor of the dearly departed Alexander MacLeod."

We all raised our glasses with him and said in unison, "*Sláinte!*"

"Thank ye, for the kind words, sir," I said in gratitude for the gesture. I thought of my father, but I also thought of Lady Margaret. We have had a great deal of loss as a family in the few months. I smiled at Duncan across the table, and he nodded his head and smiled back at me.

"Ye must know, lass, that I remember your father fondly as my dear friend, and I deeply mourn his sudden passing," he said, holding his glass before me. "He was a tribute to his profession and to his family. He was much too young of a man to pass so."

"I thank ye, sir. Losing my father was unexpected and just after that of our own Lady Margaret MacLeod, who I succeed in title as Laird MacLeod's heir. We were completely unprepared for another tragic family loss, yet here we are."

"I believe the Advocate Society will honor your father next week, and you should know that I am part of that group and hope that I will see you all again at that event," he exclaimed for all the table to hear.

The men at the table turned their heads to their host, but I was the one to ask, "The Advocate Society?" I had never heard Father mention such a group and did not know who this included or what they represented, though the name was a strong clue.

"Aye, lass," he said. "It all started as a small group of like-minded gentlemen started by yer father and his friend Master Campbell Forbes. Then it expanded to men of many professions. I join them when I can make it into the city, as some members were part of the Select Society, which is now the Poker Club. One of my oldest friends, in fact, Master Allan Ramsay, is a member and has a portrait of your father to unveil."

"Och! That is lovely!"

"I hope ye will stay long enough to attend the unveiling."

"I am certain we cannot complete all that we need to quickly, sir," I said, looking down the table at Duncan, who was listening intently to this exchange and nodding his head in silent agreement. "So, our arrival in Edinburgh is well-timed."

"I will see you all at the event then!" he said, raising his glass to me and then to the men at the end of the table. I met him upon its return and sealed our agreement with a light clink of our glasses.

The food was plentiful. Each course was better than the next. Once again, my travel companions remained mostly silent during supper, leaving me to hold the conversation with our host. It was a lovely night before a warm fire and warm food in our bellies. I could slowly feel every single cold and wet travel day finally thaw in my bones and fade from my memory.

Sir Alexander leaned to his son and said, "It is lovely having company back in the house, is it not?"

"Aye, Father," Garrick said in agreement.

"Lady MacLeod, ye have caught us at a time that my wife and other children, who are quite young, are away visiting her family in Pembrokeshire and it has just been the two of us for many weeks, hasn't it, son?" he asked, and his nodded to his father again in agreement.

"I am verra sorry to not meet yer wife this night, sir."

"Perhaps on yer way home! We would verra much like to welcome ye here on yer return to Skye," he said before sipping his wine. His tone was genuine but part of me thought he seemed quite happy to not have a house full of small children as he played host to a group of travelers, and he may not be all that bothered to not have a wife here, as well.

Garrick Cunyngham was a quiet man. He looked only a bit younger than his father, but I could not tell by his demeanor if it was life bearing down on him or his age. He seemed engaged in the conversations at the table, but said very little to be part of them. I looked at both him and his father when I spoke, out of courtesy to my hosts. It was only proper, as he was seated directly across from me.

He only asked one question to Duncan about how many days it takes to travel from Skye to Edinburgh by horse, only to stare blankly at my uncle while he answered, engaged but bored by the answer at the same time.

He fulfilled his duty, as son of the host, at the very minimum. I could not tell if he was annoyed that we were interrupting his normal evening supper in his home or if he had issues with his father, who sometimes talked to him like he was still wee Robbie's age. I am not sure I could fault him on either account.

204

"My friends, I offer ye this night a pudding that is most special here for us here at Prestonfield House," Sir Alexander said.

"Do tell us, sir!" I said as the staff put the plates before us at the same time.

"It is a rhubarb crumble," he said proudly.

We all looked at our plates and then at each other, silently asking the same question: *What is a rhubarb?* Before I could ask Sir Alexander, each of us tasted the warm dishes before us. Between the tartness of the rhubarb that none of us completely understood, and the sweetness laced in the crumble with a dose of rich cream on top, every member of clan MacLeod finished their plates quickly. It truly was a glorious pudding.

"Sir Alexander, I cannae say that I have ever had a rhubarb before, but I agree that ye gave us a fine pudding this night. What a pleasant surprise at the end of our already glorious supper!"

"Aye, you are most welcome! And with that, we are ready for the *whisky*," he said, smiling at me before standing, clapping his hands, and leading the men out of the dining room.

+++

Sir Alexander arranged for us to hear some music from a local harpist in the parlor across the entry hall and asked us to join him there for more wine and whisky to end the night. As everyone set out to the other room, I noticed that once Master Garrick stood; he did so slowly. He then grabbed a wooden cane with a silver handle from the side of the table that I had not noticed earlier.

The man had a severe limp in his right leg and walked slowly behind the rest of the group, who seemed more than eager to sample the promised drink in the next room. I suspect the whisky was a greater draw than the harpist, though I would expect that she is bonnie. Each of us was celebrating this grand house and our proximity to our destination. Full bellies and beautiful music were a bonus.

I slowed my pace to walk with Master Garrick and asked, "Have ye lived here at Prestonfield House yer entire life, sir?" Before he could answer, I continued, "It is a fine house. From what I could see on our way over the hill, the gardens are beautiful and well-tended. Yer father is quite proud of them."

"Culloden," he said, answering the question I did not ask. He did not say the words, but the look on his face told me he appreciated me walking with him to the next room. I assume he was used to being left behind.

"Aye," I said softly, acknowledging his unexpected confession.

"I was injured in a cannon blast at the verra start of the battle. The damn thing nearly killed me! My kinsman rode me out over the back of my horse as far from that bloody moor as he could and eventually brought me home by horse and cart. I dinnae ken how I survived the journey at all!"

"I dinnae ken, sir," I said in sympathy for his struggle.

"Ye ken my father is a doctor of medicine, and he restored me back to health, but I will always have this limp."

He paused for a moment before continuing, "To answer yer question, Lady MacLeod, I havena lived here most of my life. Father had a house in Edinburgh and moved out to Prestonfield when his brother died, and he took on the baronetcy in 1746. My wife and I had a small house on the way to Duddingston, and I had always tried to work at the stables here—first fer my uncle and then fer my father. I feel most at home in the stables."

"Aye sir, I have a young cousin who loves the horses," I said, smiling as I thought about my wee Robbie. Suddenly, William came to mind as he loves the horses as well. He certainly has a way with them. I had not thought about it before, but next to Robbie, William is the only man that my Munro will go with willingly. He eventually does as asked, but will sometimes fight being led by another. I take it as a sign of his own independent nature. One that I can understand and respect.

The man broke my thoughts and continued, "Our house was still on Prestonfield lands, of course, but it was our own. My dear Janet died three months before the battle, and I went to Culloden, thinking I had nothing to lose. I thought I might even welcome a gallant death fighting fer the true king, my faith, and fer Scotland."

"It takes true conviction to die fer what ye believe in, sir."

"Aye, but the minute you come close to death, ye would be surprised how much ye want to *live*. That is the only reason I am standing here with ye today."

I smiled back at him on this candid revelation and said as we reached the door to the parlor, "Thank ye for telling me yer story, sir."

"I thank ye fer listening to it. Father was correct. It has been a pleasant diversion to have company in the house—and if I may say to have a *woman* back in the house. It has just been the two of us here for some time and ye and yer men have brought laughter and conversation back within these walls."

"Well, sir, I cannae thank ye and yer father enough fer yer hospitality. As ye can imagine, we have not always enjoyed such *fine* accommodations on our travels from Skye," I said, laughing at the thought, especially since just the night before I slept against the cold stone wall of an abandoned croft.

I could tell by the look on Duncan's face when he met us at the door and handed me another glass, that he was proud that I showed Master Garrick such kindness and respect to walk with him, at his own pace, to the parlor.

The parlor room that Sir Alexander brought me to upon our arrival had been transformed. The harpist—who as expected was bonnie—was seated in the corner playing, and the chairs had all been arranged to encourage conversation while she played in the background. I had not noticed before that the room was decorated in all manner of yellow velvet and gold. The candles and lanterns again brought a new look to the room as light bounced off the gold picture frames and windowpanes. Even the gold harp sparkled from across the room. We listened to the beautiful music awash in warm, golden light.

As our evening wound down, Sir Alexander stood suddenly and bid us all a good night before finishing the last of his whisky glass. A servant tried to take it from him, but he would not allow it. He felt the need to place the glass on the table himself. He reiterated his genuine welcome to us here in his house. He also made certain we all knew where the kitchen was down the stairs if we needed anything else for our rooms during the night. We all stood with him in collective gratitude and acknowledged that we were more than cared for. He kissed the top of my hand and wished me a good night and a safe journey to Edinburgh.

"You will arrive in Edinburgh and settle the life of your father. But lass, my lady, I hope you find even more in the city that helps you be the leader that you are destined to be."

We smiled at each other on the exchange, and I said, "Ye and yer family are always welcome at Dunmara Castle on Skye. I know there may be no reason for ye to come out to the Isles, but ye—and Master

Garrick—would be most welcome! I would be verra happy to repay the courtesy ye have provided me and my kinsman here this night."

He smiled at me and took my hands in his again. "Ah, you will do your clan proud! I can see that!" He then turned to the entire party and shook each hand on his way out of the hall.

Master Garrick did the same and bid us all a good night. On his way out of the room, he told William that he would personally join him in the morning to ensure he is supported adequately in the stables.

Garrick said to me, "Lady MacLeod, I wish ye nothing but happiness. The journey ye are on is a solemn one, but I too can see that ye are prepared fer it. I hope ye and yer traveling party will think to stop here at Prestonfield on yer way back to Skye. Ye will be most welcome."

"Thank ye verra much, sir," I said as he walked out of the room, leaving me with my merry band of travelers all satiated with fine food and drink this evening.

Once Master Garrick left the room, and we were alone, Duncan turned to me and said, "Well done, *Lady MacLeod*!" Before I could tell if his response was genuine or sarcastic, he said, "Sit down, as I need to prepare ye fer the city before we retire this night."

William, Angus, and I knew immediately that his tone was serious. We refilled our glasses from the bottles left on the table and Duncan said, "If ye have not been in the city before—it can be overwhelming." We all took a sip at the thought of what was before us as he continued, "I think the only member of this travelling party that has never been in a big city is ye, Alexandra."

I looked around the table, but from the sound of it, tonight's travel lesson from Duncan is just for me. "Edinburgh is crowded with people. In fact, it is filled with people on top of other people. That alone can be overwhelming. Many of these people are poor. Everything is covered in soot and the air is thick and heavy from the fires. Add that to the stink of chamber pots. You will notice this straight away, lass."

I sat up in my seat at the thought and each of the men nodded in agreement. I was clearly headed into the squalor of the great city, and it sounded absolutely horrible. Duncan tried to further manage our expectations.

"I ken where Alexander's house is now, but I dinnae ken if it is shared or how big it is. I was last here with him years ago when he had a small set of rooms in a building near the university. We may have to split up and manage our lodgings separately. Laird Graham has given me the coin to do this. Priority will be given to ye Alexandra. If we are forced to split up, we will manage a security schedule as we have on this trip, but with each of us taking a full night's watch on rotation instead of changing in the middle of the night."

"Why would I be in any danger in Edinburgh?"

Duncan responded immediately and sarcastically, "Why is yer first response always a question, lass?"

"No one knows me in Edinburgh!" I said, ignoring his attempt at playing our old game and instead continued my protest.

"Because ye are a *woman*, lass," he said as a matter of fact and reminded us of the *real* concern. The real concern for them all along. It was not just about a hasty retreat from MacLeod lands, though at the start that excuse made sense. It was not about a woman traveling with three men, though that did present itself to be a problem along the way. It was simply because I am a woman. Period.

I was startled by his harsh response and embarrassed slightly that he was talking to me this way in front of William and Angus. I wanted to react, at first. I knew enough that what he said was true and just nodded in reluctant understanding. A young woman in the heart of the city could be a target of another sort, and it has nothing to do with her lineage or her position or being seen with three men. A woman could be a target of any unseemly man at any point, simply because she is a woman, because that alone bears its own risk.

"We will find out our situation tomorrow and adjust as we need. Agreed?"

"Aye," we all said in unified agreement.

"One last thing," he said, looking at me, "tonight, lass, I have seen that yer room is between mine and William's. Angus has determined to be in the fine stables. Christ knows I willna require a guard in this fine house, with our gracious hosts, but will ask ye that if ye need anything ye are to shout for me and I will be there in an instant. Do ye understand?"

I nodded on this ask but said nothing in response to Duncan's order. "Then haste ye all to yer bed and enjoy the warmth and the generosity of yer host. I will see ye at first light for what will be our final ride into Edinburgh."

It was an exceptional leadership moment from Duncan, and I smiled at him in appreciation for his words and his genuine care for my wellbeing. Though there was some apprehension behind his words, I felt safe with my fellow travelers and our hosts.

My bed was calling me, and I had to go. I left the men to their planning of our ride into the city or at least one more glass of fine whisky. As I walked away, I paused and turned back around to say, "I truly thank ye all for getting me here this far, safely."

Once again, overt gratitude was not for this lot. They all just stared at me. I just nodded to the silent men before me and walked confidently to my welcome bedchamber, leaving them alone to talk as men do.

+++

Seated before the warm fire in my room, my thoughts were of nothing but gratitude. My spirit was restored by the evening, and I appreciated the reception we had from our kind hosts at Prestonfield House. I am thankful to be once again clean and rid of the dust and mud of the roads leading us here. I am thankful for tonight's fine supper and drink and thankful for the warmth of this fire and the fine blankets surrounding me. Honestly, after the last few nights on the road, I am also thankful for a moment of privacy. There is much you are forced to ignore in the company of men for days on end.

I am so tired, and I am so done with the expectation of the *early start*. I dare my uncle to pull me from the confines of this warm and comfortable bliss in the morning. I can only hope that once we arrive in Edinburgh, I can sleep soundly—as long as I want—in a warm and secure peace that reminds me of my own bed at home.

As I faded to sleep in the warm comfort of my room, I told myself that I owe Angus immensely for this incredible night of comfort and safe quarter on our journey.

+++

First light came early, as it always does. But a warm night in safety, coupled with the prospect of the last ride, helped me rise and start the day without being summoned out of a deep sleep.

I did not see anyone in the house and walked outside, where I met William in front of the stone stables. He seemed shocked by my appearance so early, but said nothing to me. I handed William my bag, and he handed me a small cloth that was wrapped around a warm slice of bread with butter.

"Och, this is a fine trade, sir," I said, admiring my small parcel of goodness that I did not expect. This is one of his learnings from our travels—I do like bread and butter.

He nodded and smiled back at me before saying, "Duncan told Sir Alexander's staff that since we were so close and indulged in last night's feast, we would not need a formal breakfast."

"I took the apple from my room for my horse," he said. I nodded in agreement as I patted my pocket with my mouth full of bread.

"I did the same. The stables are fine, but I wanted to keep the special treat for my Munro."

We just looked at each other. I thought for a second to ask him his horse's name, which I should know by now, but realized now that I did not. Before I could ask, a well hungover Duncan appeared. He said nothing at first, but still loomed over the conversation William and I were having. I wanted to ask him how long he remained in the dining room or if he took a bottle to his room, but it did not matter. It was clear the man had more whisky last night than he should have.

"Has Angus already left us this morning, or is he still in the stables?"

"No, lass," Duncan said, as he glanced back at William. William said nothing, but I could tell something was amiss.

"Are ye saying we lost our advance man, then?" I asked with genuine curiosity. Surely there was more to this story. With Angus, there was always more to the story.

"I dinnae need an advance man into a city I ken. But, aye, I believe the man found some... *respite* at Prestonfield House with a lass and has the sudden need to shoe his horse."

I nearly choked on the last of my buttered bread as I laughed aloud and asked, looking between William and Duncan, "Are ye serious?"

William looked at Duncan, who refused to answer my question. I took the lack of response for what it was. Angus had found a reason to stay behind at Prestonfield House and I, for one, cannot blame him.

It is a fine place to be.

FIFTEEN
The Journey's Last

MacLeod House
Canongate, Edinburgh, Scotland
August 1766

Staring up at the building on Canongate, William, Duncan, and I stood in awe of the size of the magnificent house before us. Not far from the Holyrood Palace grounds, it seems this building should be placed behind the royal gates, not outside.

The stone building was lighter than others in this city, and it was a notable stand-out from the other soot covered buildings on top of other soot covered buildings surrounding it. The stone walk and stairs in front were spotless and clean, setting it aside from neighboring buildings again.

I was amazed at the number of people walking around us as we stood in the middle of the street with our horses. In fact, this many people around made me a little nervous. I felt like I kept moving to accommodate others walking towards me. William took my reins to help steady Munro, who was also not enjoying the commotion of the city. He was also trying to protect me from the people walking past us quickly and the occasional horses and carriages passing by us from all directions. Duncan was right, the city can be an overwhelming scene and Munro and I were reacting to it the same way. *We do not like it at all!*

Looking up at the building and then back at Duncan, I asked, "Are ye certain this is Father's house?"

"I dinnae ken, lass," he said almost apologetically.

I nodded to him but smiled as I thought that if this were indeed my father's home, the look of it would be fitting. He would have most certainly created his own version of Dunmara Castle within Edinburgh, as this grand building is a fair and bright respite within the gray city walls that surrounded it.

I had visions that he wanted to surround himself with reminders of home—the light of his home by the sea. The building also overlooked the peaceful green lands of the Canongate Kirk. Located just across the street, it looked like another welcome place of comfort and refuge within the busy streets of the city. I wondered if he spent time there and then wondered if he was buried there.

Duncan snapped me out of my own thoughts by handing his reins to William and saying, "There is only one way to be certain."

He walked slowly up the stairs and knocked on the door. A young lad opened the door but said nothing to him.

"Good day, lad! I am here to see a Missus Douglas." Duncan said. The lad just looked at him, but again said nothing. He seemed to understand the ask as he opened the door wider, just as an older woman, dressed in all black save her white apron appeared, and opened the door further to view who was standing there.

"Who is it, Petey?" she asked, touching the lad's shoulder.

Before the lad could answer her, my uncle said, "Madam, I am Duncan MacLeod. I sent ye a letter upon learning of my brother Alexander's death." He handed her the letter we received, notifying us of Father's death pulled from a small leather folio in his coat. I had no idea he had been carrying it on our journey, but could only assume he offered it as proof that he was who he said he was. Upon recognizing the letter and seal, the woman welcomed him straight away.

"Aye, Master MacLeod," she said, taking his hand and then looking at us all. "I remember ye and am verra sorry to meet ye again under these sad circumstances." The boy remained looking between the woman and Duncan as she handed the letter back to my uncle.

"Yer brother was a fine man! A *fine* man, and a kind master," she said as she brought her kerchief to her nose. I breathed in deeply at the recognition of his loss once again.

Duncan tried to move the conversation from our collective grief to the coordination of our arrival and housing. "Missus Douglas, may I present to ye my niece, Lady Alexandra MacLeod? She is Alexander's only child and now the heir and future chief of Clan MacLeod on Skye."

I straightened my shoulders on this fine—albeit unexpected and formal—introduction and waited for the woman's response. She stepped toward me, looked me in the eye, and took my hands in her own. They were rough from her work, but still gentle and warm.

"I would ken you anywhere, dearest Alexandra! Ye look exactly like yer father, God rest his soul," she said as she brought her kerchief to wipe her nose and we all bowed our heads in reverence for the dearly departed once again. "Yer father was so incredibly proud of ye, lass! And he talked about ye often to all of us in this house."

"Thank ye, Missus Douglas," I said in appreciation for her respect for my father and myself, by extension.

Duncan continued as he pointed to William, "This is our kinsman, William MacCrimmon, who, under the direction of my other brother, Laird Graham MacLeod of MacLeod, has helped me escort Alexandra safely to Edinburgh from Dunmara Castle on Skye."

I thought about how far away our home was from this busy city with his words and Missus Douglas replied immediately, "Yer most welcome here at MacLeod House, Master MacCrimmon."

William nodded in receipt of this genuine welcome to this house as the woman continued, "Just around the corner of the house there to yer left, lad, is Crichton's Close. The gate should be open. In the back, you will find our stable master, Jonny Harris. Tell him I sent ye 'round and he can tend to yer horses. The forge is further 'round to the joinin' of Cooper's Close. The smithy, Robert, is usually only here only one or two days a week, as he works for many large houses in the city. He has had no need to be here as of late but let Jonny ken if yer horses have specific needs after such a long journey. He can ensure Robert can stop in. When yer done, have Jonny send you to the house from the back through the kitchen there," she said, pointing to a door behind her in the hall. "It will be faster, and they will be wantin' to lock the gates soon. We will meet you in the front hall, aye?"

William nodded to the woman and understood her instruction, "Aye! Thank ye. Missus Douglas. I will return shortly."

He set about to guide our three horses around the corner to the stables. Before he left my sight, my Munro, who had been true to me this entire trip, bowed his head to me in reverence. I could not let him leave me without my own proper show of gratitude. William paused for me, out of respect for our ritual of affection and appreciation.

"Thank you, my dear sweet Munro," I said, and smiled at him and kissed the top of his nose over and over. I lingered for a moment as I loved him, and he loved me. We both leaned into each other. I had not fully realized until this moment how he was another male who set out on the shared mission to escort me across Scotland and deliver me safely to my father's house. I touched my cheek to his and ran my hand under his chin in appreciation for his loyal service.

"The first part of yer mission is complete, and I fully expect you to take me home, my friend," I said as I kissed him once more before letting William take him from me.

"I will see that he is fine in the stables," William said to reassure me. I nodded to him in appreciation because I knew William loved my horse as much as I did. Munro bowed his head again as he walked away from me.

Missus Douglas continued to look at me and said as she reached out her hand to welcome me into the house by way of the entry hall, "I manage all aspects of yer father's house—cooking, cleaning, and shopping. I am at yer service, as ye are now the mistress of MacLeod House."

She then said to Duncan, "We have been expecting ye from yer letter, Master MacLeod. I didna ken how many rooms to set aside, but I have all prepared for ye and yer party."

She looked at me again, my hands still in hers, and said, "Ye should have your pick, lass. You may want your father's room, as it is the largest and most fine for a young mistress—erm, my apologies. Should I call ye Lady MacLeod?"

"Thank you, Missus Douglas," I said. I wasn't sure if I should defer the main room to Duncan, but he nodded to me in agreement with her recommendation. "Mistress or Alexandra, is just fine," I said with a weak smile.

Upon my aunt's death, I became Lady MacLeod. Sir Alexander kept calling me by my title when we arrived at Prestonfield, but I suspect that it means nothing here in the city. I could not see carrying on such formality when I was still not used to myself. I will ask Duncan about what is proper later.

Once we crossed the threshold. I couldn't help looking around. I do not know what I expected when we got to Edinburgh, but this house is more than anything my imagination could have conjured on its own. It is grand in every way. All I could think as I looked around was that *this entire building was my father's.* It is the MacLeod House on Canongate.

I was still looking around as Duncan said, "That is fine indeed, madam. We left one man from our party, our cousin Angus MacLeod, at Prestonfield, south of here… erm, tending to his horse." Duncan and I both looked at each other with a slight smile on these words, as we both knew that Angus was tending to more than his horse.

He continued, "The rooms will be four. Is that something you can accommodate here? If not, we can send the lads who escorted us here to a tavern or even the stables."

"Aye, we can accommodate yer party, Master MacLeod," she said as a matter of fact and completely unfazed by the thoughts of a full house.

"Thank you verra much, Missus Douglas. Tomorrow, I will send word for Angus to join us here."

We walked further into the front hall, and I felt myself shrinking in the enormity of this massive house. I looked all around the grand hall and up at the broad staircase and the landing of the floor above. For the first time, I felt overwhelmed and unsure of my place or how to behave. And for the first time, I began to question who my father truly was on this side of the country.

Turning to me, Missus Douglas said, "Before we go through the house, what time will ye be wanting supper this evening, Mistress Alexandra?"

I was in shock and could not speak. Thankfully, Duncan spoke for me, "No, no missus! Ye have been more than generous with our late arrival at the house. We will take ye up on settling the rooms and ye may retire for the evening. We will venture out shortly. I want William and Alexandra to get their bearings in Edinburgh a little. It has been a long time since I was last here, but we can fend for ourselves this night."

"Aye, verra well, sir!" she said to him, somewhat relieved at not having to cook for us tonight.

"Ye may ken *The World's End* and a few other taverns are just up the from the house. Ye will find they all have good food and drink and are not as crowded as taverns closest to the castle. Master MacLeod preferred the *White Hart Inn* on Grassmarket, but that was near his office, the university, and the law courts, of course."

"Aye, I ken them all well. *Too well*," Duncan, always the charmer, said with a wink and a smile. "We will stay close to the house and rest after our long journey. We will be ready for your breakfast in the morning. I am not sure what Alexander expected from ye."

"Master Alexander preferred to break his fast at seven o'clock. It was usually quick, and he would try to be at his office by eight o'clock. Later and larger breakfasts were usually reserved for the weekend or if he had guests."

I looked at Duncan and before I could think about the guests my father might have here in the house. My uncle and I agreed silently for a later start. "We will be fine at nine o'clock tomorrow, madam. I suspect my travel companions may want to recover after our long journey across the country. Perhaps we can return to seven o'clock over time."

She seemed more than thrilled with no supper this evening and now a late start in the morning and said, "Aye, sir! A late morning on occasion is always welcome for a full house."

Duncan looked at me and I tried not to laugh as I figured his direction to Missus Douglas was due to our long travels, the journey's end, and his anticipated drink in the city this night.

"The lad that met ye at the door earlier is my son Petey, and this gives me a chance to spend more time with him. Ye should ken that the lad is mute, has been since he was five, but he can hear ye just fine and take any instruction ye may have. I can assure ye he does a fine job on his chores here at MacLeod House."

I smiled at her and thought, what a gift the time with wee Petey must be for a woman running this fine house. I wondered what would make the lad stop speaking, but I immediately thought about my wee Robbie, who more than capable but also had something to overcome.

"I understand completely, Missus Douglas. I have no doubt the lad will continue to do a fine job here."

"Do ye need help to dress in the morning, mistress?"

I spoke immediately, finally finding my voice for a moment. "No, I do *not*."

Duncan looked at me sharply as if I spoke in a harsh tone, and I did. But I meant it. I do not know this woman and I am grown. I can manage to bathe and dress myself. Even at home, it was only on rare occasions that Missus Gerrard would assist me.

I tried to correct my initial curt tone by saying, "But ye *can* help ensure I have plenty of water, missus. I also ken how to tend my own fire, given the wood."

"Aye," she responded in respect to me and for my preference. "Each room is set with wood. I will have the lads help me provide water cauldrons in each room that you can all heat as you wish, fresh linens, and fragrant oils."

"I couldna ask fer more and I thank you verra much!"

At that moment, William walked back in from the back kitchen carrying our bags under each of his arms and behind him came the largest dog I had ever seen. The dog ran through the house, nearly knocking William over on his way, and then stopped before me. He sat on the ground, placing his head down at my feet in what appeared to be a sign of respect.

I was startled but before I could react, Missus Douglas said loudly, "That blessed dog! Och! Stirling! Get out of this house now, ye hear?"

She continued sounding annoyed that the large dog found his way into the house and said, "I am verra sorry. This is yer father's dog, Stirling. And as much as he hates it, he has been kept in the back courtyard since yer father's death. I cannae stand for him to be in the house, but from the look of it, he clearly kens that his new mistress has arrived."

I knelt down, patted the docile but giant dog on his head and rubbed his ears with both my hands and said, "Good boy, Stirling! Good boy! What kind of dog is he?"

"He is a Deerhound," she said. "He is not suited for the city, and normally resides at Glenammon, yer father's country house. We wanted to wait for you to decide if ye will take him back there or on to Skye when ye return home."

Duncan and I looked at each other as the words *yer father's country house* still hung in the air.

"Nice to meet ye, wee Stirling," I said to the dog directly, still rubbing his head and ears. He seemed so calm and respectful for such a large dog, but I can see how a life in the city must be hard being cooped up in a back courtyard, unable to roam and do what he was bred to do. I am already in love with the lad, but Missus Douglas is right, he does not belong here. In some ways, my first instinct is that neither do I, so can only assume we will be fast friends as outsiders in this city.

"I believe we are ready for yer tour of the house, Missus Douglas," Duncan said, taking the focus off the mentions of large dogs and country houses. Stirling stayed quiet and remained in the front hall as we started the tour. But the dog never took his eyes off of me.

Off the front hall was a large dining space. It had a direct route from the back to the kitchen. While smaller than Dunmara, of course, the kitchen and storage cellar were exceptionally clean and well-stocked. Missus Douglas seemed to have little help here, but perhaps that should be expected with only one master to serve.

"This is your home now, Mistress Alexandra. I am here to help ye with all of yer meals. We can talk tomorrow about yer preferences, and I can stock the kitchen and plan meals with ye."

"Aye, Missus Douglas. We can do that… *together.*"

With my words, I suddenly felt shy about being the mistress of the house—of such a grand house. I could feel the eyes of my uncle and

William on me. I could see that she had been baking bread this afternoon, and it was all I could do to not to steal a slice from the board when she turned to lead us to the next room. If I had seen butter nearby, I might have made such a daring move.

"Lads, ye will always find food here if ye need it during the day or I can prepare something to take with ye, if ye need to be away from the house for a time."

"Aye, thank ye," Duncan said.

We followed Missus Douglas back out through the entry hall into another room with a large fireplace and chairs placed in front for sitting. I could imagine Father sitting here reading in the evening. In the corner was a large chest with glasses and bottles of whisky and claret on top. I suspect this will be Duncan's favorite room. Come to think of it, there was a similar set in the dining room. Between Duncan and Angus, this kind of free access to whisky could be dangerous.

We walked up the main stairs off the front hall to the bedchambers. All rooms were furnished with their own fireplace, luxurious linens, and fine paintings on the walls. Each room we visited was better than the next. The final room was my father's. I felt myself becoming emotional as we walked in.

"I think this chamber may be best for ye, Mistress Alexandra." She pointed to everything in the room and talked about how Father had the finest taste. The bed and linens were made from fabric he imported from France and any art that he did not gather on his travels, he commissioned from Scottish artists.

"All the art in MacLeod House is beautiful, as ye can see, but these here... these here in his chamber were his favorites. Come in, come in, lass," she said, motioning me away from the door where I was frozen and overwhelmed. "Take a look at this one here. Ye may recognize it."

She motioned me to look at a painting over a chest to the right. I stood in awe as there was the most beautiful painting of Dunmara Castle. In the distance, past all the beauty of our home on canvas, I could see the back of a young brown-haired lass seated at Cairn's Point, staring out to sea.

"Aye, I ken it well," I said, barely able to keep the tears from forming. I could not look at Duncan or I would surely cry. My father commissioned a painting to remind him of home and of me and it was the most beautiful thing I had ever seen in my life. It reminded me of the comfort that I left nearly a week ago and that I wanted nothing more than to be on that very cliff at this moment tending to my emotions with the rhythm of the sea. I loved that he wanted to remember me in that spot, and I wanted everyone to leave the room as quickly as possible so that I could cry. Unfortunately, Missus Douglas was not yet done with her tour.

"There is one other reason this is a fine room fer ye," she said, walking to a door on the other side of the bed. She opened it and eagerly motioned for me to look inside. There was a small room off the side of his chamber that held a large copper tub for bathing. There were the expected basins, linens, and chamber pots, of course. I could see Father's shaving stone and razor next to a mirror. But the crown jewel of the room was the large, hammered, copper bath at the very center of the room.

"Yer father found it in Amsterdam and had it shipped here and installed. Yer caldrons by the fire will fill the basin, lass, and the copper will keep it nice and warm fer ye. We can always bring ye more water, and Petey knows how to drain it fer ye when yer done."

Upon her words, I could see that the stone floor had a special design to direct the water at the base of the tub that when opened, drained right into a tank in the close below. I could just see the tank out of the window. I wanted to know more about how the water was used, but my head was spinning. This was all too much to take in at once!

Missus Douglas was correct. This was the room for me, but it was also the room where my father died. I backed myself into the main room and said nothing to her. Reading my mind, or just seeing the tears begin to well in my eyes, William placed my bag at the foot of the bed and quickly walked straight back to stand outside the door.

Duncan said as he walked out behind him, "Aye, ye should have this room, lass. William and I will pick one of the rooms down the hall ahead of ye."

He did not say the words, but this worked for him not just as a matter of my position or connection to my father, but for security. He has made such a point of it this whole journey. Having layers of men to get through before me makes sense to my chief protector.

I snapped out of the haze I was in and said softly, "Thank ye, Missus Douglas! Ye have taken care of us on verra short notice."

"We can handle from here and will see you in the morning," Duncan said, as he finished my statement and walked her swiftly out of the room. I could hear him asking how to secure the house at night as they made their way back down the hall together. I sat down slowly on the edge of my father's bed, staring down at the floor, overwhelmed with emotion.

"Are ye alright, lass?" William asked me quietly. I had not even noticed he was still standing by the door. I looked up at him and could not speak.

I was overwhelmed with this grand house and the evidence of the life my father had here in Edinburgh without me. I realized for the first time that I *did* feel abandoned by a man I did not truly know. His absence from my life was in service to the clan, so the sacrifice was understood. It was expected and appreciated. Now, I have a feeling I had never felt before in my life. It hurt me to think that he *wanted* his life here and not at Dunmara. All the feelings of love and loss for my father were now combined with confusion about the man and his chosen life here in the city.

I also traveled across Scotland and arrived at this magnificent house looking like a poor country relation covered in the damp muck of the Scottish roads and smelling like Munro. While the grand night at Prestonfield washed much of my journey from me, I still arrived here today as anything but Lady MacLeod—as anything but the daughter of the great Alexander MacLeod.

I could feel tears of humiliation and loss welling in my eyes once again and was lucky that Duncan appeared in front of William before I could answer his question.

"Get settled, ye two, and be quick about it. I want to go back out on the street before dark. I want ye to know where ye are and to get yer bearings. We will eat at one of the taverns Missus Douglas mentioned and plan for tomorrow."

William left immediately on my uncle's orders to whatever room he chose, and Duncan and I just looked at each other.

228

"*Duncan…*" I whispered as a waiting tear finally fell upon my cheek. I couldn't speak another word and lowered my head.

He stepped forward and briefly touched my shoulder as he said softly to me, "I ken, lass. We have a lot to talk about. Take a moment, but dinnae be long. The lad and I will meet ye downstairs."

He closed the door behind him as he left. I swallowed my remaining tears and cleaned up as much as I could with the wash basin Missus Douglas had already prepared for me. It was as if she expected that I would take my father's room. The lavender soap smelled so lovely. She also left a small pot of rouge salve that gave my lips and cheeks a bit more color and a small bottle of lavender scented oil that I put on my wrists and behind my ears, just as Lady Margaret taught me.

I did not have time to change my clothes based on Duncan's orders and hoped that my dark cloak would suitably hide the muddy and dusty travels deeply embedded within my skirts.

+++

I heard footsteps in the corridor and decided that I could unpack my bag and get more acclimated to Father's chamber when we returned from supper. I walked downstairs to find William waiting in front of the fire in the front room.

"Well, that is something!" I said loudly, causing William to turn to me suddenly. "Of course! Duncan tells us to hurry, and *he* is not even *here*!"

At that moment, I saw a single whisky glass rise above the back of the large chair in front of the fire between me and William. "Of course, *ye* are the last one down here, *Alexandra*!" Duncan said as he stood up, drank the last of his glass, and sat it down on the mantle.

He gave me a wink as he passed me on his way to the front door. "Let us go! I have the key to the house door. Missus Douglas let me ken that it is important for everything be locked up on the front and the back. There will always be someone at the stables. Master Jonny lives above them. Her own small set of rooms for her and her son, are in the back of the close. Each gate is shut at dusk. They can only be opened on the schedule of the master... erm, now the mistress of the house." He said as he tried to hand me the heavy set of keys.

I held up both of my hands in refusal of his offer and said, "Ye can be in charge of those tonight, sir."

He agreed by silently placing the keys in his coat pocket and asked, "Do ye both ken the rules of the house?"

William and I nodded agreement to the rules and the need for such security in the city. But always one step ahead, Duncan said, "I am certain you both have questions. It has been a long day. But I want ye to understand our immediate location before it gets dark. We can talk more over food and drink."

After days of weary travel, neither of us could argue with his plan. I appreciated his leadership and direction at this moment. Also, the mere mention of food made me realize just how hungry I was. I regret not taking a slice of bread from the kitchen on our house tour with Missus Douglas. We walked out of the front door, locked it behind us, and crossed toward the kirk before us.

Canongate Kirk across the street glowed in the fading evening sunlight. I could immediately see that the grounds were surrounded by lush gardens that would be a place of refuge for me so close to this house. I stopped on the side of the street and asked, "Is this where my father is buried, Duncan?"

"I dinnae ken, lass," he said, moving me out of the way of approaching horses. My uncle seemed pained by the ask and his lack of an answer. "I am so sorry. I shoulda asked Missus Douglas that verra question when we arrived. I will correct my error first thing in the morning."

I changed the subject and said, "I am definitely hungry, so perhaps we start there and can explore more of the city tomorrow." I grabbed his arm, placing my head on his shoulder, trying to get him to agree with that plan. "After Father's grave, I want to see where he worked, and then maybe we can see the castle. As close as we can, of course. Sir Alexander told me about it. Can we do that, please?"

Duncan smiled and placed his hand over mine. "Aye!" he said, but left it there, seemingly unwilling to discuss our plan any further in the middle of the street. "It has been some years since I was here with Alex. Might be good to look at a few taverns and then decide."

William spoke up unexpectedly and said, "Perhaps we choose one where we believe we can have a good meal *and* a private conversation."

"Aye, man," Duncan said in agreement.

The three of us walked up the Royal Mile together quietly. William and I followed Duncan's lead. He seemed to know where he was going and, in the hope of food and drink, we were more than willing to follow.

Much like our ride to Edinburgh, I was strategically placed between Duncan and William for protection. Occasionally, William would gently guide me by my elbow to move me out of the way of others or to keep me on pace with Duncan as I was easily distracted by the imposing buildings and the overwhelming masses of people rushing past us on every side on this street.

231

+++

SIXTEEN
The First Glimpse Of Father

We arrived at The World's End tavern first and decided to stay. It was closest to Father's house, fairly quiet at this hour, and seemed to have decent food and drink. There was no need to venture further up the street to inspect other options. Duncan secured us a table at the back of the room. We sat together quietly at first before Duncan said, "I will go order something for us to eat and drink."

He left William and me alone at the table. Even after a week of travelling together across the country, we still had occasional moments of silent awkwardness.

"Yer father's house is grand. Ye will sleep well with a warm bed and a full belly again this night."

"Aye, I suspect we *all* will."

He nodded in agreement. The truth was that we were all going to benefit from this fine house and Missus Douglas' care. No more travel, no more uncertainty about our accommodations each night, and no more being up at first light. I did not say the words, but this may be the first night on this entire trip that William no longer has to worry about security shifts or a cold night above a stable. He will surely benefit from having a fine room and sound sleep himself.

Duncan returned with three ale pots and placed them on the table, "This will hold us fer now, until I can determine the whisky situation. I have some food on the way."

Duncan sat down with us and raised his ale pot to the middle of the table and said, beaming with pride, "Well done, travelers! We completed the first part of our journey and arrived here in Edinburgh City—and to Alexander's house—safely."

"*Slàinte mhath,*" we all said in unison as we raised our drinks to each other. I am not sure I have ever seen Duncan so happy... so relieved. Once again, the weary group ate together in silence when the oysters arrived first. We were all starving after the ride today. Duncan gave us the option not to stop at mid-day to make it to the city before dark. I was so desperate to finish this trip that I accepted the offer to keep going.

"Och! Thank ye, Geordie!" Duncan said to the barkeep as he took the whisky jug from the man to pour us each a glass.

I was uncertain if I should talk about the afternoon in front of William, though he seems to have earned Duncan's trust throughout our travels. With more drink, I was starting to become agitated at the continued thought of what we witnessed upon our arrival, but I waited to follow my uncle's lead.

Duncan let us enjoy a few sips of whisky before saying, "Erm, I ken ye have questions, lass."

I did not hesitate and leaned in across the table with a fury in my eyes, "Aye, uncle, I *do*! This grand house for himself, filled with

234

commissioned art and a bespoke copper tub from Amsterdam! A full household staff! *And Christ above! A country house… with a giant dog… named Stirling?!*"

He just took my words in as I spat them out and just nodded until he finally looked at me and said, "Yer angry, lass."

"No, sir! I am not *angry*. *I am confused!*" I said, refilling my own glass this time with no concern for anyone else at the table. I drank it all at once. "I feel like I ken nothing of *my own* father! Aye, he came to the city to go to university, was here working on behalf of the clan, and all of that justified him not being with me… with *us… his family!*"

My voice broke and slowed at the last, and I tried to regain my composure. I said, calmer now. "That may have been only partly true, as it is clear to me that he had other business to keep him here in Edinburgh. And that business was financing a life we ken nothing about!"

I lashed out at my uncle, but I was overwhelmed with the unexpected world of Alexander MacLeod we all just stepped into. Duncan may be right. Perhaps I am angry. I adored my father and had always seen his absence as a sacrifice he was making for the clan, and now in this tavern came the realization that he wanted to be here. The thought of him wanting a life that did not include me hurt. I could barely breathe under the weight of what felt like rejection. *He chose to be here.*

William was gracious, as always. He filled his glass and immediately stepped away from the table to give us a moment. Duncan and I waited for him to leave to talk more.

"I am sorry. I shouldna have said all of those things to ye in front of William," I said as I looked down at my own glass, ashamed.

"Dinnae fash! I trust the lad. He has proven to be a fine travel companion and has done everything his laird asked of him. He just showed his honor and respect once again by stepping away quietly from a family conversation."

Duncan was right. William let us have our moment, and it was the right thing for him to do. I did not know about the expectations set for these men on this journey, but Duncan's assessment of the man so far seems positive. William MacCrimmon seems to be meeting his obligations on this trip, earning him even more respect from my uncles. Duncan once told William that he should be proud to have Auld Knox on his side, but I would argue that having Duncan and Laird MacLeod on your side might be even better.

"I am as shocked as ye are. I felt the same thing walking through the door on Canongate, lass," Duncan admitted to me, sipping from his glass. "I can assure ye of that! I began to question my relationship with my own brother on top of the grief I felt the minute we arrived at his door."

He paused for a moment and said, looking at me intently, "I am so sorry that the first question to Missus Douglas was not to ask where Alexander was buried. I regret it and mark it as a failure to ye. It should have been my first task when we arrived. It is the reason we are here."

"No, Duncan," I said as I reached across the table to touch his hand to comfort him. "I coulda asked the same question as his daughter and *mistress of the house* and I didna. We were all exhausted from our travels and overwhelmed by the grand house. I fear this trip may not be as fast as we hope, but I want to uncover the reality of Alexander MacLeod… and then I want to go *home*. I can already tell the city is not the place for me."

"Aye, let me bring William back over and talk about the plan for tomorrow then."

I nodded to him and sat quietly while Duncan went to retrieve William. They talked at the front of the tavern for a moment before walking back. I suspect Duncan was thanking him for politely stepping away from the table like a gentleman on our words.

I took a moment to look around at the tavern once again and the mix of people from all walks of life filling the room. It is all overwhelming, but everyone seems to be having a grand time. One of the benefits of a tavern in a populous city, seems that it can be an equalizer of many people, from different stations in life. Drink and eating food always bring people together. A tavern is not unlike the Great Hall at Dunmara Castle in that regard.

Duncan and William returned to the table with another bottle of whisky and new glasses for us. The night is still young, and we surely have more to discuss. Just as the men sat down, and Duncan poured us all another glass, we were suddenly joined by an older gentleman standing at the end of our table.

He was much older than Duncan for sure, but I could not tell if he was hunched over in age or just the drink of the evening. It may have been as bit of both as he stood quietly before us, one hand on his glass and the other on the edge of the table. He leaned in to look narrowly at us both. His white hair and beard were in striking contrast to his black clothing. He carried a black tri-corner hat, rimmed with gold stitching, under his arm. I could not tell where he came from in the tavern, as I had not noticed him before his sudden appearance before us.

Standing silently, the man had small wireframed glasses perched on his nose as he looked down at Duncan and then me, and then back again. "Excuse me, sir. I have to ask, are ye Duncan MacLeod?"

"Aye, and ye are?"

"I mean no disrespect interrupting yer conversation here, but I could not get over the resemblance between ye and the mistress to Master Alexander MacLeod," he said. "Alexander spoke of ye both so often. I surely thought the drink was overtaking me with ghosts. Ye both look so much like him and how he described ye that I kent it *had* to be ye. Erm, but please, I should introduce myself. I am Doctor Edmund Tyndall, at yer service."

We both knew instantly on the declaration of his name, that Doctor Tyndall was the one who pronounced Father dead based on the letter we received from Allan Calder. It was a shock to have the man standing at our table on our first evening in town. His choice of words were even more intriguing.

"Aye sir, I am Duncan MacLeod," as my uncle stood to shake the man's hand and look him directly in the eye. "I am Alexander's brother and please, I present my niece, Alexandra, his daughter."

"It is indeed a pleasure to meet ye both," Doctor Tyndall said as he raised his half-empty glass to us. We raised our glasses back to him in kind.

"This, sir, is our kinsman William MacCrimmon, who has accompanied us on our travels to the city." The doctor nodded to William, who nodded back to the man upon the introduction. "How incredible to meet ye here as we arrived this verra day to Edinburgh from Dunmara Castle on Skye to settle my brother's affairs."

"Well, I come to say nothing more to ye than yer brother—yer father, lass—was a fine man. His presence will be missed greatly here in the city. If I can be of any service to ye while ye are here, I am just up the street across from Bakehouse Close."

Duncan patted him on the shoulder and said, "Thank ye, sir. It is so good to meet ye."

We all nodded to the man for his kindness as he walked away from us to the other side of the tavern. Duncan and I looked at each other. Something about meeting the man this very first night in the city, and his use of the word *ghosts* made me wary. I will just add this to the growing list of clues to my father's life in Edinburgh.

+++

We were starting to be mad with drink and exhaustion. Duncan, William, and I were all so tired, so emotional, that we should have left this tavern and the bottle on this table long ago.

As the night progressed, I lost a lot of the worry and doubt that I had earlier and could not stop laughing at my companions, who were a great relief to me. Everyone was so thankful to be here finally, and the guarantee of a warm bed and a late rise that we indulged in the warmth of the tavern and the whisky a little more than we should have.

I leaned across to them both across the table and said, "Can we talk about Angus?"

"Christ above! Can we not?!" Duncan asked as he and William laughed with each other.

"He *really* met a woman overnight and decided to stay at Prestonfield?" I asked, skeptical of the timing and the outlandish story these men told me earlier this morning.

William chimed in on this one before Duncan could and confessed immediately, "It wasna overnight. He told me after supper that he would not be in the grand house and that I could have the bedchamber to myself. I must confess that the woman may have been the reason we were there at all!"

Duncan seemed intrigued by this, and perhaps dispelled some of the wariness he had about any connections to politics and the Jacobites. He asked, "Ye think that we were driven to the fine house fer a *woman?*"

"Dinnae sound so shocked, uncle," I said, dismissing his tone of slight disgust at such a moment of what could be love or, at the very basic level, physical lust. "Though I have to admit it does make ye wonder about the type of woman who would want to bed, Angus. There must be a story there."

"*Alexandra MacLeod!*" Duncan scolded me as William nearly spit out a mouthful of whisky.

I laughed and said, "Ye ken we were all thinking the same thing! I just said the words out loud!"

William said through his own laughter, "I dinnae ken for certain, but I believe he kent her before we arrived. Otherwise, the man moved with incredible speed from night to morn' and that would be a feat indeed— especially for him!"

"A feat indeed, William! She would have to find the man attractive *and* understand what he was saying in a few short hours." This time, Duncan nearly spit out his whisky and we all laughed together to the point of tears at the thought. I tried to bring us back from the brink of complete drunken silliness by saying, "Well, I dinnae ken what sent us there, it was the best night of the trip for me, and I will be sure to thank the man fer it when I see him next!" I raised my glass and said, "To Angus, *Slàinte!*"

"*Slàinte,*" my companions said in unison.

We finally left the tavern and made the short walk down the street to Father's house. Duncan fumbled with the keys at the door, but finally got us inside and locked it safely behind us.

"Och! We get to sleep in warm beds and do not have an early start!" I said as I started to climb the stairs before Duncan and William.

"Aye! We get a late start tomorrow, but ye need to be ready to set out after breakfast to Alexander's grave and then to his office."

"Aye," we all said in unison, agreeing to my uncle's plan.

I yelled back, "Dinnae be late! We must honor our commitment to Missus Douglas in the morning. She will have breakfast waiting fer us at nine o'clock."

We all walked across the corridor, and each man slipped into their rooms behind me before I finally disappeared into the warm and inviting comfort of my father's bedchamber at the end of the hall.

+++

I awoke with a slight headache in the morning but was so grateful to not have a long ride ahead of me, I actually relished getting ready at my own leisure. As much as I loved my Munro, I hoped he was as relieved as I was not to have to journey this day.

While still foreign to me, my father's house made me feel safe and happy. The bed and the bath were the best things I had ever experienced, now putting Prestonfield House as a close second for the best accommodations on this journey. After a week on the road, I moved easily from one warm comfort to the next.

My legs and back could finally take some time to recover and the warm copper bath was just the healing tonic I needed. Missus Douglas seemingly anticipated this need after a long journey and provided me with extra water for the cauldrons before retiring and I found all kinds of soaps and oils in the small chamber. Each smelled better than the next.

After my luxurious bath in the work of art that was the copper tub, I explored the room, looking for artifacts of my father's life. Outside of his beloved art, and his clothes still in the chest, I found nothing. It was odd. There were no papers, no sign of the many letters I sent him—or anyone else, for that matter. Also, I knew my father read a lot and there were no books in his bedchamber.

I told myself that he must keep them elsewhere in the house or Missus Douglas cleared the room, uncertain of who would stay in it. I dressed and went down to join Missus Douglas in the kitchen, like I used to with Missus Gerrard.

"Good morning, Missus Douglas!" I said. Suddenly, my voice sounded higher than normal. She seemed unsettled with me hovering while preparing breakfast, but I welcomed the chance to talk with her. "Missus, my uncle and I failed to ask ye where my father is buried last night."

Before I could finish the question, she answered me, "Aye, mistress! I left the house last night and realized I had not told ye. I felt horrible fer it, I did!"

"No, please," I said reassuringly. "My uncle and I walked out the door and felt horrible for not asking at the verra start. We were overwhelmed being here, in his house, finally."

"Master MacLeod is laid to rest across the street at Canongate Kirk. Reverend Gordon offered the plot to honor him for all the great contributions he made. There is something comforting about him being so close to his home."

I thought about her words and wanted to argue that his home was at Dunmara Castle on Skye, but I did not. "I believe we will go there after yer breakfast, but I will leave that direction to my uncle. If I may continue to ask some questions while ye are working, missus?"

"Aye, of course," she said, seeming more relaxed the more we talked. Perhaps as mistress of the house, she thought I was here to inspect her work or start barking orders at her. What I really want is more insight into who my father was. Who better to ask than the woman running his household?

"Aside from his clothes, I see nothing of my father in his bedchamber. No letters from me or home, and none of his beloved books. Are they kept elsewhere?"

"Aye, many of the items ye are looking for are in the parlor room at the front. His desk and books are behind the door to the right. Ye may not have been able to see since we were so quick on our tour and I didna call it out."

"Aye! I kent they had to be in another place," I said, relieved that at least one mystery was solved this morning.

"When I prepared the room fer ye, I took anything he had in his chamber and placed it on top of the desk."

"Thank ye verra much, Missus Douglas. I will go there now and leave ye to yer work. I will see ye fer breakfast shortly."

"If ye need anything, lass, just call fer me."

+++

243

Sure enough, behind the large door to the right was a desk covered in papers and books. I closed his still open ink pot and ran my hands over his quill sitting on top of a letter he had started to me, dated the day before he died. It broke my heart to see it as I read.

19 July 1766

Mistress Alexandra MacLeod
Dunmara Castle, Skye

My dearest daughter,

I have been thinking much about our all too brief time together at Dunmara and wanted to tell you again how proud I am.

Seeing you rise to the challenge ahead in service to Clan MacLeod was a proud moment for me as your father. I admire and respect the young woman you are and the lady you will become.

I am here to serve and support you for the rest of my

The letter was unfinished, but even these initial lines meant the world to me. The last line of his mail broke my heart. Just as he could not finish the thought, he had no idea that he would not have the opportunity to keep to his commitment to me. I folded the paper up and placed it in the pocket of my skirt.

Everything on the desk seemed as it should. There was a mix of personal and business correspondence. He had a calendar open to a week of hand-written appointments he would never make. The books on top of the desk were mostly legal theory and history. The one exception was a similar book of Shakespeare's sonnets that I had inherited from Lady Margaret. That made me smile. I will leave it here for now, but I hoped to take it back home with me.

In the top drawer of the desk was an assortment of new quills, parchment, wax candles for his seal, and old letters. All of my letters were in bunches tied with a blue ribbon, and I took the unfinished letter Father wrote to me out of my pocket and placed it in one of the ribbon-secured stacks. I am touched that he kept them all. I placed them back in the drawer for now but will add them to the items I will take home.

There were several small coins in the bottom drawer that looked more like he had just taken out of his pockets and thrown here instead of actually storing money. If I knew my father, he may have also kept these small coins on hand for Petey. It would be his nature to care for the lad and I will remember the coins are here should I wish to do the same.

I could hear Duncan and William walking down the stairs to the dining room for Missus Douglas' breakfast. I shut the drawers and smiled again at the thought of learning a bit more about my father this morning. I walked out of the room and followed the men into the dining room.

After a week on the road, we dined on eggs and toasted bread with creamy butter. We had fresh fruit—some that I have never seen or tasted before—and fried ham. Missus Douglas is a fine cook and suddenly I looked forward to my task as mistress of this house to plan meals with her.

We ate together again in silence. This time not as a result of our weariness, but because of the glory of the food before us. Our mouths were too full to speak to each other.

I broke the silence by saying, "I used to think that bread and butter were the best things on a table and now I ken that I was *wrong!*"

"It is fried ham," William said before taking another off the platter.

"Aye, I have never had anything this delicious in my life," Duncan said, taking his own bite of the salty goodness.

"Duncan, do ye think we can take Missus Douglas back to Skye with us?" I said, and both men laughed at the notion. He did not respond, as his mouth was full of food. Instead, he gave me a look that said we could, but Missus Gerrard might have something to say about it. He was right, of course.

While we ate, I told the men about the grave and Father's items in the parlor. Duncan seemed interested, but said nothing. I believed he would want to inspect on his own later. I declared that I would retrieve my letters at another time, but decided to keep the unfinished letter from the top of the desk between me and my father for now.

Our magnificent cook walked in to check on us and I said, "Och, Missus Douglas! This feast was wonderful, madam! Well done!"

The men at the table nodded in agreement, unable to speak, as their mouths were filled once again with food.

"Aye, ye are happy, mistress?"

"I had so many delights that I have never had before and was just telling my uncle and friend that yer fried ham has now overtaken fresh bread and butter as my favorite item on a dining table."

"It makes me happy ye are all pleased," she said with her hands clasped before her chest and a huge smile of satisfaction on her face in serving us well with her first meal. "I make the bread and butter here myself. We have a chicken coop and small garden on the other side of the stables, and of course can order anything else ye wish."

"I look forward to working with ye on menus, Missus Douglas," I said, "though I dinnae think ye need much direction from me."

"Can I get ye anything else?" she asked as she cleared the empty plates.

"No, our bellies are quite full." I said. "We just wanted to thank ye."

Finally, my companions spoke and in unison saying, "Thank ye, Missus Douglas!"

William continued, "I dinnae ken that I have ever had a better breakfast in my entire life, Missus Douglas!"

And with those words, the woman blushed, and she nodded her head to him before walking out of the room floating on air from the kind compliment from Master MacCrimmon. He certainly has a way of charming women in charge of a kitchen. I suspect we will all have fried ham often while we are in MacLeod House. Come to think of it, as the new mistress of this fine house, I will see that we do.

+++

We met back downstairs to set out on our errands for the day. Duncan stood at the bottom of the stairs with William and Missus Douglas. He was holding a beautiful bouquet of flowers tied with a blue ribbon, not unlike the ribbon around my stack of letters Father saved.

Missus Douglas walked us across the street in silence to the kirk and to introduce us to Reverend Gordon.

"Welcome! Come in, please," the reverend said as he shook each of our hands. "I am Reverend Gordon and I want to personally welcome ye to Canongate Kirk. I hope each of ye will find this hallowed ground a place of refuge and comfort while ye are in Edinburgh. If ye will, follow me."

He continued talking to us as he led us through the sanctuary, "Master MacLeod was an incredible supporter of the kirk and the charitable works we carry out in the city. His generosity helped us rebuild a damaged stone wall, and he saw to the planting of new trees at the front, which not only add beauty to the grounds but shield us from the noisy city. But the most important work he helped fund was for our charitable programs for those living on the streets of Edinburgh, especially women and children."

He did not know it, but his words added to our list of clues of Alexander MacLeod. I was gathering every single one I could to stitch together the other life my beloved father had here—the life I was not part of for many years.

"I will walk with ye to where Master MacLeod is buried and say a few words of prayer and remembrance. But I will leave ye and yer family to stay as long as ye need. Ye are welcome to come back to the kirkyard anytime, of course. I would also, personally, invite ye all to Sunday service."

We all smiled and nodded politely to his offer, but made no commitment. I thought he was warm and genuine in his welcome to us in our time of grief. However, this is a Presbyterian kirk and not Episcopalian. I can only imagine that my father gravitated here due to the proximity to his house, but he may have developed other views on religion. Perhaps this was another clue.

I could tell that Duncan's initial response was much like my own and took Reverend Gordon's comments as being a little too focused on Father's monetary commitment and not his Christian commitment. We walked out through a door on the back of the nave to the kirkyard, to a plot with a small, flat stone marker with a cross and the number three carved in it. The ground was still quite fresh. Next to the small stone marker was a small, shriveled bouquet of flowers tied with a blue ribbon, much like the one we carried with us today.

Reverend Gordon began to recite the Twenty-third Psalm. We joined him in unison, albeit softly.

"The LORD is my shepherd; I shall not want.

He maketh me to lie down in green pastures: he leadeth me beside the still waters.

He restoreth my soul: he leadeth me in the paths of righteousness for his name's sake.

Yea, though I walk through the valley of the shadow of death, I will fear no evil: for thou art with me; thy rod and thy staff they comfort me.

Thou preparest a table before me in the presence of mine enemies: thou anointest my head with oil; my cup runneth over.

Surely goodness and mercy shall follow me all the days of my life: and I will dwell in the house of the Lord forever."

We all bowed our heads in reverence, and I whispered, "*Amen.*"

Reverend Gordon continued, "While the life of Alexander Ewan MacLeod was all too short, it was full. We celebrate his contribution to his loving family, his honor and duty to his kinsmen of Clan MacLeod, and to his country. This day, in the presence of his dear brother and his daughter, we once again commend his body to the Earth and his soul to Christ Almighty."

Missus Douglas and William stepped back toward the kirk with Reverend Gordon. That is when my body told me that I could not stand stoically before this barren plot any longer. I took the flowers from Duncan's hands and fell to my knees. I placed them on Father's grave and cried. I just sobbed into my hands harder than I ever had before. I could not speak and if I could, there were no words that would mean anything in this moment. The loss of my own father was made final here at this spot where he laid alone. He died alone. He does not even have a suitable marker yet to declare this is where the man lies. At some point, I felt Duncan's hand on my shoulder and then a much-needed handkerchief was lowered down to me.

I stood up off the ground and through sniffles and, trying to clean my face, I hugged Duncan. He said softly in my ear, *"Why do ye never have a handkerchief when ye are in need of one, lass?"* He was trying to make me laugh and perhaps mask his own pain at the reality and finality of my father's unmarked grave before us. I knew his heart hurt as much as my own.

"Always unprepared, I suppose. No flask. No handkerchief," I said as I hugged him, and he hugged me back. "I will leave ye to yer own grief. Take yer time, sir."

I kissed him on the cheek as I left him by Father's grave with tears still streaming from my eyes. I rejoined William and Missus Douglas on the side of the kirk. Missus Douglas wiped her own tears away and offered me a sympathetic and motherly hug.

I felt awkward crying in front of William once again, but this was the reason we were here, and the emotion of Father's loss had to be expected. He gave me a weak smile of support and said, "I am verra sorry fer yer loss, Lady Alexandra."

I appreciated his kindness and respect for my father. I continued to wipe my nose and face with Duncan's handkerchief. I thought about returning it to him, but this tear-soaked cloth would be of no use to him in its current state. Then I saw that he had a spare when he wiped his own face with a new linen. I smiled for a brief moment. Duncan was never short of a clean handkerchief.

I said to Missus Douglas and William, "I will wait fer Duncan in front of the kirk." I knew that I could not stand here and watch my uncle's final moments with his brother. I would talk with him about it, one day. But I did not want to linger here on the outskirts of his own grief, as it was breaking my heart. I was fine to share my own with him, but men are different, and I needed to give him the room to say goodbye on his own. William and Missus Douglas followed my lead and walked behind me to the front of the building.

When Duncan joined us, his eyes still red and wet with his tears, he said plainly and without emotion, "Now we walk back to the house and Jonny will direct us to Alexander's office, lass."

"Aye, Master MacLeod," Missus Douglas said as she pointed back to the house across the street, "yer instructions were clear, sir. Jonny is waiting fer ye all just there."

Upon her words, we looked across the street to see Jonny standing with a carriage in front of the house on Canongate. He already had the door open to take us to our next appointment. None of us said the words aloud, but we were all thinking the same thing: *Of course, Master Alexander MacLeod has his own carriage.*

SEVENTEEN
Alexander MacLeod, Esquire

We arrived in front of another grand building sitting just off of Lawnmarket behind St. Giles' Cathedral. Next to the door was a small, engraved brass plate with the name, *Alexander MacLeod, Esquire.* The simple notation below his name read *Advocate.*

Duncan and I both paused to acknowledge Father's life once again. We smiled at each other, with pride that my father had done so well for himself. We also hoped that today we would learn even more about his life and his work here in Edinburgh. I ran my fingers over his name plate and thought to myself how much I admired him, but how much I also missed him. Seeing his name engraved on the brass plate was bittersweet. Despite my pride, it was another symbol of a man that no longer lived.

William spoke up from the bottom of the stairs, "I will wait out here fer ye with Jonny."

"Aye. Thank ye," Duncan said to the men beside the carriage. "I hope we willna be long."

As soon as we walked in the door, we were met in the entry by a lovely young woman with a bright and welcoming smile. She could not have been more than ten years older than me, Duncan's age. Her dress was fine and looked to be made of silk instead of wool, and she had beautiful blonde hair and dark brown eyes.

"Mistress Hay? I am Duncan MacLeod, Alexander's brother, and this is his only child, Alexandra MacLeod," he said, placing his hand behind my shoulder.

"Come in, come in, please, Master MacLeod!" she said, motioning us both further into the front hall. "I am Elizabeth Hay and I help, erm, I helped… run the office and diaries fer both Master MacLeod and, on occasion, *Master Calder.*"

The mention of the name Calder sent a chill through the room. I could see instantly that she did not seem to care for the man any more than we did just by the way she said his name. I had completely forgotten about Father's shadow and never even thought about possibly seeing him here.

"Mistress Hay, my niece and I have three goals this day."

"Aye, sir!"

"First, we want to secure any documents that relate to Clan MacLeod so that we can determine if we need to retain legal counsel here in the city."

I interrupted him by saying, "And perhaps we need to ken if my father already assigned that responsibility. He talked of his friend and colleague, Master Forbes."

"Aye," Duncan said agreeing with me and my clarification. "We also need to understand the status of Alexander's clients so that we can decide what to do going forward for his business. And finally, we need to

253

understand how to settle Alexander's affairs and Alexandra's inheritance. We welcome yer direction on all three matters."

Mistress Hay smiled at both of us and said, "Please, come with me."

We walked behind her into another room off of the long hallway that had a fireplace on one end, and two chairs opposite a desk on the other. I could see the spent candles, the quill, inkpot, and papers in my father's own handwriting atop the desk. I smiled at the thought of him working there.

"This was yer father's desk. Master MacLeod made it clear to me what to do in the event of his death," she said, as she pointed to the other side of the desk, to a grand chest bound by leather and secured with a lock.

"This chest here contains all the documents and papers related to Clan MacLeod. It is organized by year with the most recent items on top. He told me someone would collect them to return it to either Dunmara Castle or to a new legal representative. I have the key just here."

"Aye, wonderful," Duncan said, taking the key from her before handing it to me. I just nodded my head in agreement. "I will have William, our kinsman, come in and take the chest to the carriage."

Duncan left us together for a moment. I am not certain why I have gone mute, but I could not speak. It was all becoming so *final* and once again, I felt out of place and uncertain of myself. We stood quietly in the room before Mistress Hay said with respect, "Yer father was a fine man, lass."

"Thank ye, Mistress Hay," I said softly and slowly. She looked at me with a kind and sympathetic smile. "I apologize. I am overwhelmed by being here and seem to have lost my ability to speak. Or at least speak without emotion."

"Ye are doing *just fine*."

William came into the room with Duncan, who said, "Mistress Hay, this is our kinsman, William MacCrimmon, who escorted us to Edinburgh. Lad, that chest there should go into the carriage."

"Aye, sir," William said, as he lifted the heavy chest seemingly with no effort and carried it out of the room.

Mistress Hay continued, "This ledger here will tell ye everything ye need to know about the current list of clients and where we stand in our financial books. All are completely paid, but not all clients know that he passed. We have sent messages to most of those most active here in the city and have directed them to yer father's lawyer, Campbell Forbes, Esquire as Master MacLeod requested. We have other clients further from the city that still need notification. I must tell ye that Master MacLeod was removing some clients from Master Calder's responsibility, and he documented the clients he rejected in the ledger. Ye will want to look *closely* at his notes."

She pushed the ledger to me without another word. Suddenly, I found my voice. "Where is Master Calder, Mistress Hay?"

"I do not know. Master Calder has only come into this building one time since yer father died."

"How is that? Does he not still have a job to do here?" Duncan asked.

"If I may speak freely, sir?"

Before Duncan could answer, I said, "Please! We are trying to better understand my father's life and business here. Anything ye have to tell us helps understand him better and settle his affairs in the city."

Duncan nodded and said, "And if this information allows us to be of help to ye, we are at yer service, mistress." I thought this was a chivalrous take for him, but it was true. If we needed to handle Allan Calder for her, we could and we would. Duncan nodded again to her that she should speak to us openly.

"Erm, like I said, Master MacLeod was reducing the man's responsibilities. But I venture to guess that if ye met the man, ye both know that already." Duncan and I looked at each other in silent agreement and then back to Mistress Hay.

"Master MacLeod started to realize that the man was not to be trusted. That is why I kept the chest related to the Clan MacLeod business hidden. It was only moved here knowing your arrival. I was given strict instructions on this, and Master Calder didna know that I had these files secured or where. He came to the office the day Master MacLeod died to retrieve papers that I believe the man had no right to have. I only know this because he asked for yer father's most recent documents from the last trip to Skye. I told him I had no idea what he was talking about, and after a bit of an argument, he finally left. He has not been back since."

I looked at Duncan and asked, "The marriage contract?"

He said back to me, "Possibly. More if Laird Graham gave Alexander any other tasks while he was there. I dinnae ken."

"Mistress Hay, are we paying Master Calder a wage?" I asked. Duncan looked at me and nodded his head in agreement at the ask. A legitimate ask if the man has not been working.

"Aye, we are," she said.

"Well, that ends now. Duncan, do ye agree?"

"Aye, I agree and well done, lass."

Still speaking to my uncle, I said, "Want and need of money may bring him back here, or perhaps we can find him first so that he is not

Mistress Hay's problem on her own." I am not sure what we would do when we found him, but it was a fair thought to prevent him harassing Mistress Hay for this decision. It is ours, not hers.

"I have his home address, but I believe ye can find him most often in the White Hart Inn."

"Give me his home lodging fer now. We may need it, but if we can see him at the tavern, that will be better," Duncan said.

"Aye!" both Mistress Hay and I said in unison.

After a moment, Mistress Hay said, "Fer yer last request, as ye ken, Master Alexander did indeed have his own advocate and counsel. Next door is Master Campbell Forbes, Esquire. Master Forbes owns this entire building and was a trusted friend to Alex."

I thought for a moment that her reference of my father seemed suddenly informal but could not read into her words just yet as she corrected herself immediately.

"He will handle Mistress Alexandra's inheritance and settle Master MacLeod's personal affairs, including if ye want to close this practice. I will arrange a meeting fer ye."

"We will see that ye are sorted, Mistress Hay, but with no one in a position to carry on for Father, we may have to do just that."

"I understand completely," she said. And I believe she did. She knew we would not be able to keep Father's practice going on our own or from Skye and with no other trusted lawyer in employ here to carry it on in this name. The thought of closing this practice was a practical one, but it was another point of finality in ending what remained of my father's life in Edinburgh.

She continued, "I will send word to MacLeod House when to meet Master Forbes. I think he will just need a day or so to have all the documents in order."

We all nodded in agreement to this plan and Duncan said, "Understood. Ye ken where we are. Just send word and we will meet Master Forbes when he is ready."

"Is there anything ye need from us, Mistress Hay?" I asked as we started to walk to the door.

"Ye are too kind. I will keep things going here. Like I said, most of yer father's clients in the city are aware of his passing and that we are in a moment of transition. They have been verra understanding. I will follow yer instructions on what to tell them next, or his clients outside the city, after ye meet with Master Forbes. There *is* one more thing that I need to make ye aware of."

She handed me an invitation with a black seal. It had been opened, and she said, "The Advocate Society, of which yer father was a founding member, wants to honor and celebrate his life with a small event on Friday next. Master Ramsay has a portrait to unveil."

"Aye, Sir Alexander Dick, let us know about this when we stopped at Prestonfield House," I said.

The thought of a portrait of my father from the master was both intriguing and an honor. Allan Ramsay is a well-known painter and portrait artist to the Crown. He painted my grandfather over a decade earlier, and the portrait hangs prominently in the Great Hall at Castle Dunmara.

"I let them know that ye would be here in the city and ye may want to receive this honor yerselves. Here is the invitation. Take it with ye. If you want to attend, I can arrange it all fer ye, including all travel scheduling with Master Jonny and Missus Douglas. I am here to serve ye both as I served Master MacLeod."

"Thank ye," I said as I took the invitation from her hands. It was beautifully written, the paper was heavy, and the official black seal was ornate in its design.

"Ye keep doing what ye are, and we will return on yer word to meet with Master Forbes." Duncan said.

+++

Duncan and I walked down the front stairs in silence. It had been a long and emotional day for all of us. Jonny and William were waiting patiently for us by the carriage.

"Jonny, we might need to make a quick stop at the White Hart Inn before MacLeod House," Duncan said.

"Aye sir! It is close and a favorite stop fer yer brother on the way home after a long day."

"Give me a moment, will ye?" I asked as my uncle held the carriage door for me. The day had been filled with one revelation after another, but I have one more question. Before he could say anything back to me, I turned back to the front of building and ran up the stairs.

"Mistress Hay, may I ask ye?"

"Of course," she said back to me and placed her hand on my arm. "How can I help?"

"I need a new dress," I said, somewhat embarrassed and unsure of my own words. My clothes still represented my place of origin and my cross-country travels. "Erm, I feel the need to fit in better in the city, but even more so now with this request to honor my father at the Advocate Society event. I will need to be more... presentable in the fashion of the day. I may also need to ensure my uncle is also… well, as presentable as he can be."

We both laughed at the last. "I can help ye here-on both fronts! Come with me!" She walked me back to Father's desk and took a quill and paper and wrote down her instructions.

"First, ye will want to take Duncan to be fitted by the tailors at Marshall Aitken. Finest bespoke tailors in all of Edinburgh and made all of yer father's clothes. Ye will find them across from St. Giles' Cathedral."

She wrote down the address and continued, "Then ye will see Missus Helen Scott at Scott & Sons on Grassmarket for yer dress. Helen is a fabulous dress maker and seamstress. She can get fine fabrics to match any on the High Street but will craft a dress fer ye that is almost half the price of the more well-known shops. Her husband owned the business but died last year. Helen did most of the sewing work herself, and she is trying to keep her business going to feed her family. I say this to ye, not fer sympathy, but to support her. Helen is a dear friend and makes all of my dresses and ye can see she does fine work."

"Aye! She does!" Mistress Hay's fine garment was the primary reason I asked her for this particular piece of advice.

"Dinnae fash, lass," she said as she took my hand. "Ye look just fine, but if ye want a new garment, this is the place. I will send Helen word to expect ye tomorrow. Perhaps ye can get yer clothing settled and then see Master Forbes in the afternoon, but again, I will send you a message to MacLeod House to confirm yer appointment with him."

"Thank ye, indeed! I have one more question. Is it fair to think that Missus Scott could have a new dress made in time for the Advocate Society event?"

"Aye! Helen has many dresses already started and then fits them to the woman. Perhaps ye will find one that ye like. But even a bespoke garment can be made in time… for the right price, of course."

"Thank ye, Mistress Hay," I said, smiling as my confidence was restored at the prospect of new clothing.

She walked me back to the door and said as she handed me the paper with the names and addresses, "Mistress Alexandra, I only have one ask of ye."

"Aye."

"Please call me Elizabeth."

"Thank ye verra much, Elizabeth," I said as she walked me out the door and I ran down to the carriage where my uncle was waiting impatiently for me. I turned back to her at the bottom of the stairs and said, "And please, ye can call me Alexandra."

I got in the carriage and signaled with a tap on the roof for Jonny to take us to the White Hart Inn.

"What was that all about, lass?" my uncle asked once we were on our way.

"Och nothing. Just trying to help us be prepared for Father's event," I said with a smile. He just looked at me, clearly uncertain of what I was saying. "Be ready to go to the tailor's tomorrow morning, Duncan. We need to look like we belong here and can represent Clan MacLeod properly in Edinburgh City."

He looked across the carriage at William first in disbelief and then at me as if I were raving mad, but said nothing. I could only smile to myself at the thought.

+++

EIGHTEEN
Life Lessons

"What'll ye have?" asked the man behind the bar. It was then that I realized that he was only looking at Duncan, so I answered before my uncle could.

"Three ales if you please, sir," I said with a wink to the side at Duncan. I was showing him that I was not afraid to state my ask to the barkeep, but he also knows I do not like being dismissed by men.

The man never took his gaze off Duncan and never acknowledged that I was standing there before him or speaking. I could feel my jaw clenching immediately. I know I pursed my lips in a defiant stare.

"Aye, Jacob! Three ales. It is good to see you again, man," Duncan said, as they shook hands across the bar.

"It has been a long time, Duncan."

"Too long."

As Jacob walked away to fill the ale pots, I turned to the side and through my teeth said, "Ye ken, this sets my blood afire! Why will the man not even look at me?"

Exasperated by my attitude, Duncan turned to me and said, in a whisper, *"Here is an important life lesson fer ye, lass."*

I tilted my head so my right ear could receive his soft-spoken message in my ear. "First, settle yerself," he said through a laugh. My jaw got even tighter, and I bit my lip at his scolding. "Second, Jacob remembers me. I have been here many times with yer father. Finally, always ken yer barkeep's name—and, for that matter—any barmaid. Trust yer own instincts, lass! But for the most part, your barkeep and barmaids are honest, hard-working people. Come to think of it," he said, scanning the room once again and saying reflectively, "some of my best friends were made at a tavern."

"Ye dinnae say!" I said with all the sarcasm I could muster.

"Ye miss my meaning, lass, if that is all ye heard," he said, scolding me slightly again. Before I could protest, he handed me the coin to pay for our drinks and continued with his lesson. "Take a moment to be kind. Take care of them, and they will take care of ye. Ye may need them if I am not here with ye."

I realized that he was not just talking about filling my glass. He was talking about treating others the way I wanted to be treated first. And ultimately, he was talking about how these new friends could keep me safe within these tavern walls. Despite my personal confidence, no matter where you were, city or country, the tavern can be a dangerous place for a woman.

He was right. Duncan knew that if I were to be here without his protection, I may need support. I may need a friend. Our entire trip has

264

focused on safety and security for me as a woman—but we never talked of what to do if I were alone, as I have always had the protection of the men on this journey. I have *never* been alone.

"I get yer meaning," I said, looking cautiously around the room and assessing the people in the tavern at this hour. Jacob returned and put three pots forcefully on the bar with ale splashing about. Again, still only looking at Duncan, he waited for his payment.

"Jacob, this is my niece, Alexandra—Alexander's only child. And this is our kinsman, William MacCrimmon."

The man nodded to William and then, for the first time, looked at me in the eye, nodded and softly said, "Nice to meet you, Mistress Alexandra. I was verra sorry to hear about Master MacLeod's passing. He came here often after a long day's work and was always verra kind and generous."

Passing the coin to pay for our ales across the bar myself, I said in appreciation for his words about Father, "Thank ye, Jacob. This is my first time at the White Hart Inn. It is… lovely." I am not sure there has ever been a *lovely* tavern, but this one was the cleanest of any I had been in so far—at least by city standards. "I am certain I will visit again, with or without my uncle."

He seemed genuinely shocked that I would acknowledge him by name, but more shocked with that I was the one placing the money in front of him. He took it quickly, but immediately began wiping up the spilled ale from the bar and the sides of our pots with the cloth previously perched on his shoulder.

"Of course, Mistress Alexandra," he said as he leaned in. "I do have a quiet seat in the back if ye and yer uncle would like to go there," he said with the faintest hint of a smile and a flicker in his bright blue eyes, as if sharing a secret.

"That would be wonderful, thank ye!" I leaned in toward Jacob to meet him and said in confidence, "We have a lot to discuss, sir, so a quiet spot is *most* welcome!"

I reached for our drinks, but Jacob grabbed them for us immediately and escorted us to a table in the back by the window.

As we sat down, he said, "If ye need anything, ye call to me or to Hilary there," pointing toward at a young barmaid clearing the next table. "We will see to yer needs."

Nodding to Hilary with a smile, I said, "Of course! And I thank ye both!"

As he walked away, Duncan, William, and I tapped our ale pots. *"Slàinte mhath!"*

I nearly choked on the warm bitter drink and said, "Och, I really dinnae like ale."

Duncan said as he leaned in closer to me, "Ye just learned an important lesson, lass. Every person ye meet deserves kindness and respect—until they show ye, they dinnae. Ye gave respect to Jacob, and he gave it right back, didna he?"

"Aye, he did. Though I am certain yer endorsement helped."

Realizing that I had indeed learned a lesson, I articulated what I learned. "Duncan, I thought that Jacob was dismissing me as a woman, but that was not the case. I see now that I read the situation wrong." He nodded at that point but did not say a word, letting me work it out myself. I took another sip and continued, "It was more than I thought. He recognized ye and naturally acknowledged ye first as someone he kent. Not just as a man. I overreacted."

"Och! Yer a quick learner, lass," he said, laughing like a proud father—a proud father teaching his lass to navigate life in a Scottish tavern. In many ways, this whole trip has been about lessons on how to deal with life in a tavern, not just our country.

"Like I said, some of my best friends are from the tavern," he said, gulping once more from his ale pot. "The White Hart is one of the best in Edinburgh. Good people work here, lass. They work hard and if they ken ye, they will keep ye safe as much as they keep yer glass full."

It was a valuable life lesson indeed, for Jacob and Hilary never let our ale pots be empty for long. But more than that, I know that I just made two new friends in the city.

+++

With his ale pot in hand, William asked, "Was this afternoon productive fer ye both?"

"Aye, we will hear from Mistress Hay about whether we can meet with Father's advocate, Master Forbes, tomorrow or the next day to settle things. And as Sir Alexander said, the Advocate Society are honoring my father next Friday."

"That is good news—and good timing, then."

"Aye, tomorrow, we will see to the tailors, lass," Duncan said as he sat down with us.

"I am so glad yer agreeable to it, uncle!"

"I said we would see the tailors, lass," he said with a wink and a smile. "I didna say I was *agreeable* to it."

William laughed loudly and said, "I am sorry! The way ye talk to each other makes me laugh sometimes." We both looked at him and he continued, somewhat embarrassed that he said what he thought aloud, "I just mean that ye both like to tease each other—mercilessly sometimes. It is... erm... *amusing*."

"Aye," I said, and Duncan nodded his head in agreement. "We are only ten years apart and I suppose I think of Duncan as much as my brother as my uncle."

"Aye," Duncan said, "we grew up together in many ways and the manner in which we speak to each other is a little... less *formal*."

"Ye will hate this story," I said to Duncan, almost begging for forgiveness in advance, before turning back to William. "When I was a wee lass, I combined Duncan and Uncle and called him *Duncle*! He *absolutely hated* it!"

Both men before me nearly spit out their drinks on the confession. It is not a name I have said recently, but I smiled at the memory of it. Terms of endearment are special, and the laughter at Duncan's expense made me happy. He will always be my own *Duncle*!

"Och, it was horrible, Will! Here I was, a young lad trying to get the bonnie lasses to pay attention to me, and everywhere I went, this wee lass would scream '*Duncle*' at the top of her lungs and run fer me. As embarrassed as I was, I could not ignore her." He smiled with his own thoughts of fond remembrance of how we grew up together. We *love* each other.

After a moment, Duncan changed the subject, and said, "As for the tailor, I think William should go with us."

"Of course, sir," William said immediately. "I am here to escort ye and Lady Alexandra wherever ye need."

"No lad. As it looks like we have more to do here in the city, and the days and nights are only going to get cooler before we can return home, ye should have another coat and hat—suitable for events like the one for my brother. I would like ye to join us."

"Aye, sir," William said, seemingly uncertain of the ask before him.

"I have plenty of coin to cover us, as we did not have to put anyone up in a tavern during our stay in the city with Alexander's grand house. And lass, ye should see if the seamstress can also make ye a new cloak to protect a fine new dress from the rain and chill."

William and I were both grateful for this instruction, as neither of us had any means to pay for new clothes. I had not expected Duncan to insist that William accompany us, but it seems fair to ensure clan MacLeod is well represented to honor my father. Also, if his job is to keep me safe on this journey, he should go with us.

"Aye," I said in agreement.

Duncan spoke to William directly, "Lad, I want ye to keep yer eyes open for Allan Calder."

"Calder?" William asked, looking at us both with narrowed eyes.

"Aye. Ye ken the man?"

"Aye. Well, I mean, I saw him on his visit to Dunmara with yer brother. He stood out in the crowd, of course."

"I never trusted the man, and Mistress Hay says he has also stopped working since Alexander died."

"Och, but he is still getting paid from Father's purse!" I scoffed. "Mistress Hay says Master Calder comes in here from time to time and if we can let him ken that he no longer has a position in Father's employ, then I would verra much like him to hear it from me and Duncan as we made the decision this day. I dinnae want Mistress Hay to have to deal with him if we can help it."

"Aye, he was apparently being removed from any responsibility," Duncan said with a sigh. "My poor brother just didna get to finish what he started."

William spoke up and asked pointedly, "Master MacLeod was taking away responsibilities from Calder, but he brought the man all the way to Skye for one of the most important days of his only daughter's life?"

Duncan said, looking into his glass, "It is a fair question. What do ye think, Alex?"

"Fair indeed," I said. I had not thought of it before. William was correct. *Why would my father travel across Scotland with someone he did not trust and did not want him working for him any longer?*

We sat silently for a moment before I said, "Perhaps Father was remaining true to the old saying… *'keep yer friends close and yer enemies closer'* so that he could keep an eye on the man instead of leaving him for a few weeks back here alone in the city to cause trouble."

Duncan nodded and said simply, "Possible."

William thought for a moment and said, "Traveling across the country with someone can also reveal a lot about them. It could have been a test or a chance fer yer father to get to know more about the man and his intentions. Or as ye said—just to keep him from causing trouble while he was away."

I thought about the journey we all just took together. How people react to challenges on the road. Their own peculiar preferences. Or even just the unfiltered moments in a tavern over whisky. You learn a lot about someone when you travel with them. I learned a lot about these men on our journey to Edinburgh, for sure!

"Like I said, I think we will spend some time here over the next several days," Duncan said. I suspect that it will not be any great sacrifice for him to spend time in a tavern, but the task is honorable.

"If ye see Allan Calder, I want to ken," Duncan said to William. "I will also talk to Jacob about him." Duncan stood and took his ale pot to the front of the tavern to see what he could learn from the bar keep. I suspect he is also assessing the whisky situation. William and I sat quietly for a moment. Both of us surveyed the room in hopes of having the first glance of the elusive man in question.

"When did ye encounter Master Calder at Dunmara?" I asked William. His words to Duncan that he knew of the man suddenly registering in my mind.

"He came out to the stables at one point and was just lurking about," William said. "He was an odd-looking fellow with an even stranger countenance. He talked a lot but said verra little of consequence. It was like he was trying to impress anyone who would listen to him. But there was absolutely nothing impressive about him. The other lads and I just tried to ignore him and kept doing our chores."

I nodded at this fact and William's detailed assessment. Allan Calder was indeed an odd-looking fellow. I had thought of him as my father's shadow, but it appears he spent a good bit of time on his own during his short stay at Dunmara.

"He also talked to me in the Great Hall after ye were named successor and asked about ye, lass."

"Me?" I asked, nearly spitting my ale out on the table.

"Aye, he asked if ye were betrothed," he said, turning a little red in the face. "I told him that I was nothing but a stable hand and had no idea if ye were promised to anyone… and that it was none of my business."

"It was none of his, either!" I said, annoyed at the thought of Allan Calder asking about me.

Duncan rejoined us and picked up the last of our conversation, and said, "Surely, he would have kent that there was no name on the marriage contract."

Duncan was right. If Calder was involved or aware in any way of the marriage contract, he had to know that there was no name other than mine on it. I thought about the question and the reasons Master Calder could be asking William such a personal question.

"Perhaps with everything we have learned, he wasna involved at all with the marriage contract. I cannae see my father giving him that kind of responsibility based on what we heard this day."

William agreed, "Aye, I suspect that is right or he wouldna be asking questions to anyone across the halls of Dunmara."

"It makes me shiver to think of him asking such questions about me," I said, thoroughly disgusted at the thought and a little fearful of his motives for doing so. My mind raced, and I thought about the scene with Wesley and how all of these lads were talking about me, and I had no idea.

"Ye mean ye are not madly in love with the slick eel of a man, lass?" Duncan said, laughing at me.

"Duncan! Stop it! Can ye even imagine something so horrible?"

"I cannae," he said. Duncan and William laughed at me and the thought that I—or any woman in Scotland, for that matter—could possibly find Allan Calder remotely attractive, or a potential suitor for marriage.

I drained the last of my ale pot and said, "We should go home. Missus Douglas likely has supper waiting for us and we should have word from Mistress Hay about when we can see Master Forbes."

+++

"This came fer ye, mistress, while ye were away."

"Aye," I said as I took the sealed letter from Missus Douglas in hand. "This must be from Elizabeth, confirming our appointment with Master Forbes." I read the message aloud to those assembled.

13 August 1766

Master Duncan MacLeod and Mistress Alexandra MacLeod
Canongate, Edinburgh

Master Duncan and Mistress Alexandra,

I have confirmed this day that Master Campbell Forbes, Esquire, will be ready to meet with you both to settle the estate of Master Alexander MacLeod on Monday, 18 August, at eleven o'clock. He has asked for the additional time to ensure all documents are in order for your meeting.

If this is acceptable, please meet me at Master MacLeod's office just before this meeting, and I will personally escort you both over for proper introductions. If not, I await your instructions back.

At your service always,
Elizabeth Hay

"I am fine with that, uncle. What do ye think?"

"I agree. It might be good fer us to give them time. They didna ken when we would arrive exactly, and we should also ken that we cannae complete everything in a day. The city runs faster than Dunmara... but not *that* fast."

"Aye. It might be good for us to take a moment. I will send word back in the morning that we will meet Mistress Hay on this day, as expected, just ahead of our meeting with Master Forbes, and I will confirm for her that we plan to stay for the Advocate Society tribute. I will leave the arrangements to her."

Missus Douglas said, "When ye are ready, Petey can deliver yer message back to Mistress Hay. He has taken many a message to Master MacLeod's work."

"Aye! Thank ye! Missus Douglas, we will all return in a moment for yer glorious supper, and I will work on my response for Petey to deliver tomorrow."

+++

After supper was cleared from the table, the men were soon to follow. I realized that I was so lost in my own thoughts and was sitting alone in the dining room. I took my glass to the kitchen and sought out Missus Douglas.

"Missus Douglas, thank ye again for another fine meal," I said as I placed my glass in the water for cleaning. "Do ye have a carrot to spare?"

"Are ye still hungry, lass?"

"No," I said with a smile. There was no way I could still be hungry after another hearty meal in this house. "I would like to visit Munro in the stables. I am verra glad to not have to ride every day, but I admit that I am missing my friend."

"Aye!" she said, retrieving me the largest carrot she had in her basket. "Jonny usually tries to keep some carrots or apples out in the stables, but I am happy to give this to yer Munro."

"Thank ye. I ken it is late, and I dinnae want to disturb Master Jonny."

I walked out the back door and across the courtyard. The gates from Canongate onto the closes were already shut for the evening, so it was quiet.

"Och hello, my love!" I said, walking into the small stables and seeing my Munro standing in the largest stall at the end. Just then, William stood up. He was in the back refreshing the hay in Munro's stall. I turned immediately red in the face.

"Erm, I meant…"

"I ken. Ye meant that loving greeting for the mighty Munro," he said with a smile and patting Munro on the neck.

"What are ye doing here?"

"I could ask ye the same!"

"No, I mean, *why* are ye here, William? This is not yer responsibility."

"I have been feeling in need of a task, and thought I could make myself useful to Jonny. He helped the other hands find work with new houses since yer father's passing, and Petey is still quite young for such work."

I nodded in respect for his words and raised the carrot as I said, "I thought I would say hello to Munro. I have not seen him for days since we do not have to ride."

"Aye, yer beloved has likely been missin' ye as well."

I walked toward Munro and thought about William's words. He has been escorting us around town, providing protection, but that is not satisfying for him. He was used to doing more physical tasks and has to be longing to find his own role and place here. A place where he feels useful and rewarded for a job well done—not sitting idle in the grand MacLeod House on Canongate. I cannot blame him, and in fact, I admire him. A lesser man would be more than happy to sit idle in a grand house, without any responsibility, or any want for food or drink.

"My darlin' Munro, I have missed ye, my love," I said as I stroked his chin and neck. He immediately nuzzled my own neck and pushed my shoulder.

"Alex, here! Let me bring him out for ye, so ye can walk him a little in the open air of the courtyard and I can finish cleaning his stall."

"Thank ye." This is the first time William called me by the shortened version of my name, which is to be expected as he has been so used to Duncan calling me the same this entire trip, but I noticed it because of all of the men, he has always been the most formal in addressing me.

"Here ye go," I said to Munro with my carrot on offer once he was in the yard.

"He has missed ye!" I looked at him, silently asking with my furrowed brow how he knew that, and he said immediately, "Ye can tell. His reluctance to take the carrot straight away and the nudge to yer shoulder was meant to tell ye he is unhappy with ye, lass."

"No, no, my Munro," I said, moving from rubbing his neck to kissing his nose and reaching both hands for his withers. "I am so sorry that I have been so focused on other tasks here in the city. I am just as ready to go home as you are!"

It was then that my horse finally loved me back. He took the carrot eagerly and then calmly put his cheek to mine as he chewed it.

Just then Stirling came in, barking at first, before sitting quietly at my feet when he saw me. I think Munro would have gladly crushed the giant dog, but he did not. Either because I was there or because Stirling immediately sat down respectfully.

I reached down and stroked Stirling's head and said, "Settle yerself, wee Stirling! This is Munro, lad. Munro, this is Stirling. Ye are brothers, do ye ken? My giant horse and my giant dog, meeting for the first time." Munro stopped moving about and Stirling retreated to the side of the courtyard, possibly to stay out of reach of him, and sat himself down quietly again and looked only at me.

"Well done," William said. I could not tell if he was speaking to me, to Stirling for settling himself, or to Munro for not crushing the dog.

"Look at all of these lads here to protect and guide me on my journey! I cannae have ye fighting amongst yourselves."

"Aye, ye never want there to be a fight between a horse and a dog. *The largest will usually win,*" he said with a wink and a smile to Munro. I laughed back at him and thought that he was not only a kind and honorable man, but he had a keen sense of humor that I had grown to enjoy on our travels.

"Then Munro wins the day," I said, patting my horse's neck before William walked the happy lad back to his newly cleaned stall.

Once they left, I kneeled down and said to the dog seated respectfully in the courtyard, "Stirling, ye darling. Ye giant, unexpected darling. Come here, lad."

Stirling rose up slowly and, in the reverence, as has always had and I kissed him on the cheek. I looked at him and said, "Ye are in charge here in the courtyard, aye?"

William walked out of the stables at that moment, and I asked him, "All is well?"

"Aye!"

"Then let us go in for the night."

"I wanted to show ye something first," he said to me, motioning to the other side of the courtyard. We walked around the corner of the building and he said, "Take a look! This is the water cistern collecting both what comes out of yer copper bath, *and* the rainwater off the roof of the house."

I looked above at the network of connected pipes and drains leading to a large tank on the side of the building. "What is the water used for?"

"Jonny told me that the cistern has three layers of filtering to help clean the water, but it is not fer drinking. It is mostly used to clean the front walk of the building, or to help clean the stables and carriage. It is something yer father helped design and installed when he bought the house," William said as we stared at the structure in awe.

"Once again, my father was ahead of his time," I said, looking up at the cistern. "What a wonder!"

"Aye, I have never seen anything like it. We might want to learn as much as we can in case any of his incredible ideas would suit ye at Dunmara. I am interested in learning more about the filtering layers and what they are made of."

I was shocked at first by his statement and that it matched my own thinking for the future of copper baths, drains, and the capture and reuse of water.

"We could use for any number of purposes across the stables or the forge."

"We should, indeed. Christ knows we have plenty of rainwater on Skye." I said as I followed William back inside. I thought to myself again, *we should indeed.*

+++

278

NINETEEN
Acts Of Contrition

William and Duncan spent time with the bespoke tailors, getting measured and fitted for new breeches and coats. As much as I wanted to understand the process, they both seemed embarrassed to have me in the shop with them, so I waited for them outside.

Standing alone on Lawnmarket, at the top of the Royal Mile, I watched the bustle of the city before me and became mesmerized by the flow of people—rich and poor and everything in between. You could not miss the speed with which they walked, who stopped to talk to each other, and those that did not. I even thought about my own father walking up and down this street. Part of me wished that he would emerge from the crowd, so that I could share this part of his life with him. The city Alexander and the Isle of Skye Alexander were not the same. That had been made abundantly clear on this trip.

Edinburgh is a wondrous city. I caught myself slowly moving forward up the street to the castle with the crowd, but realized along the way that I better return. Duncan might panic if I were not close when he came out of the shop.

I turned and walked myself back down the hill before finding myself across the street at St. Giles' Cathedral. I have never seen a kirk this large and ornate. Once they were finished, William and Duncan walked next door on recommendation to secure new tri-corner hats to match their new coats. The men finally emerged, seemingly exhausted by the ask of them this morning. Duncan said they would retrieve the hats on Wednesday, the same day as their clothes. The men escorted me around the corner to Scott's & Sons and provided me the same courtesy of waiting outside while it was my turn to be measured and poked.

Duncan handed me a bank note and some coins and said, "I hope this will do, lass. If not, call fer me and I can spare more."

I walked away from them, standing in the street. Duncan yelled to me just as I walked up to the door, "Remember the new cloak, lass!"

I turned back to him and just glared. Of course, I remember that I am supposed to get a new cloak to protect my new dress. Why Duncan felt the need to remind me, is beyond me. I am sure it is some sort of revenge for making him endure both the tailor and the milliner this morning.

I stepped into the shop and was met immediately by a friendly, heavy-set woman in a fine silk dress. She greeted me immediately and had the largest smile filled with pure joy that I had ever seen. So much joy that she was practically laughing with her welcome, which immediately put me at ease.

"Thank ye, Missus Scott. I am Alexandra MacLeod. Mistress Hay sent ye word that I would visit yer shop today."

"Aye! Come in! Come in, my dear!" she said warmly, taking my hand and leading me into her shop.

"Elizabeth sent me word!" Missus Scott said, "She told me everything! She said ye were a verra bonnie lass, who needed a verra bonnie dress for a special event hosted next Friday evening, I believe."

"That is correct! My late father is being honored by his friends at the Advocate Society. I need something more suitable for the city, for Edinburgh society, and for such a fine occasion." I said, looking down at my brown wool skirts with slight embarrassment. While clean from the journey across Scotland, the garment was fine for Skye, but not so much for Edinburgh.

"Aye! Let's start with some of the dresses I have already started and see if any suit ye, lass," she said as we arrived at the back of her shop. Hanging across the room were no less than ten unfinished dresses, a handful of jackets and skirts, and even a few cloaks.

"Och my," I said, overwhelmed by the variety of garments before me.

"Dinnae fash, lass! Based on what Elizabeth told me about the event and yer coloring, let me present ye with the two that I think will be more than suitable."

She brought forward two dresses from the side. "Ye may like the fabric and not the style, or ye may like the style and want it in a different fabric," she said, holding both up for my inspection. "But they should do well to start our conversation about yer preferences."

"I am in awe of yer work, madam," I said, overwhelmed with choice but also the broad selection. Missus Scott's handiwork was impressive,

282

even noticeable on her unfinished garments. Suddenly, I realize that I do not fully know what would be acceptable for this type of event. Each dress was more beautiful than the next.

The first dress presented had a brown silk shell with the bodice and inner skirt in an ivory and brown design. It could have been seen as a subtle plaid but had no colors or meaning that would violate the law against clan tartan.

"I appreciate the brown dress. The fabric is fine, but as ye can see, I spend much of my life in that verra color or gray," I said. "This is my chance to be different and truly match the city and such a grand event. This is my chance to feel bonnie."

"Aye, my dear," she said. "Ye are a bonnie lass, but a new garment can give a woman *all* the confidence in the world. No matter the occasion."

"I think this is the one," I said, pointing to a dark blue dress made of silk. The dress was stunning. The bodice and outer skirts were of such a deep color of blue. The subtle bell sleeves had a visible ivory silk interior lining. But the first thing I noticed was the intricate embroidery of vines of blue and green accented by crimson and yellow flowers, hummingbirds, and even small honeybees on the ivory silk panels in the breast and inner skirt.

"A fine choice, lass," she said as she brought the garment forward and holding it up next to me. "A fine choice, indeed!"

The wonder of the embroidery on the ivory silk alone was enough to make this a fine dress. Up close, the design and intricate stitching was even more impressive.

"Did ye stitch his design yerself, Missus Scott?" I asked as I looked closer at her beautiful creation. "It is so detailed, and the colors of the

283

threads are verra fine. I am used to wool in all of its many forms, and the stitching on the delicate silk is remarkable."

"Aye. But I must confess. I fell in love with a fabric from Paris in one of the shops on the Royal Mile a year or so ago. I couldna afford it myself, but I thought about it all the time. It was so stunning! I stopped in the shop often to just touch it. I dreamt about it being in a dress like this. So, I tried to recreate the stitching from memory, though I might have enhanced some myself."

"It is magnificent, madam," I said to her with a smile. But the embroidery on ivory silk was only one part of Missus Scott's masterful creation.

"This dress is a favorite of mine," she said as she retrieved other items off of the wall of unfinished garments.

Hidden just under the bodice and folds of the skirt were small loops and she placed another ivory silk skirt panel and tied the panel to hold it in place. The panel had a more subtle embroidery pattern in ivory silk thread, and the stitching was indeed masterful. She completed the look by placing an ivory silk jacket with a peplum waist on top, creating a totally new look.

She lifted the new panel, revealing the colorful embroidered skirt once again, now with the jacket on top. I smiled at the view of another possible combination that I never expected.

"It is like four dresses in one!"

"Aye, this dress is of my own creation and provides you more than one choice. And if ye are going to spend for a fine garment like this, it helps to ken that ye can make small changes to it make it completely new."

"I absolutely love it! But before I choose, madam, do you have a suitable cloak for the garment to protect it from the rain and chill?"

"Och aye, just here, lass," she said as she pointed to a dark blue wool cloak seemingly made for this very garment. "It is a simple cloak, but will protect ye from the cool wind and the rain in the city. Ye can see that it has a crimson wool on the inside lining of the hood to match some of the embroidery, and I can also place fur around the hood, if ye prefer."

"I like the crimson lining." I said. "I suspect I may need new boots, or at least have these cleaned up, as well. Do ye have a recommendation, madam?"

"Aye! Just four doors down, ye will see Murray's. They make boots for men and women and can repair or shine anything," she said. "Cal Murray kens my work, and I can also talk to him about the final dress, so he kens what to expect, if ye like."

"Thank ye, but I fear that I am getting ahead of myself," I said as I laughed with nervous embarrassment. "I have never done this before. Every dress I have worn in my life had been made fer me. I never had the luxury of selecting my own and certainly not fer such a grand event. I am overwhelmed."

"Aye, Mistress Alexandra, let us start here," she said to me as she touched my arm sweetly. "Ye have eyed a dress ye like. Ye should put the dress on and then I can pin it to tailor it all to fit ye perfectly. It is important that ye *feel* good in the dress first! Ye may think differently when ye have it on. Follow me! Ye can change back here."

She had an area for me to take off my old dress. Once I placed the new dress on, I loved it even more! Though it did not fit in its current state, the fabric and design were more beautiful than I could have imagined.

285

She had me stand up on a pedestal so that she could begin pinning the dress to fit me. With each pin, the shape of the dress was made even more perfect. I smiled as the shape formed by her pins to the bodice and the hems began to enhance my own figure. I could see that this dress was not just bonnie, it was destined to be mine. She placed some minimal pins on the ivory silk jacket, as well.

It was quite a long process, but when it was all over, she said, "The actual sewing needed is not that much, lass. Really just bringing in the waist and bodice along with finishing the hems to match yer height."

I felt like the woman staring back at me in the mirror was beautiful, and I wished for a moment that Lady Margaret could see me standing here in such finery. That very thought made me think of the MacLeod broach.

"Och, I have a broach that I would like to wear in tribute to my father and clan. I dinnae think that it will fit on this bodice, though. And I wouldna want to ruin the silk."

I explained the shape of it to her and she said, "Aye! Bring the broach with ye for yer last fitting on Wednesday, and we can see what works best when the final dress is on ye. There is always the option to add a silk ribbon with the broach, so that is not on the dress directly, and there is also the option of placing the broach in yer hair."

I looked at her, confused at the thought, and she said, "Some women in town are using jewelry in different ways. Some are adding it to hats, to hold a sash at their waist, or even in their hair."

"Think of it as you would a fine comb just here," she said as she touched the back of my head and the network of hair pins holding my hair up. I nodded at the thought and felt confident that she could help me look my best.

286

She carefully helped me undress so that I did not lose any of her guiding pins removing the garment and I quickly put my original skirts and jacket back on and met her back at the front of the shop.

"I can definitely have it finished fer ye by Wednesday next. Ye will come back here for a final fitting on that afternoon to make certain everything is to yer liking."

"That is verra fine, Missus Scott. How much do ye require fer this bonnie dress and yer work?"

She started writing out a document where she placed my name and address for MacLeod House on Canongate. Then she added up her fabric and alterations to the dress and jacket, plus the addition of the cloak, which needed no adjustment.

"That will be eight pounds sterling."

"My uncle was right! That is exactly what he gave me!" I said, amazed that Duncan could estimate the cost of a lady's dress and cloak.

"Och no, mistress! Ye only pay me when you pick up yer dress and are happy with my work. If I were uncertain about ye, I could ask for a partial payment now and ye would pay the balance on delivery. But ye are a friend of Elizabeth's and from a respectable family. I trust ye and value yer patronage. Come back on Wednesday after mid-day and we will try it all on again to make certain it fits perfectly, then I can make any final adjustments and deliver to ye at MacLeod House on Thursday."

"Thank ye verra much, Missus Scott!" I said as I put the money back in my pocket and walked to the door.

"Ye will be beautiful, my dear!"

I smiled back at her and walked out into the bright sun, feeling more confident than ever about my choice. I looked up and down the street and saw William standing across Grassmarket from me. I waved to him, and he walked over to meet me.

"Where is Duncan?"

"He walked down to the White Hart. He was impatient and told me to wait fer ye here."

I did not say anything to William, but despite his impatience, I suspected Duncan was also looking out for Calder. Or at least that is his excuse to be at the tavern day in and out.

"Well, let us meet him there, aye? But if ye dinnae mind, I want to go up to the castle first. Will ye walk with me? I know we cannae get too close, but it is so amazing. I want to see it for myself and not just looking up at it."

"Aye, lass, but we have to be quick, or yer uncle is going to be marching up this city street looking for ye soon."

+++

"How are ye not out of breath?" I asked, nearly bent over in pain at breathing so hard when we reached the top of the hill. "That last bit nearly did me in!"

"Aye, it is a steep climb," he said, still unbothered by the ascent to the castle. I, however, was breathing heavily and sweating. I was embarrassed at how the short walk affected me so.

"Christ above! I need to walk more at home," I said through my gasping breaths and wiping my sweaty brow with the back of my hand.

"Aye, ye do," William said, as a matter of fact. I should have been offended, but only laughed at his assertion. He was right. I did need to walk more if I could not make it up a city street without being unable to breathe.

"The castle is bigger than I imagined," I said, looking around.

"Aye, no wonder ye have such a good view of it around town."

"No wonder."

We stood together and watched all the soldiers marching about. It looked as if they were replacing each other on watch at the front. I thought of all the wars and sieges these old walls had seen through the centuries. Then we turned and looked back down the busy street below us.

+++

"It is about time!" Duncan yelled to me as we walked up to the table. We barely sat down on the benches before Jacob brought new ale pots for me and William.

"*Merci*, Jacob!" I said, appreciating his speed and devoted attention.

He responded with a big smile and his false French accent, before walking away, "*But of course!*"

I smiled back at the man that I thought dismissed me as a woman on our first meeting, but who has now become a dear friend and always makes me smile with our newfound respect and shared greeting *en français*.

"Did you find a dress or were ye obliged to sew it yerself, lass?" my uncle asked, clearly exasperated with the events of the day, and having to wait for me. I ignored his insult about the time I spent with the lovely and talented Missus Scott. I did not confess that part of our delay was that I asked William to walk to the castle with me. I also know that waiting for me in a tavern is no real sacrifice for the man.

"Aye, I did find a dress! Ye will have to wait for the Advocate Society event to see it as I will go back for a final fitting on Wednesday, and it will be delivered to Father's house on Thursday." The men said nothing, as I suspect I had already lost them to the ale and boring talk of dresses. "The amount ye gave me was exactly the cost for the dress and cloak, but Missus Scott said I did not have to pay her until Wednesday if I was happy with her work."

"Then I am sure it is a fine dress! Hold yer coin for Missus Scott."

"One thing I asked her about was about our shoes and boots." Again, they both looked at me like I was speaking another language. "I do not think any of us need new ones. But we might want to go to her cobbler just up the road and have the soles checked and leather polished. William and I just passed the shop on our way here, and they look respectable and seem to do quality work." William silently nodded his head in agreement upon my words.

"Aye, on Wednesday, William and I will pick up our coats and hats and can take all boots to be shined while ye are getting yer dress."

"Thank ye both," I said with a huge smile of satisfaction. As much as I wanted to go home, the anticipation of the event in honor of my father made me happy. And shopping for new clothes has made me happy in a way I never expected.

"Any sighting of the elusive Master Calder on yer watch, uncle?"

"No, but that is one of the reasons I stopped in at this time of day. I asked Jacob about the man, and he said he hasna not seen him in many weeks. But if he comes in, it is usually mid-day with the ringing of the bells and not the evening. I have not seen him, but I am not convinced he is gone."

"He is not," William said, as a matter of fact. Duncan and I both looked at him, curious as to his opinion on the matter and that he felt the need to speak so definitively.

William just looked at us both and said, "If the man is as everyone says, then I suspect he will come back once he learns ye are here in the city.

I asked, "Do ye believe so?"

"It is about opportunity," William said, sipping his ale. Realizing we were trying to follow his logic, he continued, "When he discovers ye are here *and* he is no longer paid, I believe he will come out of hiding. The man has taken advantage of having no master, but is still being paid. Mistress Hay has no power over him, and he kens it. Ye both being here changes that in an instant."

"Interesting notion," Duncan said. "Like I said, I would like us to run into him first before he goes to see Mistress Hay."

William and I nodded in agreement on this account. After the oysters, we had bread and butter, and the three of us all had a plate of lamb stew. We knew that Missus Douglas was preparing supper for us but could not help ourselves after a long day of bespoke tailoring.

My reluctant shoppers did not say the words, but I knew that they felt proud at the thought of new garments for the Advocate Society, and we had a day that was light and happy in the city. As I sipped my ale, I felt for the first time like we were no longer a marching army of sadness and mourning, but friends enjoying each other's company in the city. I am happy to be here with both of them and I hope they are happy to be with me.

+++

"Can ye spare a coin, sir?"

"Sorry, lass. Keep movin' along," Duncan said to the lass at the end of the table. Not even looking at her, he waved the woman forward

291

dismissively to the next table with one hand as he raised his drink to his lips with the other.

The poor lass was a sight. At first, her hair and clothes looked put together. But on closer inspection, you could see that her skirts were caked in mud. Her red hair was so dirty that it looked brown.

I felt sorry for her and looked at her in solidarity as a woman. I wanted to help in some way, even if we just pointed her to Canongate Kirk. We had learned of the many community programs supporting women and children there. But before I could speak, I had a moment of sudden and unexpected recognition. The emotion of such hit me in an instant and not only set me back, but made my heart hurt.

"Mary?"

"Aye! *Alexandra?*" the lass asked, backing away from the table slowly in disbelief. I could not believe my eyes. If she were not standing right before me, I would not have.

Mean Old Mary MacAskill.

The look on her face was at first relief at the recognition of her name and then panic and fear as she realized that she was standing before me—and Duncan. He was the one who made it clear that by riding off of MacLeod lands with Wesley she was accepting his same banishment, unable to return to her home again. The fear showed in her eyes as she slowly backed away from us.

William stood up immediately from the table to take a protective stance behind me, looking around the room to see if our old adversary, Wesley MacLeod, was near. Duncan looked up at her for the first time and then stood behind me like William to complete my protective guard on both sides. Once again, I am between them both for protection.

"Aye," I said as I stood up from the table and put myself in front of these imposing and overprotective men to lessen the combative stance they had at this very moment.

Mary turned pale, making the soot on her face even more noticeable, and stepped back a bit and asked her question again with a shaky voice, "Alexandra... *MacLeod?*"

"Aye, Mary," I said, walking around the table toward her. I looked back at William and Duncan with concern that she seemed confused, before turning back and reaching out my hand to hers as I asked, "Are ye alright, lass?"

I knew the answer to my question the minute I asked it. I could see it with my own eyes, even more so as she backed away from me further and refused to accept my hand. With tears in her eyes, she looked at me and said, shaking her head, "No. *No...* I am *not alright!* I am surrounded by *ghosts!*"

I put my arm around her trembling shoulders and said as I guided her back to the table, "Sit here, Mary. Please sit and eat something." Unsure at first, she quickly overcame her fear of the MacLeod's standing before her and succumbed to her own hunger by immediately setting upon the remaining food on my plate.

She only looked at me once to say softly under her breath, *"Thank ye."*

I smiled faintly as she cleared the rest of my lamb stew and my ale pot. I stepped aside and caught Hilary in passing, asking her to refresh both for her.

"Alexandra, a word?" Duncan asked, and nodded that I join him away from the table while William remained on watch over the young woman.

"Ye must take caution here, lass," Duncan said, as he grabbed my elbow. "She has been banished from our clan lands, and ye cannae undo what yer laird decreed."

"Mary chose to follow a man banished from our lands, sir." He started to argue with me, but I shook my head, unwilling to hear his words, and said immediately, "And we are *not currently standing* on MacLeod lands, are we?" I looked down at his hands on me. Duncan tilted his head at me in defiance. I know he wanted to say something more, but I spoke before he could.

"Mary placed her trust in the wrong man and has no way of undoing what she brought upon herself. I am not changing anything Laird Graham ordered, but I will not let this woman, who is clearly in need of help, starve before me in this tavern." In an attempt to appeal to his better nature, I said, "This has nothing to do with our clan. We have a Christian responsibility to help her, do we not, sir?"

"Alex," he said with a slight tone of warning, "with yer position, by helping the lass, ye are also giving her false hope. And ye will have her on yer verra doorstep tomorrow or seeking ye out every day in this tavern from this point forward."

Now trying to reason with me and guide me, his tone softened, as did his grip on my elbow. I cannot reverse Mary's fate on MacLeod lands or send her home to her mother though I wanted to, but I could not ignore her either. She was starving, and she was beaten down by her short time in this city. You could see it across her face, her body, and her clothes. I could not find the words. It is hard to explain, but I did not feel sorry for *Mean Old Mary MacAskill,* but I did feel compassion for the gaunt, young woman seated before me. God only knows what she has had to endure on these city streets to survive. She traded a life of comfort and hope for one of desperation and fear, all because she was not a nice person and put her faith in the wrong man. You could say that she asked for it. You could say that in some ways, maybe she deserved it after a lifetime, stewing in jealousy and her constant, bitter attempts at bringing unhappiness to others.

You cannot walk through Edinburgh without seeing many women just like Mary and some with small children, in deep poverty and hunger, with no means to protect or fend for themselves. They are begging on the streets and in taverns. They are selling their bodies for coin or temporary shelter in alleyways and closes. I could not ignore her, *even her*, and not give her some grace this day.

Duncan said no more to me, released my arm, and respected my decision. Whether that was because he understood my argument or he took it as my declaration as Lady MacLeod, I may never know. He rejoined William and stood to the side of the table on watch. Hilary refreshed the plate and ale for Mary and brought me a new ale pot of my own.

I sat across from Mary as she devoured her lamb stew and asked, "Are ye alone in Edinburgh?"

For the first time, she looked at me in the eyes and I must admit her vacant look caused me more pain than I already felt upon recognizing her just moments ago. She always had bright green eyes and red hair. Now they both seemed dulled.

"Aye," she said as tears formed in her eyes. It took her a moment between the food and the drink to catch her breath and say, "Ye ken I came to the city with Wes."

"Aye, and where is Wesley now?" I asked, knowing it would reveal the answer my companions and protectors standing guard behind me wanted to know most of all.

"Wes is *dead,*" she said with a mouthful of food, as her tears fell and cut clean lines through her soot-covered cheeks.

I looked at William and then Duncan with a mixture of concern and shared relief. They both relaxed their stance and sat themselves on the bench next to me to hear the rest of what Mary had to say.

I put my hand out, asking silently for Duncan's handkerchief. He reluctantly gave it to me, newly cleaned and pressed by Missus Douglas. I offered it to Mary. She did not take it so, I left it on the table should she change her mind.

I did not even have to ask before she told us her story. "Master Duncan told me of my own banishment, and I accepted my fate. I *loved* Wes and wanted nothing but to be with him, even if it meant never seeing my home or my mother again. We rode all the way to Edinburgh on the back of his horse. I told him… I begged him… to just stay near Fort William or maybe Glasgow. He insisted. *It had to be Edinburgh.* He said we could both find work here. It wasna until we arrived that I learnt he had never even been here before," she said, taking a gulp of ale. "Ye ken, Wes! He was all talk!"

My side of the table knew exactly what she meant and believe we all nodded together in affirmation of this fact. The lad was indeed *all talk*.

"He had work for a short time out on the docks at Leith, but he went mad with drink every night. He drank or gambled nearly every coin he earned."

I looked at William as it sounded just like the story he told me of his own father. He nodded to me in understanding the connection and I hope a shared sympathy with the lass.

"I think it was easier for him to run his mouth in a tavern than to be a kind and responsible husband to me."

"Ye did marry then?" I asked.

"We were just handfast," she said as the tears continued. "I didna realize until it was too late that the only person Wes MacLeod ever cared about was himself." She looked at me and said, with regret, *"If I could go home, I would."*

I said nothing to her, as that was not an option based on Laird Graham's declaration and her own choice. I know Duncan looked at me with her words, justifying his earlier advice, but I could not look back at him.

"Wes was angry all the time. He couldna find work and if he did, he lost it not long after. He was beaten to death in a brawl outside a tavern down by the docks in Leith. I dinnae ken what the fight was about or even who it was with. I was brought to the tavern only to find him lying face down, dead in the street."

We all looked at each other in silent understanding that we knew this man's mouth and his inability to defend himself would likely get him killed one day. William predicted as much after their own fight in the stables.

"I couldna afford to bury him properly. He is rotting in a pauper's grave somewhere on the edge of the city," she said with the tears of a woman with a broken heart. Still, she never took the handkerchief from the table. She looked at all of us and said through her unending tears, "I had no way to send word to his family. Can ye please tell them the truth of it? *Please?*"

"Aye, we can," I said softly. Despite everything the lad has left her with, the shared banishment from home and the poverty, she still loves the man. *Mean Old Mary MacAskill* had a heart, after all.

"I have been on my own ever since. I came back into the city hoping I could find work as a seamstress... a barmaid... *anything!*" She sat back in her chair, more animated now that she had a belly full of food and drink and said, arms wide, "And here I am livin' off the streets, the needs of men in the shadows, and the *charity of others*."

For half a second, the original *Mean Old Mary MacAskill* showed the resentment of mercy being afforded her. But, even now, she could not maintain the audacity and spitefulness she had relied on her entire life. Her tears streaking through the dirt and soot on her face started to show both a face filled with sorrow and regret.

I thought about what she had to have been feeling in the beginning. The rush of young love, the belief that the man she was sacrificing everything for would love and protect her, and the self-determination that she could take such a risk and be just fine. I had not thought of it before, but Mary and I had that last part in common. We were strong, independent women who believed above anything that we could fend for ourselves. We would be just fine.

The reality is that I am educated, and she is not. I landed in the city of Edinburgh in a grand house surrounded by a trio of guardians, and she landed on the streets, abandoned by the one person she believed would love and protect her. It was not an even match on any score—despite our belief in our own personal strength.

The lass was doing what she had to do to survive, but it would *never* be enough. She took the last sip of her ale pot and stood up from the table. She spoke again as she wiped her mouth on her sleeve, "I thank ye all for yer kindness this day, as kinsmen. I am not sure I deserve it."

I stood up as well and did not acknowledge her last statement and asked, "Mary, do ye ken where Canongate Kirk is?" She nodded to me that she did. "Go there, lass, and *please* ask for Reverend Gordon. Ye can tell him I sent ye. They have support programs fer women on the streets. They have clothes, food, and ways to help women find work. He and the kirk will be a help to ye. It is part of their mission in the city. Will ye do that? Will ye go there?"

She just looked at me. As her faint smile faded, and her eyes went blank again, she said, "I will, but I fear I am already gone."

She calmly walked out of the door before I could try to convince her otherwise. I just sat down slowly in the shock of it all. Tears flooded my eyes and Duncan signaled to Jacob that we would have one more drink, and we sat in silence together until he brought them. True to form, Jacob read Duncan's mind, and we got whisky instead of more ale. This town loves its claret, but Jacob secured more casks of whisky once Clan MacLeod arrived.

After a few glasses, William spoke to me and said softly, "It was kind of ye to try to help the lass."

"Do ye think *kindness* is enough?"

"I dinnae ken," he said softly and shook his head. He could see that I was in pain for what we just witnessed and that I could not do more for Mary. I wanted to send her home to her mother and could not. I felt nothing but the tears retreat behind my eyes at the thought of her last words as the three of us drank the rest of our whisky together in silence.

I do not believe kindness was enough today.

+++

The next morning at breakfast, I asked Duncan, "How far is the water, uncle? I hear the cry of gulls in the city all the time, so it cannae be far. Can I walk there?"

"No lass," he said, shaking his head, "ye cannae walk to the Forth. It is too far and would not be safe fer a woman on her own down by the docks."

I looked down at my plate in disappointment before he said, correcting himself, "But Jonny and I can take ye there in the carriage. It willna be the same as Dunmara, but it is water, and a great departure from the crowded city. Once we meet with Master Forbes, we will plan fer a trip."

"I will hold ye to that."

I could tell that Duncan understood that I was not only missing home and Cairn's Point but also the simple strength and peace that only water could offer. After only a few weeks in the crowded city, a trip to the Firth of Forth would be a welcome relief.

A few days passed. I felt restless about the fate of Mary, the anticipation for the meeting with Master Forbes, and our event next week. After I planned menus with Missus Douglas, I attempted to take Stirling on a walk down to Holyrood Palace and back, only to find he was much more docile in the confines of the courtyard than on the streets of Edinburgh. The lad nearly took my arms off! We looked a fright running through the city streets together today. Just as Missus Douglas said, Stirling does not belong here in the city.

Before returning to the house, I stopped into the kirk to ask Revered Gordon if he had any record of Mary MacAskill coming to seek the services of his women and children's charity program. Sadly, there was no record in his ledger of her coming in for meals or clothing assistance. We never saw Mary again. Along with the elusive Allan Calder, I set about silently looking for Mary as well. I wanted to see her again—if only to take her to the kirk myself.

One morning at breakfast, Duncan let me know just days after our encounter that Mary's body was found floating in what remained of the Nor' Loch. The loch was in the process of being drained in order to start construction on the New Town. It was unclear if she drowned herself there, as many were known to do, or was left there by someone else. Her status in life did not warrant an investigation of any sort, and I assume she landed in a pauper's grave, much like her beloved Wesley. I did not cry before them all, but I was devastated by this news.

We only knew of the loss, as it was published in *The Caledonian Mercury*. The lass had been smart enough to stitch her own name into her skirts. Perhaps she knew what her fate would eventually be, and she wanted some record of her life.

I let Reverend Gordon know that as long as I was in Edinburgh, I would be happy to volunteer at the kirk. I was committed to cleaning and folding donated clothes for distribution—whatever he needed for the women's program. Kindness was not enough to help Mary, but at least I could try to have a positive impact on the life of another trying to survive on the streets of Edinburgh.

When I return home, I will honor my commitment to tell Wesley MacLeod's family of his fate and I can look Mary's mother in the eye and tell her of our last conversation. It was not deep in sentiment or remorse, but the story will tell her what her daughter experienced here. And it would certainly end the persistent longing that one day, the poor woman would ever see her child again in this life.

That unfortunate task will be my responsibility and duty as Lady MacLeod, and it breaks my heart.

+++

TWENTY
Father's Last Instructions

We arrived at Father's office and met Elizabeth, who personally escorted us next door to meet Master Forbes. I thanked her immediately for her recommendations and told her all about our new clothes being made for the Advocate Society event. We both agreed that Missus Scott was a lovely woman and a talented seamstress. It was nice to have another woman to talk to about such things for a moment, as I am constantly surrounded by men.

William once again waited with Jonny outside and Duncan and I waved to both of them like silly children when we walked past them, standing with the carriage to the next building. Jonny laughed out loud at our juvenile display, and William just smiled and shook his head in mock disapproval.

Master Forbes met us straight away. He was a handsome, older gentleman with a kind smile. Tall in stature, he had dark brown hair, including some gray at his temples and in his beard. His eyes were as green as the fairy pools on Skye. His demeanor was formal, almost regal, but open and welcoming at the same time. I could see how Father would befriend and trust this man. He greeted us in the front hall with a hearty welcome.

"Mistress Hay, always a pleasure," he said with a big smile to Elizabeth.

"Master Forbes, may I present to ye, Alexander's brother, Master Duncan MacLeod and his daughter, Mistress Alexandra MacLeod."

"Master MacLeod and Mistress Alexandra, ye have my deepest sympathy for the loss of Alexander," he said, shaking each of our hands. His touch sent a shock through my entire body, and I could not understand the attraction. It shocked me so much so that I stepped back away from him for a second.

"He was not only a dear friend to me personally, but a colleague that I had admired and respected ever since we were at university together. His loss has left a deep hole in our profession and my life personally. I can tell you both that!"

"Thank ye verra much, sir," Duncan said. "The sudden loss of my brother has been a shock to our entire family and our clan."

"We thank ye, for yer kind words, sir," I said. I was proud that I did not get emotional, but it was another reminder of the loss we all felt and the real reason we were all here. It was good to hear how Father had friends here in the city and served as another clue to his life.

"We have much to discuss. Please come with me," he said as he put his arm out for me to take. I was a little unsure at first at the formality of it, but willingly took his welcoming arm and his gracious escort.

I stopped for a moment and turned back to say, "Thank ye fer walking us over, Elizabeth." She smiled and nodded back at us as she walked back out of the front door.

Master Forbes escorted me to a seat across from his desk and motioned for Duncan to sit in the chair next to me. Taking his seat on the other side of his desk opposite us, he opened a leather portfolio and arranged the parchment before him. He put on his glasses, which made him look even more distinguished.

"Let me say a few words about how this meeting will be conducted," he said to us both. "First, I am going to read Alexander's Will and Testament. It was updated right after his trip to Skye." I looked at Duncan and he looked at me and I know we both wondered what would make my father update his will at that time, but we said nothing.

"This is always a hard discussion to have with the family dealing with the loss of a loved one, but I can assure you lass, your father has taken every care to safeguard your future. Of course, that is not to diminish your own loss as his brother Master MacLeod."

"I am confident my brother has done his best fer his daughter, and that is all that matters," Duncan said. And he meant every word.

"Quite right, sir! The important thing to know is that my office managed all of yer father's legal needs—both personal and in matters related to his own business, and I must say to you both, it has been my honor. I will go through the distribution of assets, any decisions you may need to make, and then I will conclude with any debts to be paid. I am here to answer the questions you have and to help you settle any of the open items—today or in the future. I am at your service. But I am already ahead of myself. Let us start at the beginning."

He began reading the document before him, *"This is the last Will and Testament and inventory of the personal estate and effects of the deceased* **Alexander Ewan MacLeod** *and items known to be belonging to him or due to him beneficially or owed in debt at the time of his death. This reflects his wishes for the distribution of his legacy and that of his estate in Scotland."*

Duncan and I looked at each other for a moment. This is all about to be finally revealed to us, and we will find out more about the life of Alexander MacLeod here in the city through the reading of this document. We have already uncovered some bits in the house, but I am so nervous. I could not tell if Duncan felt the same. He looked calm and stoic in his chair as I shuffled my skirts upon the reading.

"To my dearest daughter and only living child, **Alexandra Flora MacLeod,"** he said and paused with a look at me over his glasses and a sweet smile. I breathed in deeply, awaiting his words to me.

"I leave all of my worldly possessions in my homes on Canongate in Edinburgh and Glenammon on River Forth, along with my financial accounts at the Royal Bank of Scotland which are to be converted into a trust held for her until she turns twenty-one years of age."

"As my daughter is no longer a child and is of marrying age, I ask my brother **Duncan Baird MacLeod** *to help manage the bank account with her complete knowledge and involvement so that she is prepared for what she will inherit. She will also remain under the parental guardianship of her other uncle,* **Laird Graham Malcom MacLeod of MacLeod,** *until she turns twenty-one years of age."*

"If my daughter is already twenty-one upon my passing, I encourage her to involve both of her uncles in any decisions where she feels she needs guidance and assistance. They are my most trusted brothers and have only her best interests at heart."

Duncan and I smiled at each other on this as Master Forbes continued, *"If my daughter is married at the time of my death, her financial inheritance will still remain under the supervision of her uncle until she turns twenty-one because of her position in the clan. I expect the Marriage Contract drafted upon the announcement of her succession to be Chief of Clan MacLeod, will protect her and Clan MacLeod from any undue influence or indirect inheritance of property, titles, monies, or responsibility by her betrothed at the outset of their marriage."*

Duncan and I both looked at each other again. At first in silent agreement to the terms, and then in acknowledgement of the first mention of the marriage contract revealed at Dunmara.

"The value of the estates of MacLeod House on Canongate and Glenammon House on River Forth and home possessions—including furniture, housewares, linens, and art is approximately £5000 pounds sterling each. Costs of annual maintenance and staff are detailed below should she wish to retain either house. If not, any future buyers need to understand the commitment required with such a purchase."

"You can see at the bottom of this page Alexander has noted what the annual cost to maintain each house including staff wages is. I will continue reading so you understand why he provided such details."

*"Alexandra should determine which of my personal possessions or art within said estates she wishes to keep for herself before placing the houses for sale. The residences within the close and the stables at Canongate—under the supervision of **Missus Jane Douglas** and **Master Jonny Harris** shall remain under the possession of their current inhabitants and both shall retain their positions, pay, and responsibilities for MacLeod House. This should be a condition on the sale of the property."*

*"The Estate Factor **Master Bennett Cameron** and his wife, **Missus Anne Cameron,** shall also retain their home, positions, pay, responsibilities for Glenammon House. This should be a condition of sale of the property."*

"So that is going to be one of your first decisions, lass," Master Forbes said, looking at me over his glasses.

Before he could continue, I said, "If I may interrupt ye, sir, do ye have a spare quill and parchment so that I can record this so that my uncle and I can review all the decisions needed?"

"Not to worry! That was an essential part of my ask for a delay in our meeting today, and I should have said it from the outset. This packet here," he said, placing a hand on another leather-bound portfolio at the end of the desk, "includes a copy of everything I will read today, so that you may take and review on your own."

"Aye, thank ye!" I said as I sat back in my chair, relieved. I looked at them both and said, my voice shaking as I did. "I am a tad overwhelmed."

"It is an emotional process to be sure, Alexandra. We will see that you have what you need. So going back, your first decision is going to be to determine what you want to keep, and what you want to sell, starting with the houses and any property within."

"I understand."

"It is a kind thing to ensure his devoted staff do not lose their homes and positions with his death," Duncan said.

"Aye, Master MacLeod," Master Forbes said, "and it is a mark of who your brother was as a man. He was always incredibly loyal, and he was always looking out for everyone else. I cannae say many men of wealth in this city leave such instructions. I admire him for it, I do."

Duncan and I both smiled at the thought. We knew that my father was a kind and generous man, but it was another clue to who he was here. It is lovely to see how many he touched and cared for while he lived on this side of the country. I suppose that was the mark of a life well-lived, to have a positive impact on others and my father had, even after his death.

Master Forbes continued reading, *"My account at the Royal Bank of Scotland is current and holds a cash value of £35,500 pounds sterling."*

I looked at Duncan and he looked at me—each in complete shock at such unexpected numbers.

Duncan spoke first and said, "Please, say that again, sir?"

He repeated the line, and the figure was not any more believable to our ears than it was the first time he said it.

Looking over his glasses again, Master Forbes said, "I know you are reacting to the number, but I think you will understand when I complete the list of assets and investments. Alexander did verra well for himself."

"Christ! He *must* have!"

Duncan sat back in his own chair in disbelief. We were both astounded at the thought. This sum could keep all of Dunmara Castle and Clan MacLeod running for many years, not to mention providing for my own personal care for the rest of my life.

Master Forbes continued, *"I have provided my brother,* **Laird Graham Malcom MacLeod of MacLeod** *an annual stipend over the last fourteen years to help in the care and support of my daughter and intend to provide support for the remainder of her board until she turns twenty-one and has the means to determine and care for her own needs."*

"Alexandra, this has mostly been to fund your clothing and education materials, along with anything else above room and board that you have required at Dunmara Castle on Skye. Please understand that this will come out of yer account going forward. The sum has been £20 pounds sterling annually and is paid directly into an account Laird Graham has at the Royal Bank at the first of each year."

"I understand, and I assume this year has been paid, and we are looking at only one more installment until I am of age next year and I take over the account in full and fund my own care."

"That is correct," Master Forbes said, nodding and smiling.

"I also leave the chief of Clan MacLeod, the painting in my bedchamber of our ancestral home, Dunmara Castle, on Skye. I commissioned the work to remind me of my family and of my home on Skye. The chief at the time of my death should have it so that it forever remains within our clan."

Duncan and I both smiled at each other, and I said, "It is a beautiful painting of our home, and I will set it aside for Laird Graham and return it to Skye."

"I leave the widow of my late brother, **Sarah Margaret MacDonald,** *and my nephew* **Robert Ian MacLeod,** *the sum of £100 pounds sterling. I have also pre-paid for Robbie to attend the University of Edinburgh to continue his education when he becomes of age. The lad is bright, and I encourage him to seek further education so that he can build a future for himself and to support his own family."*

"That is so generous. I respect that my father values the role Auntie Sarah has in our family and that he knows the value of education," I said to Master Forbes, smiling and feeling emotional, thinking about my wee Robbie. "The lad is verra intelligent and we should have a new educator at Dunmara when we return home to help him advance in his learning so that the gift of a university education can be a real possibility for him."

Master Forbes continued reading, *"If I know my brothers, they will have dispatched my brother Duncan to Edinburgh and likely in the company of others to settle my estate. I would like to ensure that all who are in that traveling party are compensated for their safe arrival, their time in the city, and their safe return home to Skye. I leave each of these trusted kinsmen £10 pounds sterling."*

Duncan and I laughed at this as Father did indeed know his brothers for, they did exactly as he predicted. Master Forbes asked Duncan for the names and recorded it at the bottom of the document and in the bank ledger.

"Aye, sir," Duncan said, "William MacCrimmon and Angus MacLeod accompanied us to Edinburgh."

"Master MacLeod, you are also included in this bequest," Master Forbes said as he wrote Duncan's own name down on the ledger with the other two. Duncan just smiled and nodded his head in acceptance of this generosity.

Master Forbes continued, looking over his glasses with a sly smile. *"Knowing my daughter as I do, she likely also made the trip from Skye to Edinburgh. If the lass crossed the country of Scotland with a band of travelers, she deserves the same. £10 pounds sterling to* **Alexandra Flora MacLeod***, as well."*

I yelled with a victorious laugh and my hands raised in the air over my head, *"Equality!"*

"Aye, ye earned it, lass," Duncan said, laughing with me. Turning to Master Forbes he continued, "There is nothing harder than crossing the Highlands of Scotland with a band of men and this bonnie lass navigated everything from rowdy taverns and sleeping on the floor of a cold, abandoned croft house, to all that Scottish weather and a week on the back of a horse can offer without a single complaint."

I smiled at the thought that my uncle saw that I never tried to separate myself from my traveling party.

"I can only imagine," said Master Forbes as he recorded each recipient in both documents and handed the bank notes to Duncan. "I believe you can handle the distribution, sir."

"Aye," Duncan said, immediately handing me my note and pocketing his own. He will deliver the notes to William and Angus when we see them next and kept them securely in a different pocket of his coat from his own.

"Let me continue," Master Forbes said.

*"For my youngest brother, **Duncan Baird MacLeod**, I leave him the dominant stake, consisting of sixty percent, in the Glenammon Brewing Enterprise currently based on the docks of Leith. I know that my brother will continue to make this business viable across Scotland and beyond. I will also look to him to think about other improvements in brewing, distribution, and also the potential for a whisky distillery on Skye in the future. I trust his instincts and believe that he can make Glenammon even more successful. Should he choose to sell his stake outright or retain his ownership, he will be set for his own personal income for the rest of his life."*

I think if there was a moment for Duncan to start crying, it would be now. Like me, he was just granted his own personal fortune from his brother, and one based on a business that suited him perfectly.

Master Forbes said, "You have not asked me for legal advice, Master MacLeod, but you will want to take a trip to the brewery in Leith and get a feel for their operations and your role as primary owner. It is a successful venture that Alexander started himself and one that has allowed him to afford his life in the city much more so than his legal practice. You both hesitated at the numbers I quoted earlier, but this has been the most successful enterprise for Alexander during his time in Edinburgh and he has seen to its considerable growth over the last several years."

Master Forbes continued, "You have decisions to make here, sir. When you meet with Master James Drummond who owns the remaining share of the brewery, you can decide if this something you want to manage, how you are to be paid, and if you want to explore the potential for operations in the Isles. You may also decide to have him buy out your stake all together with one cash payment."

"I understand."

"Mistress Hay can arrange the meeting for you, and I am here to help in any way to evaluate yer options, to extend your ownership, or to end it completely contractually," Master Forbes said. "You should in fact meet here, at my office. I am happy to attend the meeting with you and protect your interests on behalf of you and your brother."

"I welcome yer advice and counsel, sir. Thank ye!"

"Until a decision is made, any income earned from the enterprise will continue to go into Alexandra's account at the bank. There is no transfer of ownership until you decide your involvement. Alexander saw to that."

Duncan smiled and said, "If there is anything I ken it is ale and whisky, but the *business* of drink and how I could possibly be of help on the other side of the country is something else."

"Alexander continued with his advice and instruction," Master Forbes said to us both, leaving Duncan with thoughts on this decision.

"My legal practice should be ceased as I have no associates prepared for succession or that I deem worthy to continue our mission under my name. I will ask that my daughter Alexandra or my brothers ensure **Mistress Elizabeth Hay** *finds new employment and is paid for the time she serves until the time the practice is officially ceased.* **Master Campbell Forbes, Esquire,** *owns the building to which he is entitled to any rents due until such time as the practice is officially ceased. It is my recommendation that active clients are informed of my passing and are offered continuation of service with Master Forbes if they wish to transfer or allow them to find other representation of their own choosing, thus releasing them from any contractual obligation to Alexander MacLeod, Esquire."*

"I must tell you that I have stopped collecting the rent on the office since Alexander passed in light of him sending me his clients. I will not collect anything further from your account Mistress Alexandra and our office is here to help move his files over. I provided Mistress Hay the language to use in the letters to your father's clients and will happily serve them with the same integrity and care that your father did."

"I appreciate that, sir. My father's trust in ye for his own affairs speaks volumes about yer legal ability and character. I will offer to help Mistress Hay with the completion of the letters myself." He smiled at me, and I spoke again, now intrigued by Father's use of language, "Master Forbes, if I may ask, does this decision to close his practice have anything to do with my father's lack of confidence in Master Calder?"

He looked at me for what seemed like a long time before responding, understanding that I was asking him to confirm something my father has alluded to but not fully expressed himself.

Before I could reassure him that we already knew some of the shared apprehension around Master Calder, he said, "Your father lost his confidence in Master Calder well over a year ago. It was one of the primary reasons for Alexander changing his instructions upon his return from Skye after traveling with the man."

Duncan and I looked at each other again on this statement, as it explained a lot. But I wanted to know more. We were all still gathering clues to who Alexander MacLeod was here in Edinburgh, and the mystery of his shadow, Allan Calder has only added to our questions.

Duncan asked, "Why do ye think the relationship was so broken, sir?"

Master Forbes said, "I am not certain, but your brother came to believe the man to be... erm, *untrustworthy*."

314

"Aye! I have reviewed Father's notes in the ledger, and it was clear to me that he and Master Calder had verra different views on which clients to accept or to reject."

"It is an important point," Master Forbes said, sitting up in his chair, seemingly impressed that I had already reviewed the ledger. "As I said, the primary change to this document upon his return from Skye was just to this section—his wishes and guidance for the future of his legal practice. He wanted to protect against questionable representation that could damage his well-earned reputation in Edinburgh."

I thought at that moment that this was likely the primary reason that Master Calder did not return to work. If he knew that my father was not going to support him and he had fewer and fewer clients, he had to know that he was not going to take this practice as his own. I am now actually wondering why the man is still lurking about on the edges. Surely, he would have nothing to gain by doing so. Well, save for a consistent wage for doing nothing.

"Calder kent his fate when they both returned to Edinburgh, then?" Duncan asked.

"Aye, I believe the man did."

After a few quiet seconds, Master Forbes continued to move us along. "That brings us to his household staff, professional staff, and professional holdings," he said, looking at the next paper in his portfolio.

*"I leave **Master Jonny Harris**, £30 pounds sterling, his home on Crichton's Close, the horses, carriage, and equipment at Canongate stables to use in service to the new owners of the property. It is my hope that he remains in employ at Canongate House. As noted, I ask that this be a condition of sale of the property."*

*"I leave **Missus Jane Douglas**, £30 pounds sterling and her home on Cooper's Close. I have the express intention that her young lad, **Peter Douglas**, is*

315

educated at Braidwood's Academy serving the deaf and dumb. I have already paid his tuition for the next two years with the Headmaster. It is my hope that the lad, who is mute, learns in an environment that can best help him. It is also my hope that Missus Douglas remains in the employ of the new owner at Canongate House. As noted, I ask that this be a condition of the sale of the property."

"I leave **Mistress Elizabeth Hay**, *£30 pounds sterling. I have noted my intent to help her find new employment but want to acknowledge the important and vital role she has played in the success of my own legal practice."*

"I leave **Master Bennett Cameron** *and* **Missus Anne Cameron** *£15 pounds sterling each, and their home on the grounds of Glenammon House. It is my hope that they remain in the employ of the new owners of Glenammon House. As noted, I ask that this be a condition of the sale of the property."*

Master Forbes said, "I will send word to all mentioned to meet with me to hear what they have been left and to distribute the bank notes. The exception being the Cameron's and it will be my pleasure to ride out to Glenammon House to deliver this bequest in person. I will confirm when the distributions are complete. And again, these have already been pulled from your father's account and set aside at the time the testament was drafted."

"Thank ye sir," I said. "These are most generous gifts, and along with the numbers ye mentioned at the start, I admit that I am in a bit of shock."

"I understand, lass," Duncan said quickly. "I am also in shock at the numbers, but *never* the generosity. That was Alexander!" We smiled at each other and nodded. It was a mark of my father to be kind and loyal to those around him. This was not a clue that needed to be uncovered here in the city. We, as his family, knew this of him already.

"It is my request that any household staff should be paid fully until the time they are no longer in the service of my family or houses. I have provided Master Campbell Forbes, Esquire signed letters of recommendation for **Missus Jane Douglas, Master Jonny Harris, Master Bennett Cameron, Missus Anne Cameron, and Mistress Elizabeth Hay** *mentioned above. They have served me well, are good at their respective positions, and are trusted friends."*

"Your father drafted and signed each of these letters of recommendation," he said as he raised the signed letters for us to see, "and I will provide them to any purchaser of the houses and work to help Mistress Hay find employment in our professional circle. He set aside three months wages from the time of his passing to each of those in his employ. If we complete sales before that time, anything I have remaining from the potential payments to staff will be deposited back into your account and if we go over what your father estimated for transition, then I will be looking to you to fund, Mistress Alexandra."

"I understand, sir, and that is only fair. You have my full agreement."

"And finally," Master Forbes continued, "*I leave Canongate Kirk, £30 pounds sterling specifically designated for their program to help women and children living on the streets and struggling to earn a suitable living in Edinburgh. The contribution is to be only used for that purpose and nothing else related to the daily running of the kirk or maintenance of the physical building and grounds."*

"Signed **Alexander Ewan MacLeod, Esquire** *at Edinburgh and witnessed by* **Campbell Forbes, Esquire,** *this eleventh day of July in the year, One Thousand Seven Hundred and Sixty-Six."*

"This makes me so proud," I said with tears in my eyes as I explained to the men before me, "that he is so generous with those in his employ. This is also Father's testament to the importance of women in his life and the support of women in this city. From Missus Douglas to Mistress

Hay, to the women's program at the kirk. I confess to ye both, that admire my own father all the more for these last bequests."

I said nothing of what we just witnessed with Mary, but I had pride that my father also saw the need to help women living in poverty on the streets of Edinburgh.

Master Forbes nodded to me, but continued, "Your father only has two outstanding debts."

"Remarkable, is it not?" Duncan asked.

"Aye, but Alexander was meticulous and never spent the money he did not have. These debts are a result of the timing of his death, and nothing more. Aside from all the committed payments to staff and management of his household and practice during this transition, noted before, he has the following:"

"One final debt is that Alexander ordered his own grave marker, which is currently being completed. Once it is done, the balance of £3 pounds sterling will be due to the stonemason. I have that money set aside here," he said, patting the folio with his bank notes, "and will complete the transaction when I know the marker has been delivered to the kirkyard as ordered."

"Do we ken when it is to be delivered, sir?" I asked. "I would verra much like to see it, if we can, before we have to return home."

"Aye, we would," Duncan said in agreement.

"It is expected next week, I believe." Master Forbes said. "Reverend Gordon will send word when it is installed, and I will inspect that it is correct, pay the stonemason, and I will then send word to you so that you can visit in private."

"That is much appreciated, sir."

I wanted to ask what the marker looked like, but decided against asking that of Master Forbes. If Father commissioned it himself, then it was of his choosing, and I had nothing to say about it now. I was saddened that he somehow knew that he would be buried here in Edinburgh to have commissioned his own marker. While he could not have known the time or day of his death, he knew he would never return to Skye. And that made me sad.

"The last debt is for a portrait commissioned with Master Ramsay and the very one the Advocate Society and members of the old Select Society will present to ye next Friday."

"Aye, Sir Alexander Dick of Prestonfield, let us ken of the painting from Master Ramsay," I said.

"Alexander only owed Master Ramsay £20 pounds sterling, as the last payment from the original commission. It was to be paid upon delivery of the painting."

"I am so looking forward to seeing it and meeting more of his friends and colleagues later this week."

"Like I said, I have all the funds here to clear these debts," he said, patting his portfolio once more. Finally, Alexander has provided this letter for you, mistress. He added it when he made his last changes."

He handed me a letter written in my own father's hand. I did not expect this and breathed in deeply as I broke the wax seal to open the letter before these men. I read it out to my trusted companions in this room.

"My darling daughter,

If you are reading this, then I am gone from this world, and I have sadly left you behind.

Master Campbell Forbes will take care of you, the remainder of my family, and my dearest friends. I have disclosed in my last Will and Testament my own wishes for the distribution of my personal estate and business holdings.

You will be cared for, but I want to let you know that there is more.

Within the house is a small wooden box. The lid is carved with my own initials. This box includes the reminders and memories of my life that only you should have.

You will find my gold watch, your mother's wedding ring, my original MacLeod broach attached to a small remnant of my plaid, and a necklace made of pearls my mother left me to give my wife one day. Sadly, I waited too long and never had the chance.

These precious treasures of mine are now yours. I hope that you cherish them as much as I have.

I am so incredibly proud of you and all that you are. But most of all, I am proud of all that you will become.

Your loving father always,
Alexander Ewan MacLeod, Esq.
> *Signed in Edinburgh on the eleventh day of July, One thousand seven hundred and sixty-six years in the presence of witness*

Campbell Forbes, Esq.

We all sat in silence for a moment at the words. I teared up at the end and wanted to cry, but my emotion was overcome with the mystery of the unknown box. Drafting this letter must have inspired him to send me my own letter that I found on his desk, as the sentiment and words were much the same. He would have no idea when I would see this one and that he would not finish the other.

"I am currently in Father's bedchamber at MacLeod House, and I have not seen any such box," I said to the men before me, "but I was also not looking for one. I will check again once we get back."

Duncan said, "To be fair, lass, he didna say which house the wooden box was in."

"Aye, he didna," I said in agreement, looking at the letter again. It only says, *within the house.* "I guess I assumed that the watch would be something he kept on his person each day and that it would be in the city."

"Aye, ye are right, lass."

"Duncan, did ye notice if he had his watch at Dunmara?"

"No, I didna. But, like ye said, I wasna looking fer it."

We all sat in silence for a moment, thinking about the mysterious wooden box and its family treasures.

"Master Forbes, thank ye for taking such care of my father's last wishes. We have much to consider as we decide what to do to settle his business and his life here before we return to Skye. But there are two other items not mentioned today that I would like to know more about."

"Tell me, lass," he said to me, hands folded across his papers, awaiting my questions.

"The first is the marriage contract Father presented when I was named successor. We have all the Clan MacLeod documents from Mistress Hay, but the contract is not amongst them."

Duncan just looked at me. Partly out of amazement that I had already gone through the clan files and with a bit of a smirk that of course I was looking for the one document I found most contentious.

"Interesting indeed. I helped Alexander prepare the contract for his trip, but admit that I did not see it again after he returned. When he came to change his will, I was so focused on that task I did not ask him about it. Perhaps this is another item to look for in the house."

Duncan and I nodded to each other in agreement. We must look at the house—or the houses—closely now that we have to think about all of Father's possessions that we want to keep.

"But dinnae fash, lass!" Master Forbes said as he stood up and showed us another portfolio. "I helped Alexander draft the original document and have the responsibility to execute the document. I have a copy of the document here. If we need to replace your copy, we can in short order."

"Thank ye, sir! And finally, how are his household and staff paid?" Before he could answer me, I said, "I have two reasons for this question. First, we have determined that Master Calder, who has not returned to work since my father died, should no longer receive a wage. And the second is, ye said that you have the money for three months for staff. I ken I have a responsibility to pay the household staff after that time, but on what schedule? I do not want anyone working in service to our houses or to Father's law office to miss any payments."

"Great questions, lass. It shows your heart to look out for those in your employ, much like your father. This is another example of Alexander being ahead of his time. Your father set up bank accounts at the Royal Bank of Scotland for everyone in service to his houses or to his practice. Payments distributed monthly are direct from his account to theirs based on a schedule that we reviewed at various times throughout the year. By telling me that Calder is no longer to be paid, I will cease those transactions immediately on your behalf."

"Thank ye, sir," I said, looking at Duncan, who nodded his agreement. "The man should no longer be paid."

"Consider it done," Master Forbes said, as he took the note in his ledger. "I will contact the bank straight away. Calder's funds, set for the months ahead, will be put back into your account. The payments for the next three months for everyone else have been deducted from the balance I quoted from your account earlier. Anything after that will be taken from your account as it is today. You do not need to do a thing until we note that a sale is made to cease payments from you and transfer to the new owner."

Looking back up at me, he said, "The last thing for you, Alexandra, is that we will need to go to the bank to transfer this account to you. We will also record your signature and, of course, Duncan's on the account at that same time, which will remain essential for any transactions until ye are twenty-one."

I nodded in agreement and understanding as I smiled at both men before me.

"Duncan, when you make your decision about the Glenammon Brewery, I can also help you get yer own account at the bank, if that is your wish."

"I thank ye, sir! I think that would be best. Let us complete both tasks at the same time."

"I will send you both an appointment time at the bank."

We left Master Forbes and stopped once again at the White Hart Inn before our return home. Duncan was now obsessed with finding Calder in the tavern, though we were both relieved that we officially stopped his wage.

William was touched by the inheritance my father left him as a guardian on this journey and seemed proud to have money in his pocket. I know Angus will feel the same when he joins us in the city.

We had no luck catching the elusive Calder on this night, and headed home in silence after a long and emotional day.

+++

TWENTY-ONE
An Unfinished Life

The days passed slowly and started to blend into each other with our quiet and simple daily tasks. Missus Douglas and I planned menus and discussed household needs for the next week. We were in a full house now with Angus' arrival from his Prestonfield bliss. I had so many questions for him, but never had the courage to ask. I likely would not understand his response, anyway, so will see what gossip I can get out of Duncan.

The full house for Missus Douglas meant that she had more work to do to keep the lads fed during the day and the rooms clean. I tried to reassure her that no one should be making extra demands of her. I told her that if she needed help on this, I would gladly set the others right in an instant. She just wanted me to know Angus was being a little demanding of food and drink—often at odd times. She told me that she kent enough Angus' in this life and could keep him fully in check. I believe she could, in fact. She agreed, however, to send him to me with the next ask.

I also tried to keep my own bedchamber and bath clean and tidy for her so that her work in my room was primarily about the exchange of linens, refreshing of cauldrons, and wood for the fire. I spent some more time searching for the wooden box Father mentioned, but I never found it. It was not in any chest in his room and Missus Douglas had no knowledge of the box, but was fairly certain he had his watch on him the day before he died.

I poured through the ledgers, trying to understand more about his legal practice and his clients. He had quite the eclectic mix and was serving many more Scottish clans than I would have expected, knowing what was asked of him from his own brother.

His notes on his clients—or even the clients he rejected and his rationale for doing so—were extensive and thoughtful. In most cases of rejection, he tried to offer people an alternative option or guidance. I could easily see how he could be respected in his profession, as he treated each case, and each person, with care and respect.

+++

One day, I met William, Angus, and Duncan for another one of Missus Douglas' incredible suppers. We all ate together, and the conversation invariably turned to home.

William asked directly, "Do we ken when we will return to Skye?"

I looked at Duncan, assuming he was the one to make this call. He looked at me, assuming the same about me. I understood that I was mistress of the house but did not know that I was in charge of this journey, but I said, "Well, it is a fair question and one I have asked myself

326

for weeks. We have the Advocate Society event on Friday evening, and should detail what is left to do, including selling the houses—one of which we have not even seen—and Duncan still needs to evaluate the brewery he has inherited."

Duncan nodded, and said, "My biggest worry is that if we get late into October or November even, we could be up against harsh weather on our return."

I gave him a sideways glance to indicate that I was not some delicate flower that could not cross the country in the cold.

"Ye ken how ye felt traveling in August, lass!"

"Aye, but that doesna mean I want to be here until the Spring or Summer of next year, uncle! We all are ready to go home, but I ken we have a lot to do. Perhaps we can sit together tomorrow with the papers Master Forbes provided and start checking off the things we need to ken more about and the decisions we need to make."

"Aye, and one of those has me going to Leith, and I can then travel to Glenammon to assess the other house, unless ye want to go yerself, lass. We could divide the tasks."

"Aye, I would like to see the country house. Perhaps William can escort me and help take wee Stirling home."

William spoke up and asked, "Ye think to take him back there and not to Skye?"

"Aye, I ken nothing of the country house, but based on Missus Douglas' opinion, I suspect that is where the lad belongs. And Duncan and Angus can evaluate the brewery." Thinking better of the words I just spoke aloud, I said, "Though I feel like there is some danger in sending the two of ye to a brewery together."

Angus, as incoherent as ever, mumbled something about the worthless drink of ale versus the mighty whisky on his way from the room. It was hard to tell what he said, but despite the risk, I was somewhat relieved to send them to a brewery and not a distillery.

"I have no idea what the man just said, but believe he proved my point." The minute I said the words, William coughed and nearly choked on his own drink as he laughed at me.

"Duncan, ye promised to take me to the water, so perhaps we see both sites together," I said, thinking that it was likely improper for me to suggest that William and I should go to Glenammon House together.

"I did! Let us go together then. William, lad, let Jonny ken that we may need to be prepared to travel on Saturday morning to Leith. Have the man tell us what he recommends. I say horses are fine, but he can determine if carriage is best. We will take a day on the shore and see what we think of this brewery before I meet with Drummond and Forbes next week."

"Aye, I will do that for ye sir," William said.

"We can see about Glenammon House after that meeting and the Advocate Society event."

I smiled at them all and said enthusiastically after my last sip, "Aye! We all get our new clothes on Wednesday!"

Both Duncan and William looked at me as if I were raving mad. I am quite used to it, with this lot, but priorities are priorities. The healing power of water first, then the confidence building of new clothes to follow. I smiled at them both at the thought of exciting days ahead and the feeling that my spirits were already being lifted.

+++

After a day on the shores of the Forth and the distinctive sounds of the water and the smells of a maritime coastline, I was restored. I relished the smells of salt, fish, and water on the edge of the docks.

William asked me, "Not the same, but still comforting, aye?"

Nothing could compare to Cairn's Point and the churning sea below the rocky cliff, but it was a marked difference from the dark, confined, stone-walled inner city of Edinburgh. In fact, even just standing on the docks, breathing in the air of fish was a welcome and familiar smell from the reeking streets of the city and the nightly yells of *'Gardy-loo!'* signaling the collective emptying of chamber pots onto the streets. No wonder Father preserved water to clean his own walk and stairs.

"Aye it is! I thank ye and Duncan fer bringing me here today," I said, staring straight ahead to the water before me and closing my eyes again to listen to the lapping water, the circling gulls, and the shouts of the fishermen on the docks.

We ventured to Leith to see about the brewery. The buildings were massive and dominated the shoreline. The name of the brewery was painted on the stone building in large black letters on both sides, so that all who walked by or passed by boat or ferry on the water could see this was the proud home of Glenammon Brewing Company.

The number of men coming and going from the buildings showed that it was a sizable operation. Horse-drawn carriages carried wooden casks of ale out to places within the city or beyond. Flatboats waited to carry more casks out to larger ships, anchored at the end of the Forth, bound for England and France.

"Impressive," I said as we stood together watching the comings and goings at Glenammon Brewery. Once again, this was a much bigger enterprise than any of us could have imagined.

"Aye!" Duncan yelled, calling to a man, leaving his shift, and walking past us. "Is this a fine place to work, lad?"

"Aye, wage is good fer a man, but the ale is even better," he said as he walked past us with a smile.

"There is a tavern across the street there," Duncan said, "perhaps we can taste the ale they brew fer ourselves."

William and I followed him willingly after a long day. We were certainly hungry and wanted to settle our own curiosity on the prospect of the ale on offer. The tavern was quiet at this hour and was filled mostly with shift workers from the brewery on their way home for the evening and perhaps a few preparing to start. We secured a small table in the corner and Duncan brought us our ale pots. Sipping together, we all looked at each other in amazement. The ale was good. Really good!

"I like it, Duncan!" I said. "Most ales are so weak and sometimes bitter or stale."

William spoke up after taking a large gulp of ale, "This tastes fresh and... well, like proper ale should."

"Well, it *is* made across the street, lad," Duncan said, laughing at him. "Ye never ken how this travels in the barrels to its final destination. And sadly, sometimes taverns water it down to make it last longer."

We nodded our heads, but drank more, enjoying each sip more than the last.

"One thing we have learned about Alexander MacLeod on this journey has been that he was ahead of his time. Duncan, ye may learn that Father crafted a brew beyond any other. And he may have given ye the greatest gift of yer life! It is fine ale, sir! Get in there and see what ye think of the books, the work practices, and the potential for the future.

Ye dinnae need my advice, but I wouldna let such an operation go easily."

"Aye, I thought that I wouldna want to maintain this being on the other side of the country and may still choose to have them buy me out or focus singularly on future whisky operations on Skye, but I am proud of what Alexander has done here."

"To Alexander MacLeod," William said, raising his ale pot in tribute. We met him with ours and quietly celebrated the life of the dearly departed and a man who was clearly ahead of his time.

+++

I spent all day preparing for the event this evening. Missus Douglas sensed that I was nervous. After learning that she did not need to prepare supper for anyone but Angus, she volunteered to help me dress. I took her up on the offer as I was intimidated by the lovely garment hanging in my bedchamber and knew that I would need her help to secure the broach in my hair.

"This dress is beautiful, mistress."

I stood before the mirror and smiled. "Aye! I have never been in a dress this fine, and I am a bit frightened of it. But Missus Scott and her wondrous hands have made me feel worthy of my father this night."

She smiled and said, "This is as much for ye, as yer father. Ye wanted a dress to help ye with Edinburgh society and ye got it."

"So I did!"

The dress was such a perfect fit, but it was the placement of the broach in my hair that took most of our time. I gave Missus Douglas all the instructions Missus Scott provided me. We settled on a small bun at the base of my neck and placed the broach at the top. Unlike my normal pinning, this seemed a more elegant way to display the broach in my hair. Like Missus Scott said, it looked like an ornate comb when placed correctly. We just had to work the pins to keep it secure. Standing before the mirror, we both looked in awe at such a lovely dress. I felt confident in my choice and Missus Scott's handiwork.

"I will take the cloak and meet ye downstairs with the lads," she said, touching me gently on my shoulder. "Take yer time, but Jonny is ready fer ye all with the carriage in the courtyard."

"Thank ye again, Missus Douglas. I will be right down."

Once she left the room, I put on a little lip stain before I walked down to meet William and Duncan in all their new wool finery standing at the bottom of the stairs holding their hats.

"Well, well! Who are these two distinguished gentlemen before me?" I said as I came down the stairs, stopping at the middle landing. The men seemed unable to speak for a moment. I continued down the stairs. Missus Douglas helped me put on my cloak to cover my bonnie dress.

"Ye look stunning, lass," my uncle said as he kissed me on the forehead.

"Aye, bonnie," said William with a broad smile and his own voice of approval.

"She has a proper garment for Edinburgh society, lads," Missus Douglas said to them, beaming with motherly pride.

Duncan turned toward the back kitchen door, headed straight to the courtyard and the waiting carriage. William, however, put his arm out for me to take and escorted me to the carriage like a proper gentleman should.

+++

Jonny delivered us to the event, and we walked into a front hall of the Advocate's Library filled with an incredible amount of lit candles within lanterns. With the large candle chandeliers hanging from the ceiling, the impressive room positively glowed.

I took both Duncan and William's arms as my escorts for the evening. Looking at each of them with a smile, we walked forward as a tall and handsome trio in our new city finery. We were here to represent my father and our clan and did so proudly. I felt honored to walk in with both of them by my side.

Master Forbes was the first to greet us at the door and said, "Welcome, Master MacLeod and Mistress Alexandra."

"Thank ye, Master Forbes! May I present our kinsman and friend, William MacCrimmon," I said, bringing William forward with my hand on his back.

"William has been essential on our travels to Edinburgh, under the direction of Laird MacLeod," Duncan added.

"It is my honor to meet you Master MacCrimmon," Master Forbes said, shaking William's hand, "and I respect your role on this journey."

"The honor is mine, sir."

Tonight, William was our kinsman and friend and not our protector or stable hand. I am happy that Duncan wanted to include him in representing Clan MacLeod at this event. Angus would have never agreed to attend such a spectacle.

"Please, if you will," he said to us, "we lose some formalities in the Advocate Society. You may call me by my given name—Campbell."

"Aye," Duncan said, "then ye can call us by our given names as well."

A young man in a dark jacket came up to us and said, "Sirs, if I may take yer hats, and mi'lady, I will be glad to take yer cloak."

Duncan and William handed over their hats instantly, seemingly glad to free up their hands to hold a drink as they came by frequently on silver trays. I would be glad to rid myself of my cloak so I could show off my new dress, but it was new as well, and I hated to part with it.

"How will I get my cloak back, sir?"

"Ye are the only woman here, mistress. I think I can find ye," he said, smiling at me.

I laughed and said as I took off the cloak to reveal my new dress to the room, "I suspect ye can at that, lad! It is yers!"

Based on the reaction from Master Forbes, along with that of my uncle and William once again when I shed my cloak, I believe that Missus Scott and I did quite well for ourselves with this bonnie dress.

"Beautiful, lass," my uncle said with a proud smile, touching my elbow.

Master Forbes smiled at me and offered me his arm to lead us all into the larger room. I had not given any thought to the fact that there would not be any women here. I should have suspected that a group called the *Advocate Society* did not include any women members, but thought perhaps wives would be included in a special event such as this. I did not even ask, but I also assumed Elizabeth would be here. I would have included her in our own party had I known.

Leading us into a room filled with men, Master Forbes said loudly, "Gentlemen, if I may interrupt your conversations! I present to you Lady Alexandra MacLeod and Master Duncan MacLeod. As the daughter and brother of our dear friend Alexander, they, with their kinsman, William MacCrimmon, join the Advocate Society this night in his honor."

All the men raised their glasses in celebration of my father. I could not help but smile. Throughout the night, each man made their way to me and Duncan to tell us stories about Alexander. They gave us even more clues to who he was as a man, a friend, a colleague, and a leader in his profession. Every interaction gave me another glimpse into who he was, the respect he earned in his profession, and the help he gave freely to others. I had a lot of attention from Master Forbes and all the men in the room kept my glass full. I lost track of Duncan and William at some point and followed Campbell's lead throughout the room.

"Lady MacLeod, ye look beautiful this night," said our new friend, Sir Alexander Dick of Prestonfield House, as he walked directly to me and warmly took my hand in his. He immediately offered me a new glass of wine.

"Good evening to ye, sir! I hoped that we would see ye here this night!" I said, taking the glass of wine he offered and placing my empty glass on a passing silver tray. It warmed my heart to see my new friend.

"I told you that I would not miss this occasion for the world. And I could not pass up a chance to see my dearest old friend, Master Ramsay," he said loudly as a man walked straight to us.

"Sir Alexander," Master Ramsay said warmly, taking the man's hand before embracing him.

"Allan, have ye met Lady Alexandra MacLeod?" Sir Alexander asked.

"I have not had the pleasure," he said. The man took my hand warmly and continued, "but I would know ye were Alexander's daughter in an instant if I passed ye on the street, my dear!"

I was in dumbstruck awe of the man before me, and not just for his talent. He was a remarkable presence in the room. That was saying a lot in a room full of men who also think they are all remarkable. He matched Sir Alexander in that regard, so it is no wonder they were such friends.

"Then you are in for a treat, my friend. Much like her father, she is strong, intelligent, and kind-hearted. She is destined—as Lady MacLeod—to lead her clan on Skye."

"Master Ramsay," I said, with my hand still in his, "it is my honor to meet ye, sir. Ye painted my grandfather beautifully and I expect nothing less than perfection for my father this night."

"Aye, I remember Norman!" Leaning in, with a wry smile he said, "I had to do most of it from memory as the man had no patience for the process of portraiture and could not stand still for very long."

"I barely remember him myself but believe my uncle Duncan in this verra room would tell ye that describes his father perfectly. He was known to be pulled in many directions on a whim. I cannae imagine him ever having the patience fer a sitting."

"Yer father, however, was a most interesting subject and one that I hope ye see reflected back to ye on the canvas we give ye this night."

I smiled at him at his words, as I hoped the very same. I certainly missed my father this night and while I worried about an emotional reaction to seeing him again, even on canvas, I could not wait!

"If I may ask, sirs," I said to Sir Alexander and Master Ramsay over my glass. "Ye seem like dear friends. How long have ye known each other?"

"Aye, what do ye say, Allan? Forty years?"

"Och my! I did not expect that answer! How incredible to have a friend that long!"

Master Ramsay said immediately in agreement, "That is about right. Old friends are the best friends."

"'Tis true, all solidified after an eventful and adventurous trip we took together to Italy and back. When was that, Allan? 1736?"

"Aye! We were so young!"

"Some younger than others," Sir Alexander said as he leaned to me to share, "I am ten years older than this man!"

"My uncle Duncan is the same—ten years older than me. Though I confess that sometimes I feel ten years older than him!"

Master Ramsay and Sir Alexander laughed with me at the notion. They had only known Duncan for a short while, but my declaration was all the more obvious by the man loudly extolling the virtues of whisky amongst the group he was seated with on the other side of the room. I could not help but smile at him.

Master Ramsay said to me with a sly grin, "Lady MacLeod, ye should ask Sir Alexander how he fared on his travels to Italy."

"Och! It sounds like there is a story there!" I said, smiling at them both and eager to hear whatever tale they wanted to share. I looked at Sir Alexander and asked formally, "How did ye fare on yer travels in Italy, sir?"

"Och Christ! There is a story indeed!" Sir Alexander said, shaking his head at the memory of it.

"Ye have to tell the truth of it to Lady MacLeod, now," Master Ramsay said, laughing at his friend.

"Let me get us new drinks first," he said, stopping the man with the silver tray immediately and commandeering three new glasses of claret. We all took a sip and awaited his story.

"So we arrived in Genoa, and we lodged at the Croce Di Malta and had occasion that first evening to sup with some kind and considerate French and Spanish officers. We sat with them until it was pretty late."

"Too late! And too many bottles of wine!" Master Ramsay added.

"Aye! Too many! Master Ramsay and I were then directed to a very noble apartment of two beds that would be better for us."

"Being a very particular traveler, Sir Alexander naturally chose the bed closest to the door," Master Ramsay said, sipping his glass with a judgmental smirk.

"Aye, I know my preferences for lodging and dining, that is for certain," Sir Alexander said unapologetically.

Master Ramsay just shook his head and sipped his glass, smiling at his friend. I suspect, like my own journey, you learn a lot about someone when you have to travel with them. You can tell these two are good friends.

"The servant who lighted us up to our chamber I remember was dressed in green and a very genteel fellow of which some notice will afterwards be taken; for during the night was stole out of my breeches that were hung upon a chair *fourteen* Louis D'Or gold coins by some rogue who got into the bedchamber. This rogue had the arrogance to not only steal the coin, put in its place some brass coins which scarcely had the value of our half-pennies."

"No!" I exclaimed to them both. I was captivated by this tale and the brilliant telling of it. I thought that Sir Alexander was coming the closest to Grant MacAskill in the dramatic delivery of a good story.

"Aye, lass! The rogue did not touch my gold watch or signet ring— just the gold coins in my breeches."

"Tell her how you found out your gold had been stolen," Master Ramsay said, trying hard to stifle his own laugh once again.

"I did not come to discover this deception until Master Ramsay, and I were going to pay the bill to Seigneur Martelle, the landlord. I made a great noise when I brought the coins out of my pocket to find I had no gold at all—only brass. The landlord seemed to be an honest man and was much concerned for the credit of his house. He found the matter most unfortunate."

"What did he do?" I asked.

"I gave him the brass money and desired him to at his leisure to make an enquiry after the rogue. Not thinking it worth my while to spend money or time prosecuting the theft, I told him I suspected some of his own servants and if he found the truth to write me at home."

"Did he discover the thief, sir?"

"He did indeed, lass! Many months after having taken the utmost pains for the sake of his house only to discover the criminal happened to be that very servant in the green clothes who lighted us up to our room. He had seen me take some gold out of my pocket the day before."

Before I could ask how the thief was discovered, the man continued, "The landlord made the discovery by the fellow losing Louis D'Or coins at the playing of cards and could give no account of how they were in his possession."

"That is an incredible story, sirs!" I said, smiling at them both.

"Och, just wait! There is more," Master Ramsay said, nearly doubling over with laughter now. I just looked at them both, amazed that there could be *more*. Master Ramsay was laughing, and Sir Alexander looked embarrassed. "Go ahead! Ye have gotten yerself this far, friend! Prepare yerself, Lady MacLeod. There is a poetic lesson with this story."

"A poetic lesson?"

"Tell her the poem ye wrote about it all," Master Ramsay said, clearly enjoying every minute of openly teasing his friend in front of another.

"Och my! I am most intrigued now, sirs!"

"Very well, Allan!"

"Prepare yerself, lass!" Master Ramsay said to me, thoroughly enjoying his friend's story and the memory of their travels together. Sir Alexander released his embarrassment and started laughing with his friend.

"I wrote this to a friend traveling to England after my trip to Italy, but could apply to any traveler, anywhere."

Sir Alexander stood tall and squared his shoulders to share his verse. If Grant had been here, he would most certainly be impressed with the delivery of the words.

> "Be sure, dear friend, when ye go to bed, to lay yer breeches snug beneath your head;
>
> Throw them not off with a neglectful case, if ye regard your money and your keys;
>
> For many a thief will rob them on a chair, though to disturb your pillow would not dare!

I started laughing at the last and took another sip of my drink before Master Ramsay said, "Wait! There is more!"

Sir Alexander nodded and continued,

> "Think because yer at inns that you have naught to fear?
>
> Has the host no antipathies to bear?
>
> Has the brisk waiter got no paramour?
>
> Has the boot catch taken the vow of being poor?"

Breathing in deep, Sir Alexander continued, "It is about learning a lesson from such a horrible event, aye? Let no one who travels be too ready to show their purse, which all chancers when they have once observed will think of fifty ways to come for it."

340

"Och! That is a most entertaining story and a most valuable lesson learned from the trauma ye endured! I have just traveled across Scotland and stayed in many a tavern. Of course, my uncle has all the money, but he should heed your advice, sir! I cannae wait to tell him!"

Master Ramsay said, with all the sarcasm he could, "Sir Alexander is always here to help travelers, Lady MacLeod."

We all laughed together and suddenly I realized that we were now the noisemakers in the room. Our trio laughed heartily at Sir Alexander's misfortune and enjoyed being in each other's company. I looked around and saw that Duncan was staring at me. He nodded, silently asking me if I was fine, and I nodded and smiled back that I was. I was quite comfortable with my company this night. Master Forbes came to join us, and the men started talking more amongst themselves. I looked around the room and saw that William had retreated to the corner. He was standing alone, his hands clasped in front of him. He looked as if he were a soldier standing at attention.

"If ye will excuse me, gentlemen," I said, as I left a discussion between Master Forbes, Sir Alexander, and Master Ramsay. I grabbed two new glasses of claret off of a passing tray and walked over to him.

"Why are ye here standing guard alone on the side of the room, William?" He just looked at me as I handed him one of the glasses. He reluctantly took it from me but said nothing. "Do ye not like being here at such a grand event?"

He kept staring at me and only moved to sip from his glass. He finally said, "I just want to stay out of the way."

"Out of the way?"

"Aye! Sir Alexander, Master Ramsay, and *Campbell* have yer attention this evening and I *as yer kinsman* ken my only duty. That is just to see ye to Edinburgh and back to Skye, lass. Nothin' more. I dinnae ken why I am here tonight at all, other than to see ye safe back to yer house."

Adding to his own self-imposed misery, he pulled on the collar of his new coat and said, "And this blasted coat itches something fierce!"

I almost laughed at the spectacle of a grown man in a new wool coat, brooding in the corner but stifled it quickly, knowing William was in no mood for my humor or my judgment.

"Ye are here, William, because my uncle and I *wanted* ye here. And I believe I made it clear on introductions this night that ye are our friend and not just our kinsman." I said, hoping he would see that with this trip he was part of our family, whether he wanted to be or not.

He looked at me but said nothing. He knew that what I said was true and I had never dismissed him as nothing but a protector and stable hand. We became better friends on this journey. I can say that with certainty that William MacCrimmon is *my friend*.

"Please! Join us and celebrate why we are *all* here," as I pointed to the room and the men before us. "We are here for one man and one man only. Ye honor my father being here tonight, and I would prefer ye not do that here in the corner alone. Please, come back into the room with me and try to enjoy this special evening."

He looked immediately shamed that he was insulting me and perhaps my father. He bowed his head and walked back into the room with me. I put my hand on the back of his arm for support and smiled at him. He did not smile back, but nodded in resignation.

Campbell played the host perfectly and introduced us to everyone in the room. William followed me but held his own and covered all manner of topics including architecture, politics, religion. He even taught me an important skill that when you know little about a topic, just ask an intriguing question. In a room of well-known and well-educated men, asking them a question they know the answer to—or have a strong opinion about—will ensure lively discussion and make the evening all the more interesting.

Every man had some amazing story to tell about Father, and each of them warmed my broken heart and made me proud. Once William connected with the other men in the room and stopped brooding about being an outsider in the corner, he had a much better time than he expected. I would even gather that by the end of the evening, he determined that he liked Campbell Forbes as much as Duncan and I did.

+++

The room quickly became quiet as Master Allan Ramsay, Sir Alexander Dick, and Master Campbell Forbes stood before the attendees at the front. Next to them was a painter's easel holding a framed portrait covered by a black cloth. We all awaited the anticipated reveal.

"My dear friends, I had the great honor of painting a commissioned portrait of Alexander MacLeod—our friend, father, brother, and kinsman. I only had two sittings with the man before he unexpectedly passed and can tell ye that even in those short sessions, I got to know more about him as a man, his love for his family, and the beauty of his home that he missed dearly on Skye."

He took the black cloth off of the painting, and I immediately teared up seeing my father's face again. Duncan grabbed my hand in his not just to steady me but because he was also moved seeing his brother staring back at us. Some elements of his clothing and the edges of the background were incomplete, with brushstrokes exposed. But his face, and his eyes, were alive on the canvas. The simple words in white at the top corner read, *Advocate Alexander Ewan MacLeod, Esquire.*

"This painting is unfinished because I felt it was fitting, as Alexander's life was unfinished. It is a creative risk to put a painting out there with my name on it and leave it incomplete. I am convinced, however, that it is a perfect representation of a life that ended too soon. Lady MacLeod, Master MacLeod, my colleagues and I, along with members of the Select Society and Advocate Society—both of which yer father was a member—have framed this portrait as our gift to yer family and to yer clan."

"It is magnificent, sir," I said with tears in my eyes as I looked at a proud Master Ramsay. I breathed in and turned to say to the room, my left hand now taking Duncan's steadying myself again, "Ye all have not only honored my father, but ye have honored our family, and our clan this night with this gift. Thank ye! Tonight, ye have told us all incredible stories of what my father meant to ye as a friend and as a colleague. Master Ramsay, this portrait will forever remind us, and the generations of Clan MacLeod to come, of my father's place in this world. I thank ye again, sir! I thank ye all fer this tremendous gift!"

Everyone applauded as the room moved to have a closer look at Master Ramsay's work. All I could do was hug Duncan as I whispered softly in his ear, *"I am so proud of him."*

"Aye, lass! Alexander has made us all proud."

William came up to us both and said with a definite change in his tone from before, "It is wonderful, and I am verra proud to be here to see it. I never met him personally, but saw him on his last trip to Dunmara. The painting looks exactly like the man!"

"Thank ye," Duncan said, shaking William's hand.

"Aye, thank ye, it does looks like him," I said, still overcome with emotion as I stepped forward to the painting to connect for a moment with my father and so that I could hide my tears from Duncan and William.

+++

It was clear as the room thinned that our portion of the evening was over. Groups of men were sitting in corners, talking to each other. Likely, discussing and debating something well beyond our ability to contribute.

"Campbell, thank ye fer this event and fer hosting us. We are most honored, sir."

"It has been my absolute pleasure Alexandra," he said, taking my hand in his before helping with my cloak retrieved from the lad who knew to find me. "I will see that the portrait is delivered directly to MacLeod House tomorrow."

We all nodded in appreciation. Master Forbes shook the hands of Duncan and William and then said, "I am at your service and that of your family and clan always."

"Then ye may have yer work cut out fer ye, sir," Duncan said with a laugh, patting him heartily on the shoulder.

We got into the carriage as Duncan yelled, "Home, Jonny!"

We rode in silence through the city streets, in awe of the night we had and the incredible man we honored. I felt grateful for my company this evening. William smiled weakly at me, seemingly still apologetic for his behavior earlier. Then Duncan and I looked at each other and smiled, thinking of my father... and perhaps the unexpected thought of MacLeod House on Canongate being *home*.

+++

TWENTY-TWO
What I Could Not See

MacLeod House
Canongate, Edinburgh, Scotland
October 1766

**We have gone well beyond our expected time in Edinburgh
City.** Following the Advocate Society event, Duncan and I knew we had
more work ahead to complete our tasks before we could leave. Alexander
MacLeod has proven himself to be much more of a force on this side of
the country than either of us could have imagined. The weather is also
turning colder, and the days shorter. I worry we were headed into a
period that would keep us here in the city even longer. I know Duncan
and our band of travelers share the same concern.

Missus Douglas and I continued to connect and manage the needs
and demands of the house. That included our menus and understanding
of our schedules, which invariably meant the occasional tavern stops on
days we were about the city. This was especially important, as Duncan
has made it his mission to intercept the elusive Allan Calder at the White

Hart Inn. The woman learned that she did not need to plan on any mid-day meals for us when we were out of the house, and we would never return to a seven o'clock breakfast.

+++

Being the mistress of the house, allowed me to surround myself with family and friends, share good food and drink, and have conversations that stimulated both my mind and spirit. This differs from Dunmara Castle, where my role is truly about more operational matters and always in deference to Laird Graham. I felt empowered to lead here in ways I never expected.

Tomorrow is the anniversary of my birth, and I decided to have a supper party. This day has always been a quiet matter with family if it was acknowledged at all. In fact, it has barely a mention in the most recent years. Only Missus Gerrard celebrated the day by leaving me a little cake or a note in my bedchamber. But I am mistress of MacLeod House and I want to celebrate! For all the pain of the last few months, I *needed* a reason to celebrate. After all, you only turn twenty, once.

The guest list was small and specific. It included my MacLeod travel party, of course—Duncan, Angus, and William. And it included our new friends in Edinburgh—Master Forbes and Mistress Hay. Missus Douglas and I planned the menu. She taught me about the variety of linens and the place settings, along with the food and drink options available to us in this house. She also showed me the porcelain plates and cut, crystal glass that were stored away for special occasions.

I ordered oysters to start and requested plenty of bread and butter, of course. We decided to serve roasted venison along with peas, potatoes, and carrots from the garden or preserved in the storehouse. We settled finally on cheese and a small chocolate pudding for dessert. Claret, whisky, and ale rounded out the shopping order.

"I would verra much like ye, Jonny, and Petey to join us, Missus Douglas."

"Aye, mistress, yer most kind to include us, and we will all celebrate yer day with ye. But it isna proper for us to share the table and we will have much work to do fer yer party."

I nodded in understanding and asked, "Can we come to an agreement then?" She just looked at me and nodded her head, unsure of what I was about to ask her. "Can we ensure that we have prepared enough food for ye all to share in our celebratory meal even if ye are not at the table with us?"

"That is verra kind, mistress. I can agree to that. I will make certain that Jonny, Petey, and myself mark yer special day with good food and drink once ye all are taken care of. They will be thrilled, lass! Especially Petey! He adores ye so!"

"Then it is settled," I said with a smile to match her own.

"And ye should be seen by them on the day after. They will want to wish ye well for yer birthday and thank ye for the meal shared in celebration."

"Aye, and seeing them will make my special day complete."

Despite the bounty of food and drink and general celebration, at some point the conversation at the table turned. The room grew quiet as William said sternly to me down the length of the table, "Let's be practical here. Scottish law—and ye should ken this by now, Alexandra—is supportive of women, but not always in the way ye are speakin' of."

"What say ye, Master Forbes, on the mention of Scottish law?" I asked the one true expert on matters of law at our table and intentionally noting that this is not where William MacCrimmon should weigh in.

Master Forbes knew better than to jump into this debate and said plainly, "Scottish law tries not to meddle much in matters of love."

I smiled and nodded my head at his very measured and diplomatic response. Campbell Forbes would make a fine politician with such an answer.

"Alright, so it is not a matter of *the law*," William said, correcting himself briefly. "Ye are making an argument on ideals that contemporary society doesna support."

I responded to him immediately, "But that is my point exactly, William! No woman should have to marry if she doesna want to and especially to someone *she doesna love*."

This comment got jeers from the supper table, which skewed male. I am certain I made a face dismissing their base, albeit expected, response.

Duncan and Angus have heard me say these things before, and declared, *"Here she goes!"* in unison as they focused on pouring more wine and whisky for the other guests—silent guests—at the table. My captive audience does not know what to make of this hearty debate but seem content to drink their way through the spectacle of it.

"Och, like ye two get a say here! When either of ye find a woman that will have ye, ye can speak up! Until then, keep your focus where it is most valued at this table—the drinks!"

A sentiment met with genuine laughter, including from the two targets of ridicule themselves. I could barely hide my slight smile forming at the corner of my mouth at their reaction. These two could always make me laugh, even when I want nothing more than to kick them both in the shins.

I looked back to William to continue our conversation, "There will come a day in this world when women are not just revered as wives and mothers—or whores—when it suits ye," I said to challenge him, with my intentionally frank speak, "but respected for their own thoughts and contributions to society and ability to define their own futures based on their independent hearts and minds."

I saw Master Forbes go ashen, but concluded, "Having a say in who they love or who they marry will be part of that transformation. It is about respect for their own wishes and desires. But we must work together—men and women—to make the laws *and society* in Scotland change."

I suddenly realized that I was actually just talking to myself and William. The entire table was focused on their plates or drinks, and no one was volunteering to be part of our conversation.

"What say ye, Elizabeth?" I asked, trying to enlist some female support at the table—my only female support at the table. She took this moment to sip blithely from her goblet while staring, wide-eyed, at Master Forbes seated across from her. I pursed my lips in disappointment and resignation at this obvious lack of solidarity.

"Come now," said William admonishing me more, "how do these women who *choose* their lot expect to make a living or care fer themselves? Let us talk of Mary MacAskill, shall we?"

I looked up at him immediately in pain at his words. He knew full well what we just went through with the poor lass. He flinched for a moment at my reaction, but it did not stop him. "She chose her own path, a path of *love*, as misguided as it was. And that path left her living off the streets and drowning in the Nor' Loch!"

He knew he crossed the line of decorum as soon as Mistress Hay placed her kerchief under her nose and Master Forbes bowed his head. He made his argument all too real and disturbing at the supper table. Duncan and Angus were already lost to the whisky and did not seem to notice.

Before I could speak that this was an unfair comparison, he continued, "Not every woman has the *luxury* to have such a fine roof overhead, money in their pocket, and a staff to support them in their *independent endeavors!*"

His frustration with me was showing on his face for all to see as the vein in his forehead, hiding beneath his dark curls, looked as if it were about to burst at any moment. William MacCrimmon was an imposing figure on any day, but when angered, even more so. He realized immediately that his words of admonishment were not only painfully received, but harsh among a broad audience. But, like me, he does not know when to keep his mouth shut.

"Yer independence is yer own curse, Alexandra! And my word! I have to say ye are *most stubborn and disagreeable* tonight!"

Upon these words, the man sat down in his chair quickly as he gripped the end of the table with both of his large hands—to the point you could see his knuckles turning white. He did not just disagree with me, he was angry. And it was on display for everyone at the table.

A debate is a debate, but now I am frustrated at this public scolding from my friend. I looked at Duncan, and he nodded to me to shut this conversation down. As hostess, I had to recover this evening from the negative direction and tone it had sadly taken.

Laughing, I said in my own clumsy attempt to hide my own embarrassment and frustration through humor to those before us, *"Disagreeable?* First, *stubborn,* and now *disagreeable!* You have an extremely high opinion of me, sir!" He opened his mouth to respond, but before he could speak, I quickly added, "Thankfully, as you said yerself, I have that *luxury. In. My. Own. House."*

William cocked his jaw and closed his mouth. It took him a minute to release his hands gripping the edge of the table. Despite his anger, he retrieved his glass and leaned back in his chair, resigned to the fact I had just stopped this debate by making it clear that I was not interested in his opinion any more this night.

I returned my attention to the guests at the table and the rest of supper was uneventful with talk of future construction in New Town and how my father and Master Forbes were some of the earliest investors. In fact, Master Forbes informed us all that my father had planned to move from MacLeod House on Canongate to New Town. He had plans to build a grand house near the proposed Charlotte Square. He just did not have the chance to complete the contract for the building.

This served as another clue to Father's life and a sad confirmation of his desire to remain living in Edinburgh. I already knew that the purchase of a stone marker was commitment to stay, or at least a safeguard, but it hurt my heart to think of him wanting another home here. His life ended too soon, but somehow I always thought that he would eventually return to Skye. But all the clues we gathered told us that he had no intention of being anywhere else than Edinburgh.

We discussed other topics including the current state of Scottish politics, the Advocate Society event, and reminiscing on Skye's views of the sea and dramatic cloud formations and rainbows—which all the MacLeod's at this table agreed were the most incredible in all of Scotland.

William must have slipped out of the room at some point. As far as I could tell, he did not speak another word to anyone else through supper, nor did he say the customary parting words to me as hostess. I could only take from this that his own anger was standing in the way of decorum and friendship. And for that, I was disappointed.

With the last of the toasts in my honor, one by one, the guests departed. Master Forbes, ever the gentleman, offered to have his carriage take Elizabeth home so that she did not have to walk in the damp night air. They both thanked me at the door for a lovely supper and for being included in the celebration.

Master Forbes said, leaning in toward me before kissing my hand, "You made your argument and defended your position admirably, lass. You would make a fine advocate!"

I smiled at his kind words but knew that the debate with William was not as smooth and polite as I would have liked, but appreciated that Master Forbes did not shame me for it.

"Good night," Elizabeth said as she kissed my cheek. "Thank ye for including me. It was a fine supper party and the happiest of birthdays to ye. Twenty is a fine year, lass."

"Thank ye and good night to ye both. Please get home safe."

+++

I gave the remaining whisky set aside for supper to Duncan and Angus, the last guests, to encourage their own departure. These two would never leave this table if there was still whisky to be had. I also knew that for them, the night was young, and they would soon be headed out to a tavern somewhere. I was tired and more than willing to encourage their departure.

"If I might have a word, before I go, lass," Duncan asked. Angus, eagerly coveting the whisky bottle, said something to Duncan before grabbing the door. I lifted my glass to Angus on his way out, not knowing half of what he said, but thought to myself that his tone sounded serious.

"He will wait fer me at the door with the whisky," Duncan translated.

"Ye hope the man will! Let me thank ye again for this beautiful flask, uncle. I cannae wait to fill it and carry it," I said, admiring my own initials carved in the pewter flask my uncle gave me for my birthday. "It will come in handy on our return to Skye. Ye taught me that this vessel is essential for crossing the cold and damp Highlands of Scotland."

He nodded to me on this point, but said nothing. He just looked at me in the eyes, and I braced myself for an imminent scolding as he said, "Ye ken, it wouldna hurt ye to take it easy on William once in a while, lass."

"What is that supposed to mean?"

"Why is yer first response *always* a question?"

"Are ye talking about tonight's debate at the table?"

Slowly, he said with a smirk over his own glass, "That is yer second question."

He knows this game makes me irate. I was immediately frustrated and defensive about the question game, but instead of fighting, I explained myself.

"Duncan, William's response to the conversation was blown completely out of proportion. What I said about the hopes that women could control their own destiny and marry someone they love—or to have a way to care fer themselves if they dinnae marry—shouldna come as a shock to any of ye! I dinnae understand why the man was so angry... but... but... *he* was the one calling me names in front of the *entire* table!"

"Well, m'dear, I dinnae think *stubborn* and *disagreeable* count as name-calling if the descriptions... are true."

"Well, *m'dear*," I said mocking him now, "perhaps, I should keep the remaining whisky fer myself, after all!"

Calling my bluff, he just looked at me with his piercing blue-gray eyes, knowing I would eventually calm myself with some sense of decorum and reason. *Eventually.*

"Wait, one minute," I exclaimed as I grabbed him by the arm, staring at him sideways and with suspicion. "Since when are ye an advocate fer William MacCrimmon?"

"Well... not exactly an advocate. I just..."

"Ye just... *what?* Say what ye must!"

"It is just that the lad... is clearly... *fond* of ye," he said as he immediately sipped his whisky, uncertain of how I might react to both his words and the notion.

"Och, *stop it!*"

I fell into my chair by the table out of mental and physical exhaustion. I have no desire to fight all the men in my life this night!

Duncan then sat down in the chair next to me and said, "I am just saying that maybe ye should open yer eyes and ears instead of yer mouth once in a while. There could be worse things than being loved by a friend."

He shocked me with this talk, but I didn't flinch. "Och, here we go! Now we have moved from being *fond of* to *love*. Where are ye getting this notion?"

I raised my eyebrows in anticipation of his explanation, as he said unconvincingly, "Erm, a man as old as me can… see such things… plain as day."

"Christ above! Now I ken I *must* take the whisky back! If Angus has not drunk all of it in the hall, that is! Ye clearly have had enough this night because ye are absolutely raving!"

"Listen, lass, I promised yer father I would protect ye since the day ye were born, and I am lookin' out for ye now."

"Are ye sure ye are not just looking to marry me off so some other poor soul can do yer job for ye?" I said with scathing indignation not at all deserved in the moment. I felt the regret of my words immediately.

"I say it once again for ye plain, lass," he said as he raised an eyebrow in consternation. "*Stubborn* and *disagreeable* are not insults *if… they… are… true.*"

Duncan would never let me be disagreeable for long. "I am sorry for being disrespectful, Duncan. Forgive me. I just do not understand where all of this is coming from. I can tell there is something more to your correction this night. Please say to me what ye need to. We have always been honest with each other."

"Alright, but if I hear this story back to me again, I will not only deny it, but I will call ye a liar. Understood?"

"Understood," I said, smiling slightly at him. Duncan has always been a mighty good gossip, but this was the first I had heard of such a half-hearted threat. He took a moment and refilled both of our glasses. I slowly sipped my newly refreshed wine, fearing what he might say.

"Ye ken I cannae keep anything from ye, lass. And while I wouldna want to betray another man's confidence, maybe hearing the truth of it will help."

"Help?"

"Aye! It will help ye see what is happening around ye, that ye choose to ignore."

Before I could argue or question him more, he continued, "A week or so ago Angus, and I were at the White Hart. William came in with another lad. They had a few drinks together and his friend eventually left."

"Who was this person?" I asked honestly, because I could not account for anyone else that William could possibly know in Edinburgh other than our traveling party.

"I dinnae ken and it doesna matter," he continued, with another sip of his own glass. He saw my face and mind still thinking about who William could have been with and said, "Alex! It coulda been anyone he met on his way into the tavern and the other man left. William continued to drink alone."

I got up to retrieve the remnants of a near-empty wine bottle across the table so that I could make it through the rest of this tale as I kept nervously sipping from my glass.

"We didna think much of it at first, but Angus and I said to each other that we had never seen William in such a state. The lad was staring at the bottom of many a glass, ye ken?"

I nodded to him on this thought. William never seemed to drink that much. Duncan continued, "So, after a few more drinks ourselves, we were telling stories, laughing, and getting loud in the corner."

"I cannae *imagine*..." I said with the level of sarcasm he should expect. He gave me a smirk and then a shrug, signaling he would like to continue his story if I would allow him.

"Please," I said and smiled at him while I took another sip from my glass. "I won't interrupt again. I promise."

He looked at me in disbelief at this assertion by cocking his head at me.

"I promise!"

"So, William recognized us and came over, and the lad was as drunk as we were. We enjoyed seeing him in such a state, to be honest, and kept filling his glass with even more of our whisky, singing songs, and telling tales as men do. I have to say, the lad is a lot more fun when he has a few drams in him."

"Yer point, sir?" I asked while seeing his immediate disapproval at my interruption after my promise. "Sorry! Sorry! Go on…"

"So, suddenly the man went deathly quiet, and he leaned across the table to me while Angus was belting out a song about… erm, well, an inappropriate song… and he said, *'Duncan, ye must help me! Ye are closer to Alexandra than anyone. I love her and dinnae ken how to compete with Master Forbes fer her heart.'"*

I know my both my mouth and my eyes were wide open on this unexpected confession. I collected myself and sat up straight up in my chair. I could feel my face burning red and hot with embarrassment at the thought of his words… the thought of either man being a potential *suitor*. I was also embarrassed at having a conversation about suitors with my uncle.

I swallowed a gulp of wine from my glass and calmly said, "Erm… well… what did ye say to the man's drunken blethering?"

"First, I want ye to ken *how* he said it. The man wasna just drunk on whisky lamenting ye, lass! The man was *in pain fer it!*"

I do not know what to make of this description, but before I could ask, he continued, "There was something about the *way* he said the words. I *felt* his heartsick sorrow. It gave me chills then, and it does again in repeating the story now. The man was in agony and drowning in pain and drink." I could not speak. I just bit the corner of my lip as he continued, "I saw the same pained look on the lad's face when ye spoke to him this night."

Duncan took my trembling hands in his own and broke the spell his revelations had on me. His words made me feel shame, but looking at him now, he said, "I am telling ye this, so that maybe ye will see what is in his eyes fer yerself before ye stomp on his heart again—in front of others and Master Forbes, no less!"

"But I didna…"

"Ye didna ken, lass. Now ye do."

We sat quietly for a moment as I replayed the evening and other conversations with William since setting out together for the city. I thought about any clues to his intentions from the beginning that I missed, or even how I might have encouraged him unknowingly reading sonnets and talking with him. I said nothing to Duncan because I had no words for it all. My head was swimming with memories and my own drink this evening.

"I dinnae ken how ye feel about the lad or if there will ever be anything for ye in the future. But, have a care! Have a care with the man's heart, and aye, even his pride… as hard as that can be for ye sometimes. Do this if for no other reason than ye are friends, and he has seen us here to Edinburgh safely. The lad is also bound by oath to his laird to get you back to Dunmara."

I nodded slightly to Duncan on his words. This is the first I was hearing of expectations Laird Graham gave the men ahead of our journey. I expected as much, but did not know of the specific terms.

We sat quietly for a minute as I tried to take it all in, before asking, "What did ye say back to William after his... *confession?*"

"I told him that only ye kent yer heart and when ye were honest with yerself, ye would be honest with him," he said while finishing the last of his glass and setting it on the table. "I told him everything would work out as it should. He seemed to accept this response and didna say another word before excusing himself. Tonight was the first time I had seen him since."

"I am not sure what to make of that response, but I thank ye for helping me see what I couldna see myself. Ye ken that I would never want to cause someone else heartache or pain, but I suppose I have missed the signs that Master Forbes and William had any intentions other than friendship."

"I ken that lass. Ye are a kind-hearted soul and will do the right thing. But..."

"But?" I asked as he seemed to hesitate on his words. He might as well just say what he wants at this point. It had all been laid bare in a way we never had to deal with before.

"Sometimes I just want ye to get out of yer own way. As intelligent as ye are, ye are still naïve to the interests of men, and to what that kind of love can mean to yer life." He knew me well enough to not give me any room to respond, and even if he did, I did not have the words at this moment. "Now, I had better see if Angus drank all my whisky and leave ye fer tonight. No need to worry about us. I will take the keys and will lock the door behind us when we go."

We stood up together and walked out arm-in-arm to the front hall. I placed my head on his shoulder for the short walk, in loving gratitude to my uncle and friend. Angus was half-asleep on a bench in the hall and woke up immediately on our approach.

"Christ, man! Finally! I saved the whisky for ye!" he said as he held up the bottle carefully with both hands.

"That is a good and loyal friend right there!" Duncan said to me before kissing me on the forehead. "Thank ye for a wonderful supper and the whisky. Remember, lass, everything will work as it should."

"Good night, gentlemen! Get home safe! I expect to see ye both at breakfast," I said with a smile both ignoring his sentiment and laughing as I could already tell there was little chance that Missus Douglas or I would see either of these two at breakfast in the morning.

+++

It was strange, feeling like Father's house on Canongate was my home. It came to me first when we left the Advocate Society event and then again when I said the words to William tonight about being in my own house. I had become more comfortable inside the walls of this grand house.

Outside, I do not feel as comfortable. I cannot get used to the confines of city life and the volume of people crowded into one space. I missed my true home on Skye and especially my beloved Cairn's Point! I missed the ebb and flow of the sea as a point of refuge, but I learned to be happy here. I learned how my father was happy here.

Despite the debate with William, it was a good supper, but it was late. However, the thought of one more glass of wine called to me before my bed. There was no way I could sleep now that my head was spinning with the words Duncan just shared.

"Aye, thank ye, Missus Douglas," I said to her as she was clearing the table. "Ye can clean up the rest in the morning, madam. I have kept ye too late as it is. Go to Petey. I have just come fer one more glass of wine and will take it upstairs with me."

"Aye, I will put the food away, mistress. Ye are right that the rest can wait until the morning, and I thank ye fer thinking about Petey."

"How was yer supper missus?"

"Aye, we had a fine feast! Jonny and Petey were so happy with yer selections, and I thank ye fer yer generosity."

"I am glad fer it and ye are most welcome."

"This was left in a chair, mistress," she said, handing me a small book wrapped with a light blue ribbon.

"Thank ye. I will sleep in tomorrow and tend to my own fires, so no need to worry about me," I said, headed to the stairs with my unexpected gift. "I may not make it to breakfast. Ye may want to just have small bites fer the men to help themselves. As expected, they have all left to complete their evening at the tavern so I wouldna expect them fer breakfast either."

She nodded that the likelihood of a grand breakfast tomorrow was not needed, yet she has learned that the magical combination of fried ham and tatties would be most welcome after a night of indulgence for the MacLeod clan.

I made it to my room and stood before the glowing amber light of the candles throughout my chamber and the blazing fire. Missus Douglas was perfection! Anticipating my needs, she gave me extra cauldrons, water, and a small sugar cake on my bedside table. She left me a note in her own hand wishing me a happy birthday from her and wee Petey. I smiled, thinking about how I had grown to love each of them in such a short time.

The last moments of my birthday were as glorious as they were confusing. After my bath in the wonderous copper tub, I wrapped both hands around my wine glass and stared into the flames of the roaring fire. I tried to process the story Duncan told me and the notions of William MacCrimmon as an unexpected suitor... and perhaps similar intentions from Master Forbes.

I looked at the small book of Shakespeare's remaining fifty-four sonnets, gifted to me by the angry man who left supper early. His neat handwriting on the inside cover read:

More for us to read together—
William

I thought about walking down the corridor to his room to thank him, but I knew that would not be proper, especially at this late hour. My face grew red hot again at the thought of our exchange this evening. I did not know what to make of Duncan's words, or the thoughts of declarations of love, but I knew only one thing and that was that I sad to cause someone else pain. I was sad to cause my friend pain.

+++

My uncle and I sat across from each other at the dining table and ate in silence. We were the only people to show for breakfast this morning… and a late one at that!

"What time did ye and Angus come back to the house? I didna even hear ye!"

"I dinnae ken, but I slept like a bairn when I finally made it to my bed!"

"I didna expect to see either of ye this morning, to be honest, so I told Missus Douglas to keep it light."

"Angus doesna yet ken that fried ham will cure a night of drink!"

"That is a fact, sir," I said in agreement as we both laughed, and I reached for some more fried ham myself. The ham and tatties were already working on my wine-induced headache. I needed them both and was more than happy to keep this secret combination reserved for just Duncan and me this morning.

"I didna hear William either. Though I am not sure if he left at all. He may have been in his room the whole time after he slipped out of supper without saying a word to anyone."

Duncan looked at me with these words and put his knife and fork down. He had something to say, but seemed unsure if he should.

"Tell me, sir."

"Alex, Will took a room over the White Hart Inn last night. He is no longer staying in this house."

"What...?"

Duncan bowed his head, almost weary of the expected questions surely coming his way.

I continued, almost yelling at my uncle, "Why would he do such a thing? Is he not supposed to be here to protect me? How can he fulfill his obligation from the White Hart Inn?"

"Always a question," he said, shaking his head, "and in this case, four in a row."

"Tell me what ye ken, Duncan," I demanded. I tried to sound calm as I sat back in my chair, arms crossed, ready to receive whatever news he had for me.

"Angus and I saw the man last night. Jacob warned us when we arrived that he was in an awful state in the back and the lad was. Will said he felt that he shouldna be here in the house, based on his feelings for ye. He didna think it proper. And then after yer... erm... conversation last night, the lad decided it was time for him to go. He left during supper, took his things, and went straight to the tavern. He worked out lodgings with Jacob."

Duncan bowed his head and awaited my response. I could not speak, and my hand was wrapped tight around my own fork at the side of my plate. I felt terrible that William was spending his own money—money he inherited from my father—to stay above the White Hart Inn when he had a perfectly comfortable room and ample food and drink here in this fine house.

"Then I have to respect his decision," I said without a shred of emotion. Duncan looked at me, confused, perhaps thinking that I would argue that he should be here. But I could not argue... with Duncan or William. I have grown tired of arguing.

"I would like to have supper together tonight. I will ensure Angus is cared for here, but just us, please? Maybe we go to the White Hart, even at risk of running into William, but I dinnae want to be in this house. We have to plan what is left to do here so we can go home. I am *ready* to go home. I am *ready* to go back to Skye."

Duncan was sympathetic about my first sign of wearisome emotion and only said, "Aye! Just us tonight, lass."

+++

TWENTY-THREE
Confessions At The White Hart

Jacob greeted us at the door of the White Hart Inn the minute we walked in. He must have known that we wanted a moment together and escorted us immediately to one of the quiet tables in the back. A bottle of whisky and glasses were already waiting for us. Hilary followed quickly with cheese, bread, and butter on a board. I surveyed the tavern looking for William, but did not see him anywhere. Part of me was relieved by this and part of me was sad.

"Was all of this yer doing, Duncan? Or have Jacob and Hilary come to anticipate our needs so well that we dinnae have to ask fer what we want anymore?"

"I might have told Jacob we needed a quiet space. The rest was his doing."

"I thank ye, both!"

"*But of course,*" Jacob said in his best French accent as he and Hilary walked away, leaving us with our bounty.

We ate a bit and Duncan poured us each a whisky before I said, "Uncle, I need yer advice and counsel."

"Is this about Will, lass?"

Taken aback by his direct question, I took another sip and said, "Aye, and perhaps some other things."

I looked at him for a moment before I continued, "I confess that I am not sure what to do with yer revelations yesterday. Fer certain, I dinnae see Master Forbes as anything more than a friend. And not just my friend. Our friend. *My father's friend.*"

Duncan looked at me with suspicion at the depths of my ignorance. He knows more about the nature of men than I do, but my words were true. While Master Forbes was an attractive and successful man, I only saw him as a friend, not a suitor.

"Aside from his genuine kindness and support, Master Forbes has declared no other intention. He has represented Father's interests, as he was bound to do. Nothing more. If there *were* more, the question is easy to settle! Master Forbes is here in Edinburgh, and I am going home to Skye to serve my clan. Should he say anything to me—and so far, the man has not—we have no future together. I believe the man has just been kind and has treated us all with care here in the city, out of respect to my father, and his obligation as our advocate."

Duncan remained quiet. I knew he was listening to me, but he let me continue.

"As fer William, I feel sad that he thinks he needs to stay here, at the tavern, and I...," I paused, thinking to myself, '*I dinnae ken what to do with the information that he loves me.*' I have fought for so long to be on my own that the thought of a man loving me is not something I could ever fully understand.

369

I finally spoke again, "I dinnae ken what to do about him. He also has not made any declaration to me, but he has to ye, and now I ken it. It changes *everything!* It changes *everything* between us!"

Duncan just looked at me as I sipped from my glass and tried again to control my emotions.

"It is not right fer him to spend his coin to stay at a tavern when we have MacLeod House. He earned his money from Father and should save it all! But to have him come back to the house would require a conversation that I would verra much prefer *not to have.*"

"*Alex,*" Duncan said softly, but stopped himself and let me continue.

"I have rebelled equally against the notion of my personal worth being restricted to a man's property or being forced to lead quietly in the shadows, as most strong women do."

He looked at me with some understanding of my role in the clan, but said nothing. "I have lived my entire life protecting my heart and preserving some basic sense of *belligerent independence.* I have also thought about the heartbreaks I have suffered—some ye dinnae ken—and how I have let them falsely tell me I am not a woman that deserves love."

I stifled the tears forming in my eyes and said, looking into my glass again to avoid his stare. "It is *verra easy* to act like ye dinnae want love when ye feel like ye have *been deprived of it.*"

Duncan took a massive sip of his whisky and poured himself another before he said, "If you remember nothing of me, Alex, please remember this piece of advice. Ye should *find* love, ye should *celebrate* the love around ye, and ye should keep *showing* yer love to others more than ye do. Not just kindness. Not just friendship. But pure *love.* Do ye ken the difference, lass?"

Shocked by his words and his tone, I just stared at him. I wanted to argue that I knew perfectly well the difference, but I let the man continue. He clearly had something to say to me.

"Ye have been insistent on being alone, and we, yer family, have respected yer decision to be as ye said, *belligerently independent.* But I have to say, ye can only declare such a bold thing, because what ye are trying to reject is not really lacking in your life."

I bit my lip to keep from crying or speaking, but I could not argue with him. He was telling me something I had not thought about before, and I could not find the words to object. Not now.

"Marriage is one thing, to be sure. But *love* is another and, in that case, yer rejecting in yer words something ye already *have in abundance.* Something ye are constantly surrounded and supported by. Ye have the love of yer family and friends and ye give your love back to yer family and friends. We all feel yer love. I feel yer love. Lass! Think about what ye have done fer wee Robbie alone! It is not only admirable as a leader, and kind as a cousin, but it is based on yer *pure love* fer the wee lad. Living this solitary life, this targe and shield ye place between ye and everyone around ye, *is nothing but a lie.*"

I was shocked at his words, yet he continued, "Being alone is a lie ye tell yerself every day to protect yerself from *heartache, rejection, or the pain of loss.* Think of what Lady Margaret said to ye. Aye! Ye ken it! In a way, lass, ye are living the same lie she did."

I could not speak. I wanted to argue, but the words would not come. I wanted to cry but tried hard not to in his presence. As of late, I had cried in front of my uncle more than I should.

"Unless ye plan to live in a cave, with no human contact fer the rest of yer days, ye will experience those things in life. Trying to avoid the pain along with the joys and blessings of love is a fool's errand. The two are intertwined in ways we have to accept. Not to mention, ye would miss all the joys of this life... having another love ye for who ye are, to care for ye, and aye, even make love to ye!" His last remarks were said with a wink and a smile.

My eyes widened that he would say such a thing to me, but again, I could not find my words. Duncan knew he was being provocative and figured that such frank talk would make me think even more about the decisions before me.

Finally, after a few sips of my own, I found my words, "Duncan, why are ye not married?"

He looked at me and said with a sly smile as he filled his glass again, "Well, Alex, some people like ye try to avoid love... and some like me want too much of it to settle down with just one other."

I shook my head at him in mock judgment before saying, "I appreciate ye telling me what I needed to hear. I will have to determine what I want for my own life before I can respond to William."

Duncan just looked at me with a smile as he repeated the direction he gave William, "Be honest with yerself and then be honest with the lad. It is that simple. Everything will work as it should."

When we returned to the house on Canongate, I left Duncan at the bottom of the stairs, and said as I kissed his cheek, "I love ye. I do."

"And I love ye, lass," he said while hugging me tight.

+++

Nursing a bit of a whisky-induced headache and general apprehension for the day ahead, I was glad to have my room to myself and arise on my own time. William was gone from the house on

Canongate, and I knew that Missus Douglas could handle Duncan and Angus on her own for breakfast this morning.

I took a moment to go downstairs for water and my beloved bread and butter, when Missus Douglas met me in the kitchen to let me know that William sent word by messenger this morning that he would like to meet me at the White Hart Inn for supper this night. His formality just gave me even more reason to worry myself sick in my room all day in anticipation of a discussion I absolutely dreaded.

I retreated to the warmth of my linens straight away. I spent most of the day in bed, in fact, agonizing over imaginary conversations to be had and often added claret to my glass—which was the only thing to cure my aching head.

What would I say about the last time we talked... erm, argued?

What would I take from Duncan's advice into this conversation?

How would I get there and get back home to MacLeod House safely?

What do I want for myself?

At some point, I got up to wash and get dressed. I chose intentionally not to take the carriage, but walked all the way to the White Hart in the Edinburgh damp, so that I could have the time to perfect my responses and maybe sober up from an afternoon of courage drinking.

I know that both Duncan and William would be furious at this decision. There was risk in walking through the city alone, but I told myself that since it was not yet dark, I could just wrap my new cloak around me and walk up the hill with purpose. I arranged for Jonny to bring me home in the carriage. I did not dare look behind me, but believe our honorable stable master slowly followed me up the hill to see me safely to the White Hart. I smiled to myself at the thought of such chivalry. Again, I have honorable men around me that are solely focused on my care and protection.

+++

William was waiting for me when I walked into the tavern. I immediately took his warm and welcoming hand as he led me into a corner table that positioned us out of earshot of others. As I am uncertain of the expectation tonight, I might have preferred to talk in the open. But at least there was a fire nearby to keep us warm. And after my slow walk to the tavern, the warmth was much needed and welcome.

We were so quick to sit down, I did not see if I had any friends in the room. *Where are Duncan or Angus when ye need them?* We ordered our drinks and food immediately with Hilary, and beyond the basic pleasantries as old friends, we quickly found ourselves in silence until our wine arrived.

"*Slàinte,*" we said in unison, taking our first sip of our glasses, while smiling at each other. After a bit, the silence became uncomfortable. I knew I had to speak to break the incredible tension hanging in the air.

"Thank ye so much fer the invitation, William," I said, being intentionally formal with my friend. "It is good to see ye again. I want ye to ken how verra sorry I am that we argued. I hope my belief that…"

Thankfully, food arrived at this very moment to save me from a shaky and perhaps half-hearted apology.

"Yer supper, Mistress Alexandra and Master William," Hilary said as she placed our plates before us and refilled the wine glasses from the jug at the end of the table. Once she was done, she asked, "Will ye be needing anything else?"

She nodded to me as I looked at her. I nodded back. She wanted me to signal that I was alright with my company, and I was. William thanked her, and we kept conversation focused on all the small things—how supper tasted, how the claret was not as good as we remembered, and how the heat of the fire at this table was welcome at first but was slowly becoming almost unbearable. We moved quickly from supper to the whisky that appeared at the table. Once again, Jacob and Hilary knew that Clan MacLeod was here and accommodated us fully.

After a bit more silence, William grabbed his glass and leaned forward with his elbows on his knees, staring at the floor. I braced myself for what might come and tried to keep Duncan's words in my head—*Have a care with the man's heart, and aye, even his pride.'*

"I ken ye were interrupted earlier, but I have to ask ye, Alexandra," he said in his own formal manner that matched my own just moments ago. "Why did ye think to scold me in front of the entire table at yer supper?"

His voice suddenly turned low, husky, and even slower than usual. He raised eyes to mine for a response, and immediately unnerved me. His bright blue eyes showed me his heart and his pain—the same pain Duncan mentioned. Even when he was telling me on our journey about his family and the trauma inflicted by his father, the man did not show such sadness in his eyes. My initial response was defensive, to be sure.

"Scold? My God, man! Have ye been worried about that conversation and debate this whole time?" My poor attempt at diminishing his feelings rebounded on me quickly.

Determined eyes locked on each other. No one was going to back down now. He tried to speak, but his jaw was locked. As was mine.

"Christ! Ye just seem to take satisfaction in making me suffer!"

"*Suffer*!? How do I…?"

"Ye disrespected me at yer own table," he said, interrupting my indignation.

"I didna…"

Before I could fully respond, he said as he sat back in his chair, defeated, "The last thing I need is for Master Forbes to see such a display."

"Display? Disrespect? Forbes? I feel we are having two verra different conversations, William. How is my having an opinion on female independence and marriage—while granted, different from yers—a personal affront to ye? Ye ken me! I speak my mind."

"Aye! Ye do. More than ye should sometimes," he said in open and vocal judgment. Now, I am uncertain who is scolding who. His bright blue eyes were now aflame with both his masculine jealousy and frustration. They were made even more dramatic with the reflection of the roaring fire before us.

"Och well now, who is being *disagreeable*? William, this debate is being blown out of proportion! I *may* speak my mind! It never seemed to bother ye before. In fact, ye said once… that it was a trait ye… *admired*."

In that moment, he seemed to remember our conversation at Cairn's Point before setting out on this journey, where he had said those very words. I had not put it all together until this very minute that he was speaking with a broken heart. I had not noticed his affection for me or that he saw Master Forbes as a rival. His sulking on the outskirts of the room at the Advocate Society alone should have told me that plain enough. But I did not see it at the moment. Instead, I just thought he was a man who felt out of place with the other men in the room. And now, the debate I saw as lively supper conversation with friends to him was disrespectful, as it wounded his heart, and shamed him in front of his perceived competition.

Also, the topic was about women not marrying someone they did not love or not marrying at all. Perhaps he thought I was sending him a direct message with my own words that night that I did not want his love or that he was worthy of my love. When he looked back at me, he no longer looked as angry but sorry for his harsh words and the frustration that he shared so openly.

Immediately, I could feel my cheeks absorbing the heat of the room and William's pained stare. I gripped my glass tighter, but he stayed quiet for a little too long. Duncan was right. I did not see what I did not *want* to see. William was laying it all out before me if I would simply notice and accept it.

Looking directly at me, he took my empty hand and pulled it toward his chest. He said in a pained whisper, *"Alexandra."*

As he said my name, I immediately pulled my hand away from his and turned my eyes back to the fire. I did not dare look at him when I said, *"No! Do not!"*

"Why?"

I shifted my eyes to look at him only for a moment. The emotion was apparent in his face and the accusation was pointed in his tone, just as Duncan described. But I could not help myself.

"How much drink have ye had tonight, William? Ye dinnae seem to be yerself. Perhaps we can talk tomorrow," I said, trying to settle this conversation for now. "Aye, please come to the house tomorrow for supper. I ken ye decided to stay here, but I have to tell ye that ye are missed at MacLeod House. I promise ye we can talk more there. This is not the place, *and it is not the time.*"

"Why do ye continue to push me away? I thought… I thought we… could make each other happy. But ye willna allow it. *Why? Am I not good enough fer ye?*"

I closed my eyes and breathed in every ounce of shame that could only come from knowing you were hurting someone you loved and respected. This must be what Grant felt at Cairn's Point and my heart broke at the thought. I did not want to think of it, but now it was now my turn to hurt a friend, and it felt *absolutely dreadful.*

'I dinnae ken!' was the answer I wanted to yell loudly hoping I could excuse myself and never come back to face him. I had not yet processed what I heard from Duncan just two days ago and was now being asked to account for it before William at this very moment. I am not ready! *I am not ready for this conversation… not here… not now!*

Duncan was correct. I would have to be honest with myself first and I did not yet have the words for myself, let alone William! I stood up and said, "I will see ye tomorrow. Same time. Missus Douglas will make us a fine supper."

He nodded to me silently and said no more. Perhaps there was some hope for him since I was not rejecting him completely and offered another chance to talk tomorrow. But he would not look at me. I placed my hand on his broad shoulder briefly and, looking at the wall behind him said, "Thank ye fer supper tonight."

As soon as I could, I left the tavern. I am certain I heard Jacob wish me a goodnight, and I did not reply. I walked out of the door and straight into the carriage Jonny had waiting for me.

I could not account for my thoughts. I was all over the place and unable to focus between what I felt in the moment and what I needed to solve for. I would have to be ready to answer my friend's questions at supper tomorrow.

I thanked Jonny as I ran for the back door off of the safe courtyard. The warmth of the house, even as I stepped inside to the kitchen, snapped me out of my confused thoughts.

I said to Missus Douglas who was cleaning the kitchen, "Missus, I need to have a supper here tomorrow for me and one other. Can ye help me?"

"Aye! Anything for ye, mistress!"

"I will see ye after breakfast to plan, but tonight, I am spent."

TWENTY-FOUR
To Know Your Own Heart

MacLeod House
Canongate, Edinburgh, Scotland
October 1766

After clearing breakfast, Missus Douglas immediately set the dining room for two. We worked together all morning on the menu and our plans sent her out for shopping at the market for some final items. Planning for supper was a welcome distraction from the anticipation and worry about my impending conversation. I bought myself a little time, but I knew I was going to have to say something more to William this night.

I made it clear to Missus Douglas that I did not need attending this evening. If everything was set in the kitchen and dining room, I could certainly take care of managing a supper for two. We also arranged for Angus and Duncan to either have supper in their rooms or to find their own on a night out. As expected, they chose the night out.

Duncan did not ask me about the planned supper with William tonight. I suspect he felt as if he had been involved enough at this point or that I would come to him if I needed more advice. He knew I would tell him everything eventually, anyway.

I came downstairs to the hall and said, "Thank ye for everything, Missus Douglas. We are set. And I ken my way in the kitchen if we need anything else. Go be with wee Petey tonight!"

"Aye, mistress! The lad is happy that I will share supper with him this night. I made a small venison pie fer us to match yers and I have seen to Master Jonny having supper, as well."

"Well then, that sounds fine!" I said, smiling at her while unnecessarily adjusting a random glass on the table. "I expect a difficult conversation with my friend, so it is probably best that we are alone."

She looked at me with sympathy but did not say a word. She would not give her opinion here without being asked directly, and I am not looking for any additional advice this evening. My mind is already conflicted enough.

Looking at her, I added, "Och, and I will sleep in tomorrow. I will come down when I am ready. No need to send anything up or tend the fires. If ye can ensure I have extra wood and fresh cauldrons set aside in the room tonight for the copper bath, I can manage myself."

"I will make that happen right now, mistress and we will leave you for the evening." She directed Petey instantly on the water and the wood for my room. She paused for a moment before asking one question that is fair as the only other woman in this house, "Ye will be safe, lass?"

"Aye, I will be safe. It is *just* William," I said. I had not realized that in all of our planning, I never said who was joining me for supper. She just knew I was planning supper for two and that she and others were gone from this house. I tried to see if her face changed at that mention, and it did. I would say for the positive.

"Och! Master MacCrimmon, then?"

I nodded in agreement.

"All will be well, I am certain. But take care of yerself, lass," she said, both in relief and in support and with a wide smile. I suspect this was another affirmative vote in favor of William MacCrimmon as a potential match.

I suddenly began rethinking this supper plan. I had not thought about the appearance of impropriety in clearing the house. I simply wanted to have an open and private conversation with my friend that was not in a crowded tavern. I told myself that I was justified in taking such a risk and that no one, including Duncan, tried to talk me out of it.

She was beaming on her way out the door and wished me a good night. She was half-way across the courtyard when I finally replied to her, "Good night, Missus Douglas!"

I said a quick prayer to myself, *"Please Lord God… give me the grace I need to get through this evening… and help me keep my heart and my ears open."*

I ran upstairs to change my dress and check my hair and face in the mirror. Petey brought me two more cauldrons and returned with a new basket filled with wood, before stoking my fire for me. Despite his silence, the lad does an incredible job in service to this house.

The anticipation is the true agony. I spent the entire day occupying my mind about what we would eat and drink, what place settings we would use, how best to ensure I could manage without help, and never once did I decide what I would actually say to my guest. When I did think about it, I kept changing my position and the words. I played the conversation over and over in my head, yet each time, my response was different. I was still conflicted and tonight may very well be a surprise to us both.

+++

I met William at the door when he arrived and took his coat with an enthusiastic welcome and in a higher pitch in my voice than I had ever heard before. I can only put it down to nerves.

"Och my, William! I hope ye didna walk here in this weather! Yer coat is absolutely soaked!"

"Aye 'tis," he said, shaking off his dripping coat all over the entrance hall. "It is pissing down! Believe it or not, this is just from just coming in and out of a carriage. I did not walk here from the tavern. I woulda never made it!"

"Go straight to the parlor and warm yerself by the fire, friend," I said. I took his coat and hat back outside the door and shook them furiously before bringing them back in to dry on the hook in the hall.

I walked back into the parlor and retrieved the wine glass I had already poured myself, "Are ye warm? Or better yet, man! Should I ask if ye are at least starting to dry yerself?"

We both laughed and he said, graciously with a warm smile, "Aye, to both! Thank ye!"

"Let me help even more by offering ye a whisky, sir," I said, pouring him a generous glass. "As Duncan says, let the whisky warm ye from the inside, while the fire warms ye from the outside."

I handed him the glass as we both smiled, recalling our travels and all of the tavern stops on our way to Edinburgh and while here.

"*Slàinte*," we said in unison as our glasses touched.

In an attempt at small talk, I said nervously, "I walked to our supper last night and half-way there, thought I would surely freeze in the damp. And now ye are soaked to the bone! It will be a wonder, friend, how we do not both catch the death of the chill."

William noticed my use of the word *friend* for the second time, and it brought about another smile to his face. I took this conversation as a good start to the evening—true friends connecting with each other once again.

I remembered how William told me that his upbringing and his own size set him apart from other lads. He felt different from them and while I know he wanted more from me than I could give in the moment, I know he valued our genuine friendship. As do I. I am also not unlike him in that I never had many friends myself and can admit that William MacCrimmon has truly become a dear friend on our journey.

"Ye did *not* walk home in the night from the White Hart!" he said, lightly admonishing me for walking alone on the city streets.

"No! Jonny brought me home in the carriage. I only walked *to* the tavern. It was still light."

"Och! Thank Christ!" he said, noticeably relieved. "Duncan would surely kill me! But, even in the light of day, walking all that way alone was a risk, lass."

"I wondered," I said with a sly smile, "how ye let me walk through the city streets with no protection."

He took the bait I offered in challenging his role here as he stepped closer to me. He wanted to respond but was speechless at the accusation. I can only assume that was because of the oath he made to my uncles to serve as protection on this trip.

"Supper is ready if ye are, shall we?" I said as I escorted him to the dining room. "I hope you dinnae mind that we are on our own tonight."

Before he could say anything, I grabbed his glass out of his hand immediately to refill and I continued, "After the hectic supper party earlier this week, I wanted to give Missus Douglas a break fer tonight. She is thrilled to be with wee Petey fer their own supper as a family, so it is worth the small sacrifice."

"That was kind of ye."

"I feel I keep her from the lad too much as it is. And I ken we can find our way around a kitchen, can we not?"

He did not respond directly to this statement but seemed to respect the decision when his newly filled glass was handed back to him. "Aye, I believe we can."

+++

We ate the meal before us, commenting pleasantly on the food and drink we were sharing. We started talking of our favorite foods, trying to top each other with what made us nostalgic about our home, childhood, and family.

"My ma used to make honey porridge," William said, fondly remembering his mother. "I always hated porridge, but she would find honeycomb and make it sweet, so I would eat it. It was a rare treat, but to this day, I like a sweet porridge."

"Ye ken my tastes are fairly simple, as I am certain I could live on warm bread and creamy butter alone, but Missus Gerrard makes the best fish pie I have ever tasted."

385

William nodded and laughed at my simple tastes. He learned quickly on our travels that I have an affection for bread and butter and often gave me the last of both if either were left on the table.

"I tried to get her recipe to understand why I loved her fish pie so, but can ye believe that the woman wouldna give it to me? She said it was a *secret* family recipe from Ireland."

William laughed as he said, "Well, to be fair, lass, the woman kens that as Lady MacLeod, ye will never *actually* have to make a fish pie yerself."

"Aye! I never thought about that."

Slowly, the tension that was there at the start faded. We were just old friends talking, laughing, and reminiscing during our time together. Both of us dreaming of home and a simpler time. The wine and whisky were also helping to dull some of the stress and strain of the conversation we had last night and the impending conversation ahead.

"Och, I remember one summer at Dunmara. The lads found some mead in the kitchen. But, mind, we were no smarter than our boots and didna realize there was a *process* to making mead."

"Och no! Tell me you didna drink it too early," I said while making a face of disgust at the thought of mead, but unfinished mead had to be horrible. "Though I suspect that if ye like sweet honey, ye would like mead."

"Erm, just wait," he said with the same look of disgust at the memory and turning slightly pale. "So, here we all go to drinking somethin' that was in the early stage of completion. *Christ above!* I have never been so sick! Four lads, including myself, were retching our guts out. They called the healer... the Beaton. What was his name?"

I shook my head and said, "I cannae remember the name. We just called him *the healer*. I do remember, however, that he was verra old and mean."

"When the man found out what we had done, he put up his hands in resignation and told us we all deserved our fate. The Beaton said, *some of ye lads may live and some of ye may die.*"

"Well, that is not verra encouraging," I said, laughing at his story.

"Every lad, including me, thought fer sure that we were to be the ones to die and honestly, we almost welcomed it."

"Ye lads probably did!"

We continued laughing, filling each other's glasses, thinking of the misery the boys endured. I thought to myself that it was nice to have my friend back. Even for a moment.

"Horrible! Who started the raid on the mead? Please dinnae tell me it was ye."

"Aye, no! It was Wesley," he said as I sat up straight in my chair. This must have been how William knew Wesley had been at Dunmara before when he talked to me and Grant on the old stone wall.

"I am so sorry, Alex. I didna mean…" he reached his hand across the table toward me.

"No, dinnae think about it. I just caught a chill for a moment," I said with a half-smile of reassurance that the mention of *Sir Wes of the Stable Ashes* and what we just experienced with *Mean Old Mary MacAskill* weeks ago was not the cause of my physical reaction to his name. I did not want that to be the reason, anyway.

"Like I said, I walked to the tavern in the damp air yesterday."

"Well, 'tis no wonder, lass! The fire is nearly out! If we are done here, we should go to the front room. I will tend to the fire there and ye tend to the whisky, and we will both be recovered in no time!"

William jumped into action and led me to the parlor. I poured the whisky and watched him as he rolled up his sleeves to tend to the fire. William MacCrimmon was always handsome, a memory I had long forgotten or ignored. Despite his size, he has the most graceful arms and hands.

I watched him and remembered distinctly a time I saw him years ago in the Great Hall at Dunmara Castle. He came to the aid of a wee lad running from others who were teasing him. The poor boy tripped over a bench and landed hard on the flagstones beneath him.

"Och, lad," William said, as he pulled the boy up effortlessly by his collar and sat him on his lap by the fire. His large thumbs gently and reassuringly wiped the lad's tears from his face and smoothed out his hair, which was wet with sweat. I am not sure what was said between them, but soon the young boy smiled up at William, jumped down from his lap and was off running once again. I was in awe of William's gentle touch and his kindness.

William yelled after him with a laugh, "Yer most welcome, lad!"

Returning from the long-forgotten memory, I looked over at William staring down into his glass, held in the same large but gentle hands. We sipped from our glasses in silence for a moment as I tried to catch my breath and settle my nerves.

Whether it was the comfort I felt talking to him this night, the warmth of the room, or the drink in my glass, I decided now was the time to finish the conversation we started yesterday. I knew he was going to wait for me to start this topic again, especially within the walls of this house. I breathed in deep and sat my remaining drink on the mantle.

"William, ye asked me a question last night that I wasna ready to answer." He kept his gaze down in his glass uncertain of what direction my words could take us, as I continued, "Thank ye for the gift of time to think about what I wanted to say."

If this was not having a care and protecting a man's pride, I do not know what is!

He looked at me, and suddenly his eyes were bluer and brighter than before, and he unsettled me. In that instant, I formally traded my hard-fought independence for *acceptance*.

Acceptance of the loneliness that had always been lying underneath the surface—never acknowledged and never resolved. The unintended consequence from my own decisions and declarations to remain alone. I realized what I had been depriving myself of—something I would not let myself have or even feel worthy of—the respect and love of another person. The respect and love of *this man*.

Until this moment, I did not realize that my heart ached for my friend, and that I was tired of fighting it. I wanted nothing more than to feel safe. To feel connected. To feel loved. Just like Duncan said, it is a gift to be loved by a friend. I chased such a promise with the one friend that could not give me what I was looking for and, in my stubbornness, I ignored the one that could.

He came to stand next to me as I stood in front of the fire. I could barely breathe, let alone speak. Finally, my face showed my transition when I offered my hand back by taking his instead. I looked at my friend intently and quietly. It seemed an eternity before he would join my gaze. I waited patiently until he did and then I spoke again.

"William, I am so sorry to cause ye pain. I see it in yer face. I hear it in yer voice. And I feel it in yer touch now." I gripped his hand between both of mine, tighter as I went on.

"The simple answer to yer question yesterday about why I push ye away is that... I am *afraid*."

"I am *afraid*... *every day*," I said as I breathed in, and I could feel my eyes mist with the resignation of my own confession and his sharp and concerned look back at me. I closed my eyes again to steady my breath and my words.

"I found it verra easy to walk a lonely path in my life. To combat rejection or the fear of loss and heartbreak with defiant resistance built upon an acceptance of unworthiness. I fought the notion of the woman I should be by society, the role I must take within our clan, and my own desire to claim my true self. I have been fiercely independent and indignant in this stance, as ye ken."

He smiled to me in understanding of my words, and I continued, "So, I built every wall and raised every shield I needed to in order to *hold fast* to my heart, to keep myself safe, and to keep people—even people I *love*—at a comfortable distance."

William said nothing, but kissed my hand in his.

"I dinnae want to lose ye... ye are my *friend*. But ken that I dinnae want to lose myself along the way. That is not what is expected of me as a woman, but it has to be as the next clan chief, and I take that responsibility seriously. I want... to be with ye, but I... I honestly dinnae ken how. I am *afraid* to let you in. I am afraid you will hurt me or that I may hurt ye. That is the simple truth of it."

The tears that welled up during this speech dropped one by one onto my blazing red cheeks, and I took a second to breathe. I paused for a moment and raised my head up to him, awaiting his response.

"I have always admired yer independence and strength, Alexandra. Now, I am glad to finally have a look at yer heart. That heart hidden under all of yer armor is a beauty to behold."

I bowed my head in appreciation of his words. Just as another tear fell, I said, "Sometimes I feel so independent and strong. But sometimes I just feel *alone*."

Will stepped closer, placing both of his hands around my face, and softly wiped away my tears with his thumbs, just like the wee lad running through the Great Hall. He leaned down and kissed me. His lips were soft. He smelled of the fire and even hints of his shaving soap. I could taste the whisky we were drinking mixed with the salt of my own tears, but I did not kiss him back. I have never been kissed lovingly by a man and was shocked that he was this close to me. I did not know what to do.

What I kept hidden deep down in the core of my heart for so long left me stunned, having just said it all out loud. Just as I predicted, this conversation had been a surprise for us both. William standing this close to me and touching me, bewildered me even more. He made my knees weak, and I could not find my words.

He moved his hands from my face to my shoulders and whispered, *"I never want ye to be anything less than ye are. I understand that ye have a task ahead with the clan, but I love ye, Alexandra. I love ye. And I want to be a support to ye if I can. Not just as yer kinsman and not just yer friend."*

I immediately turned to face the fire with my back to him, embarrassed with his kiss still on my lips and that he just said he loves me. I have to decide what to do next. I had just confessed my true feelings, and that I did not want to lose him, but I had not given myself the time to think of what comes after such a declaration.

William stood behind me and put his hands on both sides of me as he gripped the mantle. He whispered into my ear from behind, *"What do ye want, Alex?"*

I closed my eyes and thought of what Duncan said about getting out of my own way. William MacCrimmon became more than a friend on our journey to Edinburgh. I had not seen it before because I stubbornly kept him at a distance in my head and my heart. But I see it all now. On this journey together, I *have* grown to love him, his honesty, and his humor. I just never had to account for such feelings and emotions for myself, let alone say the words—to him or anyone else.

I turned to him, with our faces close again. He kept his arms firmly placed on both sides of me, still holding onto the mantle as I whispered, *"I want ye, Will."*

He smiled and said, "From here on out, ye ken my heart and I yers."

"Aye," I said as I pulled his face down to me for one more kiss. This time he knew I was committed, and his passion left me even weaker in the knees. In fact, if I were not holding on to him, I am not sure I could stand. We looked directly into each other's eyes and smiled at each other—friends with a new understanding.

He kissed me quickly once more, through his smile. Embarrassed again, I pulled back.

"We have more to talk about, but I think we should say goodnight, sir."

"Aye! We should, and quickly," he said breathlessly, his forehead on mine, "or I swear, by Christ, I could never leave ye."

We walked in silence, hand-in-hand, to the front hall. I wished more than anything that he was not staying at the tavern, but for tonight, it was best that he return there. I bet that Duncan and Angus were waiting for him to walk through the doors at the White Hart to interrogate the man.

"Ye have given me hope," he said with a smile as he kissed the top of my hand quickly out of respect as I ushered him out of the door with his still dripping coat.

I shut the door, and said to myself, *"Aye William MacCrimmon, ye have also given me hope."*

All this time, I had feelings I did not understand or acknowledge. I sat before the fire as the tears flowed once again at the realization. Soon, my thoughts turned to all of the men I love and respect. I am not alone in this life. I never have been. I am surrounded and supported by good men. Good company.

+++

GRATITUDE

While this book is not about me, I cannot separate some of the personal characteristics I share with **Alexandra Flora MacLeod.** Alexandra is stubborn, head-strong, and fiercely independent. She is a perfectionist who holds herself and others to an almost unachievably high standard. She does not suffer fools gladly and yet she can be a bit of a pill herself. But she is a loyal friend with a wicked sense of humor. I do not know if I was born with these traits or if they formed over a lifetime of constantly moving and starting over, reinventing myself along the way. Perhaps it is a bit of both.

I would like to thank **my parents Larry and Cathy Harris**, who gave me an adventurous and somewhat nomadic childhood across America. North, South, East, or West, the constant exposure to new people, new places, and new schools, shaped my opinion of my myself and my country. It also made me an enthusiastic and confident traveler, always eager to learn more about the people and places I fell in love within my beloved history books and travel guides.

Oh, how I obsessed over travel guides! Particularly ones about Scotland and England. I memorized maps and the beautiful and historic places that I hoped to one day see for myself. While there is always more to learn, I am so fortunate that my life and my work afforded me the opportunity—on more than one occasion—to visit places I dreamt about as a young girl and to see more of the world than I ever imagined I would.

Much like Alexandra, I was told by my parents, teachers, and those that nurtured me throughout my life that I could be anything I wanted to be. I just had to believe that I could find my way. I realize what a privilege that wide open space is! It led me to an incredible career and this book—its contents, and its completion is manifestation of that promise. I am forever grateful.

I would like to acknowledge **my paternal grandmother, Thurza Godwin Harris,** who died on 5 October 2021 at the age of 93. I will never forget the call from my mother as I prepared to leave my hotel in London for the airport. Grandma Harris was an amazing woman who never completely understood my strong sense of independence and often lamented openly with me—and anyone else who would listen—about her hope that I would one day find someone to take care of me. She knew I could take care of myself, and I know her thoughts were not just a generational point of view, but that she believed I was worthy of love in my life.

Pulling into the red clay drive of her house in Mineola, Alabama, where my parents now live, made me feel safe. We were not always anchored as a family to one place, but my grandparent's house was a constant. I did not fully belong there as a *'city girl,'* but I loved being in the country as well. I could appreciate this amazing place at the heart of the Harris Clan—a kinship that I am deeply proud of—and I thank my entire family for their continued support and encouragement.

I would like to thank my friends at **Matts' Rotisserie & Oyster Lounge** in Redmond, Washington. My dear friends, **Jacob, Hilary, Hannah, Kayli, Mikey, Nissa, Dur, Yonatan, Kendrick, Greg, Diana, and many more** for their support over the last few years. While some others have come and gone, this team not only kept the wine spritzers[1] coming when needed but were never short of words of

---

[1] My version of a wine spritzer is a 'lesson in thirds.' As a writer who knows the 'power of threes,' I expect nothing less in my glass! Mix a third Sauvignon Blanc (or Pinot Grigio or Sancerre), a third soda water, and a third ice.

encouragement. My friends raised my spirits and my confidence more than once. They gave me the space to work (in my preferred seat), celebrated milestones with me, and kept me laughing and smiling as much as they kept my glass full!

They all gave my wings the air they needed to fly through both my demanding day job and the start of my books. But they also inspired me through their own resilience during COVID lockdown after lockdown. I will be forever grateful, and they should know that they all infused the personality and spirit of every tavern owner, barkeep, and barmaid mentioned in this book. To each of them, I say a heartfelt, *Slàinte mhath!*

In completing this book, that fast became a series, I spent nearly a month in Scotland in September 2021 to research as much as I could. I followed with another month-long trip in November—December 2021, only to return in April—May 2022. During all of my trips to this beautiful country, I met so many new friends who made my journey rewarding while continuing to make the books and my story richer.

I already knew that the people of Scotland were gracious, and kind based on my first visit in 2010, but every single person I met on these trips either added to my research, helped point me in the right direction, or provided positive encouragement for my journey. Scotland is indeed *one big village.*

Living up to this reputation, my new friend, **Natasha Howard,** from the **Marmalade Hotel in Portree, Skye,** connected me with her friend **Ellie Macpherson,** who helped me with the Scots Gaelic translation of the very first line of this book. I had two translations of the line that did not match, and Ellie quickly clarified for me in a simple email. I cannot thank Natasha or Ellie enough for their kindness in helping a stranger.

At **Gleneagles Hotel & Resort**, the Playground Planning Team is five stars all the way! You get the first hint of this incredible team in prep for your trip. It starts with all the basics of dining reservations and events, including golf and spa, but it is also paying attention to the clues of why someone is traveling. In this case it was a big birthday and research for my books. From the very start, I was treated like everyone was celebrating with me and cheering me on.

I want to call out **Mhàiri (Gleneagles Stables)** and **Katie (Bob & Cloche Spa).** The stables tour was essential to my research and helped me rethink and rewrite Alexandra's beloved horse Munro—not only the type of horse he was—but the incredible connection humans and horses can have. I also tried to name and give character to the other horses in the series ahead based on my learnings. I am not sure I have done her lessons justice, but she helped me correct my original drafts and taught me more than I could have ever imagined about these wonderful and powerful friends. I spent much of my life being afraid of horses and grew to love them in an instant with her tour.

Katie asked so many interesting questions about the books and writing that I felt proud talking about it. For the very first time, I had to articulate what I was doing to someone outside of my friendship circle. With her support, she reminded me that I made the right decision on this adventure and why I wanted to write for myself. I hope she and her fiancé finally got to have their wedding after multiple postponements because of COVID pandemic lockdown restrictions in Scotland. She deserves every happiness.

I would like to thank **Alan McGuiggan**, the General Manager at **Prestonfield House, Edinburgh**. He was so kind to me and while I know I am not the only person to learn of the *Wells of the Weary;* he gave me another gift to honor this home and its history in a way that made my story real. As a descendant of the Cunningham family, I fell in love with this place in an instant! It immediately felt like home, and I thank him and everyone on the staff that supported my research and writing. I had the great opportunity at the **National Library of Scotland** to read **Sir Alexander Dick's** hand-written journal of his trip to Italy with Allan Ramsay. The story of his stolen money and his poem come from his actual notes—which were a joy to read.

I would like to thank **Lauren Hughes** for her editorial assessment of this book. Lauren was the first person to read this novel in its entirety. As a first-time author, she helped me see where I made simple mistakes that could be easily corrected and her reading of the first draft was important because it opened my thinking about expanding from a trilogy to a series. I am certain that I did not correct everything she hoped, but I thank her for her immediate support of my story and my characters.

I would like to thank **Jared Frank** for his incredible art for the cover and a design that will translate across all of my books in this series. He embraced what I was doing from the very start, and I want him to work on all of my books. His incredible artistic vision and talent are visible, and his collaborative spirit has been a blessing to me. He is another friend cheering for my success and helping me realize my dream. I must thank **Elisabeth Kaczmarek**, my dear friend from my XBOX days, and his partner, for making a connection to a talent that has been so good for me and my work.

Finally, I would like to thank **Georgia Bain Marra**, who has been an incredible friend and colleague for over a decade. I am forever grateful that work brought us together and I cherish her friendship and support. She has also helped keep me honest (more than once) when my fiercely independent streak mentioned earlier got in my way personally and professionally. Georgia was my biggest cheerleader in retiring early, taking the time to finish my books, and live my passion. I worried I was putting my future at risk by leaving a stable career at Microsoft, but her encouragement that I should finish what I started—and do what made me happy—helped me.

Georgia has inspired some part of Duncan's character, always encouraging the benefits of an open heart, just as she has done for me. I am proud that I could share the legend of her own Scottish ancestor, Gillies MacBane, in this novel.

ABOUT THE AUTHOR

Cynthia Harris is the author of *HOLD FAST*; her debut novel and the first installment of the historical fiction *HOLD FAST Series*. She is also the author of her first contemporary romance novel, *Fun & Games*.

All of her novels are available in paperback and Kindle eBook versions on Amazon.com.

Cynthia built a career in storytelling. From leading advertising and marketing strategy for some of the world's most recognized consumer brands, international news organizations, and major league sports teams—to leading internal and external communication strategy and speech writing for technology, human resources, gaming, and entertainment executives—words have not only been her passion, but her livelihood. With her novels, Cynthia now focuses her time on finding and sharing her own voice.

As a proud graduate of The University of Georgia, she made a home in the Pacific Northwest over sixteen years ago. She keeps her gas tank full and her passport current, so she can escape to the incredible places near and far that allow her to revisit history, fuel her creativity, and find peace. But Scotland is calling, and she is currently looking for a new home in the country that she loves.

FROM THE AUTHOR

Thank you for reading! But don't worry! The next two books in the *HOLD FAST Series* will follow closely, so you can follow the rest of Alexandra's story.

If you liked the first book in the *HOLD FAST Series* (or even if you didn't), I'd appreciate a quick review on Amazon, so I know how to make my books better, and what you want to read from me in the future. Your feedback also helps other readers discover my work.

If you want to preview some of my writing, get sneak peeks of future work, or learn about my journey as an author, visit me at cynthiaharrisauthor.com or follow me on Instagram at cynthia_harris_author.

Cynthia Harris Novels

Fun & Games

HOLD FAST
Book 1 Of The HOLD FAST Series

A STRENGTH SUMMONED
Book 2 Of The HOLD FAST Series

RAISE YOUR SHIELD
Book 3 Of The HOLD FAST Series

Made in the USA
Monee, IL
01 May 2023

32738435R00246